BORDER LAND,
BORDER WATER

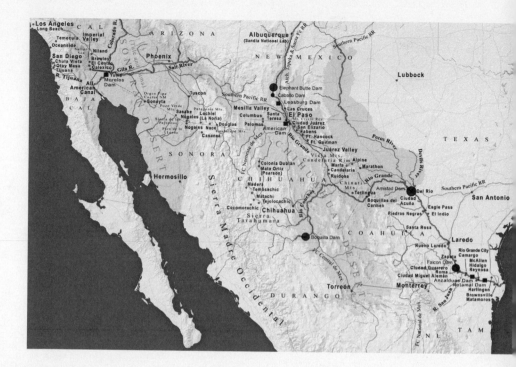

BORDER LAND,

BORDER

WATER

A HISTORY OF CONSTRUCTION ON
THE US-MEXICO DIVIDE

C. J. ALVAREZ

UNIVERSITY OF TEXAS PRESS ᐁᐁ AUSTIN

Parts of chapter 3 will be published as "Police, Waterworks, and the Construction of the U.S.-Mexico Border, 1924–1954," in *Western Historical Quarterly* 50, no. 3.

Requests for permission to reproduce material from this work should be sent to:
    Permissions
    University of Texas Press
    P.O. Box 7819
    Austin, TX 78713-7819
    utpress.utexas.edu/rp-form

♾ The paper used in this book meets the minimum requirements of ANSI/NISO Z39.48-1992 (R1997) (Permanence of Paper).

Library of Congress Cataloging-in-Publication Data
Names: Alvarez, C. J., author.
Title: Border land, border water : a history of construction on the U.S.-Mexico divide / C. J. Alvarez.
Description: First edition. | Austin : University of Texas Press, 2019. | Includes bibliographical references and index.
Identifiers: LCCN 2018055236 | ISBN 978-1-4773-1900-0 (cloth : alk. paper) | ISBN 978-1-4773-1902-4 (library e-book) | ISBN 978-1-4773-1903-1 (non-library e-book)
Subjects: LCSH: Mexican-American Border Region—History. | Mexican-American Border Region—Environmental conditions. | Building—Mexican-American Border Region. | Public works—Political aspects—Mexican-American Border Region—History. | Waterworks—Mexican-American Border Region—History.
Classification: LCC F787 .A48 2019 | DDC 363.6/109721—dc23
LC record available at https://lccn.loc.gov/2018055236

doi:10.7560/319000

For my mother, sister, Ružica, and Nadežda

CONTENTS

BORDER LAND,
BORDER WATER

INTRODUCTION

This book is a history of the United States–Mexico border told through construction projects, the built world of the border region.[1] Each genre of construction on the line has embedded in its physical form deep meaning about some of the fundamental dynamics of postcolonial North American history: the territoriality of the nation-state, the centrality of private property to capitalist accumulation, US economic and military dominance, the authority of governments to coercively regulate the movement of people and goods, and the conviction that both the unpredictability of the natural world and its "resources" should and could be bent to anthropocentric aims. The narrative in the pages that follow is about the transformation of border land and border water through the accumulation of structures, and the implications of these building projects for people as well as the nonhuman world.

The spaces through which the international divide passes are not well known to most Americans or most Mexicans. The majority of people in either country have never been to the border, or if they have, their familiarity is often confined to one or two border towns. This has the effect of making the border zone a hard-to-read space, a little-known area, but nevertheless a region that has often been both invisibly and overtly integrated into mainstream markets, politics, and institutions. The opacity of the border has been further compounded by the fact that when the border has entered national-level debates about trade or security, especially in the United States, it has often been discussed as a single place, a single thing.

The natural landscape through which the border was drawn defies this reductionism. There are six border states on the Mexican side and four on the American side, though contemporary ecologists divide the border region into six "floristic provinces," or biogeographic regions. The variation in flora is astonishing, including Mediterranean-climate grasslands, two lowland desert regions, two highland desert regions, semiarid scrub, and riparian woodlands throughout.[2] The region teems with highly specialized life. Also, the erroneous but often-held notion that the border zone is synonymous with the desert—and that deserts themselves are dead zones—is immediately refuted not only by the diversity of living things but also by even the most cursory study of climate along the line. The weather, too, is highly variable in the border region. The rainy months come at the opposite time of year in the big bend of the Rio Grande (the river is known as the Río Bravo in Mexico) and the west coast, and the driest month near the Gulf of Mexico still receives more precipitation than the wettest month in parts of the Sonoran Desert.[3]

The built environment of the border also defies reductionism. In fact, the heterogeneity of building projects along the international divide echoes the diversity of the natural landscape and speaks to border builders' recognition of the complexity and unevenness of the natural world. Hence, a common theme I develop throughout this book is how both federal agencies and private contractors have encountered the natural landscape of the border region and sought to respond to it through a built environment customized to its topography, composition of the earth, and hydrology. Every aspect of their work took the natural world into account, not out of a sense of communion or stewardship, but rather out of necessity. Building required local expertise down to the level of rocks, soil, sand, and sediment. In some cases, such as the first boundary surveys in the nineteenth century, construction was carried out in spite of the scarcity of water and extreme heat, while in other instances, such as dam building, the built environment was meant to sync with local environments and channel them toward human ends.

Construction took a variety of forms. On border land, early examples of building projects included survey markers, railroad crossings, and vehicle and pedestrian ports of entry. Surveillance infrastructure soon followed, mostly situated on the US side of the line. American immigration police first built lookout towers—the most rudimentary technology of observation—and eventually replaced them with high-tech, multimillion-dollar systems designed to detect vibration in the ground, body heat, and unauthorized air traffic. And finally, the long history of fence and barrier construction along the border includes dozens of different styles, configurations, and materials meant to impede the movement of humans, vehicles, and animals.

With respect to border water, construction often took less obvious manifestations, though in some ways was even more invasive and transformative. The waters of the Tijuana River, the Colorado River, and the Rio Grande bear little resemblance today to their nineteenth-century iterations. They have been dammed, channelized, canalized, straightened, relocated, pumped, and, in some places, lined with concrete. Even the composition of the water itself has been completely transformed over the course of more than a century of human intervention. Due in large part to high-intensity irrigation in drylands, the mouths of both the Colorado and the Rio Grande have been choked with salt for over fifty years. Diminished flows caused by massive diversion of water to crops on both sides of the line have created irregular plant growth and clogging in certain sections of the rivers, which in turn triggered massive, ongoing vegetation removal campaigns. And finally, especially around El Paso–Ciudad Juárez and Laredo–Nuevo Laredo, border industrialization since the 1970s has led to various forms of chemical contamination in the river that divides them.[4] Even taking into account the large-scale barricade construction authorized by the Secure Fence Act of 2006, border rivers have sustained more profound alterations due to human intervention than has the western land border.

It is not enough, then, to think of the international rivers as simply arcifinious frontiers, convenient, ready-made lines to demarcate the political geography of North America. The rivers have also been construction sites, and though the hydraulic building projects have differed from the land projects in both form and method, a common ideology has shot through the entirety of the larger border construction zone. Border building, taken as a whole, has been predicated on the conviction that the movements of both people and water could be controlled, influenced, guided, or halted by physical structures. Elected officials, soldiers and officers, hydraulic engineers, and others did not always advocate for *total* control, nor did they often believe such a thing was even possible. They did, however, usually subscribe to the idea that *any* modicum of influence over what they perceived to be intractable or undesirable movements in the border region should include a built environment of some sort. This ideology of control was also accompanied by an ideology of permanence. In the minds of those who erected the border survey markers in the 1890s, for instance, the obelisk-shaped "monuments" indicated the perpetuity of the nation-state itself. Similarly, for water engineers, dams and other river engineering projects often represented definitive conquests over the unpredictability of the natural world.

In the pages that follow, I lay out a *longue durée* narrative meant to capture the full life cycle of border building.[5] I explain how initial groundbreaking transitioned to greater and greater faith in the capacity to control the movement of people, goods, and water using physical structures, and why policing and waterworks were connected. By the 1960s, the boundary's built environment began to show increasingly obvious systemic flaws, especially with regard to border water. The response was more construction, which led to what I call *compensatory building*, or construction designed to mitigate the unsustainable results of previous building projects. Barren agricultural fields or those threatened by salinization, for instance, were side effects of irrigation infrastructure, the hallmark of early twentieth-century water engineering in both the drylands of the American West and the Mexican North. Compensatory building was also a response to unrealistic and increasingly punitive policies, especially those pertaining to immigration and black markets. Unnecessary and gruesome migrant deaths from drowning and exposure in the border region, as well as the unfathomable casualties within both US and Mexican societies produced by multiple "wars on drugs," were met with reckless and incoherent public spending on police barricades and surveillance on the US side of the line even as both governments established new ports of entry and refurbished and expanded old ones to accommodate the increased traffic generated by the North American Free Trade Agreement (NAFTA). The story I tell begins amid the breathless ignorance of exploration, and it ends in the willful ignorance of the overbuilt border of today.

Who were the builders on the border, and why did they dedicate themselves to the types of structures that have accumulated on the line? The US Army, the Immigration and Naturalization Service (INS), and its subsidiary, the Border Patrol, have been among the biggest builders on the international divide. The objective of these organizations has been to control peoples' movements by force, and through road building, fence construction, and the installation of ever more sophisticated surveillance infrastructure, they have advanced that goal. The built environment of policing demonstrates how coercion has been an ongoing component of the international divide's history and shows the extent to which that power, often state-sanctioned, depends on physical construction to exert influence.

Yet despite the history of barricading that now spans over a century, the border region has always been a space of movement. Since the end of the Mexican-American War in 1848, the border has been crossed hundreds of millions of times. The overwhelming majority of this traffic has been legal. Local border dwellers often cross the line nearly every day to work, shop, or see family. Those who cross the border as long-distance travelers have often been people from farther south in Mexico, headed to work in the United States. Yet the built environment of policing often emphasizes stasis, not mobility. And insofar as barrier infrastructure, especially in remote regions, argues for an interpretation of the border region that revolves around clandestine and suspicious activity, it disregards the complex set of incentives that have drawn people north.

Private industry has also shaped border construction. Commercial agriculture and mining stand out as particularly influential. Capitalists and sympathetic politicians have taken great care over more than a century to ensure the safe and efficient passage of goods across the border, first with railroads, then with highway systems.[6] Their objective has been to facilitate the accumulation of wealth and manage a cross-border workforce. Since the completion of the first cross-border rail lines in the 1880s, some of the most durable features of the border's built environment have in fact been perpendicular to the international divide. Truck and train drivers have also crossed the border hundreds of millions of times carrying commercial goods between far-flung locales. For them, the border line is a waypoint in a much larger continental system of exchange. In other words, though there is now over a century's worth of various border fencing and barricade building projects designed to emphasize territorial sovereignty, there is also a long and simultaneous tradition of building *across* the border. Whether in regard to moving heavy loads of metal and ore from the mines in Sonora to the foundries of the American Northeast; transporting agricultural workers from the Bajío to the fields of Texas, California, and beyond; importing electronics and vehicles from Mexican assembly plants; or importing contraband for black markets, all of this movement has been facilitated by built spaces—rail and road ports of entry.[7] From this perspective, the built environment reveals the extent to which long-distance markets have been a central force in organizing the border region, and how the westward push of nineteenth-century US history gave way to a northward pull in the twentieth.

But perhaps the most important border builders were not armed agents of the state or capitalists. They worked for the International Boundary and Water Commission (IBWC), an agency that was jointly established by the US and Mexican governments in 1889 as the International Boundary Commission (IBC) to adjudicate boundary disputes as the region became more populated and people dedicated more and more land to agriculture and mining. It was also responsible for the land boundary survey in the 1890s, the line we still recognize today. In 1944, when the agency was renamed the International Boundary and Water Commission, its responsibilities were expanded to include major dam construction along the border. It is unique among federal agencies in that it has a Mexican counterpart, first called the Comisión Internacional de Límites (CIL), and then in 1944, renamed the Comisión Internacional de Límites y Aguas (CILA). All official documentation of both organizations is bilingual, and for all major decisions both commissioners must be present.

Though the border region has often functioned as a police zone and a space for capitalist development, it has also been a site of contest between human beings and the natural world. The climates and rivers of the border region have been hard for humans to navigate and manage, and building projects reflect the difficulty people have had interacting with border environments. In this context, the IBWC emerged as a key agency. By the early 1980s, the boundary commission, often in concert with the US Army Corps of Engineers, the Mexican Secretaría de Recursos Hidráulicos, and many other government agencies on both sides of the line, had carried out twenty-six projects along the border.[8] From their point of view, the international divide was a blend of political boundaries, hydrological features, treaties and river laws, and individual construction sites. And even though the two sections of the boundary commission were federal agencies, they maintained intimate contact with their jurisdictions. They were headquartered not in Washington, DC, or Mexico City, but rather in El Paso and Ciudad Juárez.

Though other scholars have referenced it, the only historical monograph about the commission was published in 1941. The book's foreword identifies one of the study's central contributions as the explanation of the "political, economic, and cultural importance of one of the most intractable river systems in the western hemisphere—the meandering, vagrant Rio Grande."[9] The motif of intractability in the foreground relied on the widespread premise that the natural world of the border region was out of control, but with the right know-how, could in fact be dominated. Also, the river was described in the same terms often used to address the perceived transience of cross-border Mexican workers of the same period—unmoored, wandering, in constant and unpredictable motion. What is left unsaid is how this comparatively obscure, bilateral federal bureaucracy, prized by legal and diplomatic historians but more rarely discussed by cultural or social historians, came to play a central role in border policing, or state-sponsored measures to coercively regulate the movement of people across the international divide. One central purpose of this book is to make those connections.

The IBWC had multiple objectives, many of which concerned construction on the border. It was tasked with building dams for both electrical production and flood control to accommodate urban expansion and commercial agriculture. Commission engineers built two massive storage dams on the Rio Grande, akin to riverine construction carried out in the interior of the United States, as well as big damming projects in Mexican watersheds. Its engineers also devised ways to channel, canalize, straighten, and, in some cases, completely relocate sections of the Rio Grande. They managed massive excavations to clear vegetation and desalinate the Colorado and Rio Grande Rivers. They built sections of international bridges and maintained the border markers that were footed in the 1890s and even added new ones as late as the 1970s. And, importantly, the US section also constructed border fencing in collaboration with the INS and the Bureau of Animal

Industry (BAI), beginning in 1939. Though the IBWC had no policing component, its engineers supplied construction support to federal law enforcement. Not only were they instrumental in facilitating barrier construction in the mid-twentieth century, they also shared a variation of the ideological presumptions of border police: they aspired to control not people, but nature itself.[10]

Historians and social scientists writing about the US-Mexico border region have demonstrated how the border is a social and political construction. We have learned about the border region as a space of cross-border capitalism, finance, and infrastructure; a space of both white and mestizo supremacy; and a space of transit for labor migration. Historians have explained the evolution of vigilantism and policing to regulate these racial and economic orders, and social scientists have elaborated on how casting the border as a dangerous place carried with it political gains, and how these gains have been accompanied by expansions of policing, especially in the late twentieth century and into the twenty-first. We have also learned about the emotional complexities of migrants, how they expressed agency in unexpected ways, and how border populations have formed communities that spanned the international divide. And finally, we now have a good sense of the hypocrisy embedded in border regulation, rooted in the tensions between territorial sovereignty and economic circulation.[11]

Meanwhile, environmental historians writing about the American West and Northern Mexico, as well as social scientists whose work engages the nonhuman world, have explained the historical conflicts between rangeland science and ranching, as well as the related environmental degradation due to grazing. We now have narratives detailing the relationship between social inequality in the arid West and the rise of large-scale hydraulic engineering, the diplomatic tensions and legal nuances of water law and use as it pertains to cross-border rivers, and the development and expansion of large-scale capitalist agriculture in both Northern Mexico and the southwestern United States. We have seen the extent to which energy production and consumption has a racial component, as well as how hydraulic engineering expertise circulated between the American West and other parts of the globe. We have even come to understand the extent to which the Manhattan Project can be thought of as both a cultural and an environmental history of the border region.[12]

Most of these analyses and narratives rest upon the notion that racial hierarchies, class stratification, and environmental degradation are generated by specific policies and ideologies. In other words, the border and its environment are social and political "constructions," the products of human intervention based on deeply held beliefs in the premises of the territorially bounded nation-state and of environmental instrumentalism.[13] From this vantage, we can understand that the asymmetries between the stock categories of the border region— the United States vs. Mexico, Americans vs. Mexicans, the rich vs. the poor, depletion vs. preservation—are not found in "nature," but rather exist because political and economic policies maintain them.

Building on the insights of these diverse historiographies, this study offers a different but complementary perspective on the border. A core purpose of this book is to advance the notion of the border as a literal construction site. Whereas border historians have often ignored the built world, and environmental historians have often ignored the border, this book harnesses the contributions of these largely distinct literatures and places them into conversation on the international divide itself.[14] Paying attention to the built environment of the border can help us understand the way it functions, and for whom.

For instance, different kinds of border construction have been undertaken for different reasons. This is partly explained by the divergence, and sometimes conflict of interest, between police and industry. Railroads, roads, and ports of entry were designed to facilitate long-distance transport, whereas fencing and surveillance infrastructures were designed to achieve operational control over specific places on the border itself. Meanwhile, hydraulic engineering of various sorts was intended to control flooding and provide for local irrigation. This meant, in some cases, forcibly displacing entire towns and neighborhoods, but it also meant saving others from catastrophe. In these ways, along with many others, the history of the border region has in part been the history of tension between local spaces and far-flung connections, and the built environment makes this particularly legible. Who paid for each of these projects is also important. Many railroads in Mexico were financed by Americans, and the first large-scale border fence, constructed between 1939 and 1951, was built almost entirely by private contractors under the supervision of the IBWC, but at the behest of the INS and the Bureau of Animal Industry. All the major projects on border rivers were carried out by civilian and military branches of public agencies, though local residents made many minor alterations to border rivers as well. The built environment embodies the blurred lines between public and private goods, as well as between civil authorities and the armed forces. The built world also lends a physical form to the abstractions of sovereignty, the privatization and militarization of law enforcement, and the role of government in environmental degradation.

A brief word about what this book is not. It is not a comprehensive history of policing organizations or bureaucracies, but rather an analysis of what a constellation of government organizations and private contractors have built on the international divide. Is not a history of urban development of border towns.[15] A significant part of the built environment in the border region is the rapid expansion of urban space, especially on the Mexican side, since the 1970s. And though urban ports of entry make frequent appearances in the pages that follow, my aim is to demonstrate how they are connected to construction projects in rural and remote areas along the line to give readers a sense of the diversity of the entire border landscape, not just the cities and towns around the ports. On a related note, this book is not a history of broader building projects in the border region. The history of mining in particular, an extractivist industry that requires enormous capitalization, has produced one of the most important built environments in the border region and has significantly shaped the organization of cross-border space, though the landscape of mining, like the development of commercial agriculture, exceeds the scope of this study.[16] This book is not a diplomatic or legal history. Good histories of the sort have been written, both about border policing and about water politics.[17] Finally, this is not a story evenly weighted between the United States and Mexico. A history of building on the Mexican side remains to be written, seen from the point of view of the CILA. Also, as in other aspects of border policy, Mexican businesspeople and politicians have exerted influence in various ways on nearly every border construction project, especially those along the river borders where Mexican engineers and bureaucrats played a concrete, day-to-day role. Nevertheless, when one includes the massive accumulation of police and fencing infrastructure on the line, it becomes clear that the United States has carried out the bulk of border construction. I have followed the path of the building projects themselves, the majority of which have accumulated on US territory. Drawing on Mexican archives, however, I have tried to include the perspectives of Mexican engineers, communal landholders, and government officials wherever possible.

This book focuses on the largest, most technically complex, and most expensive construction projects along the border. A central purpose is to recover the heterogeneity and diversity of a space often cast as monolithic. I do this by focusing on multiple regions and attending to their idiosyncrasies while still underlining the basic concept of the border as a purportedly unified federal zone. Another purpose is to demonstrate how politics are embedded in physical forms. This is most evident in the fact that police have been among the biggest advocates for border construction. Law enforcement officials have often explained their activities in political terms, justifying their tactics in terms of national security, as measures either in concert with or opposition to commercial agricultural interests, as antiterrorist measures, or as public health campaigns.[18] From this perspective, a built environment analysis is a way of understanding the mechanisms of state power and the evolution of its targets, self-justifications, and side effects on people and the natural world. The structures that have been erected on the US-Mexico divide render these ideological presuppositions most legible.

Throughout this study, to help illuminate the nature of border construction, I use images, many of which were produced by the government agencies that oversaw the building. In this sense, maps, photographs, and blueprints function as political fragments, components of both border policies and institutions. Much of the visual material I reproduce here was found in the archives, some in the original, unopened boxes the IBWC sent to the National Archives and Records Administration. They were intended to be viewed by only a small subset of government employees, legislators, and subcontractors. As I explain in this book, images performed a variety of functions in these contexts, sometimes contributing to efforts to demarcate the international divide itself, while other times they were part of the process of choosing and preparing construction sites. Some, too, were used as confirmation of the efficacy of a given building project after the fact.

Some of the images offer a vision of the border unfamiliar to many readers accustomed to thinking about the border as an exclusively political or cultural domain. Hydrologists and engineers in particular often saw the border as a constellation of watersheds and geological formations, more or less ideal sites for surface water "reclamation" and dam construction. In these maps, water gauging stations and limestone classifications take precedence over human settlements and political jurisdiction on either side of the line. Even the US military and federal police understood that their operations in the border region required close attention to physiography, and maps they made reflect this.

Insofar as visibility has been an enduring theme in border history—government agencies' intention to patrol, guard, surveil, record, and monitor the passage of people and things across the line—we can also think of many of the images analyzed in this book as extensions of this preoccupation with sight. Maps produced from a top-down perspective in the style of Western (nonindigenous) cartography, as well as oblique-angle photographs taken from government planes or even satellite images, convey by their very position the privileged status of their authors. It is important to hold in mind, then, that despite the level of detail and care with which the majority of the images in this book were originally produced, that is, with great attention paid to the minutia of the environment and subtleties of place, many of the archival images exist to reinforce a particular vision for the border. They, too, are loaded with many of the same modernist and statist commitments to sovereign territory, science and technology, and anthropocentrism, as are the various pieces of the built environment situated out there in the border landscape.

The chapters are arranged chronologically rather than by agency or building project. This is because construction was often taking place simultaneously at multiple sites on the border, but toward different ends. Nevertheless, common themes emerge, and an overarching story materializes, despite the diversity of building sites. The book follows a long narrative arc that tracks the evolving meaning of building on the border from the nineteenth century to the twenty-first. Initial groundbreaking transitions quickly to overweening optimism, followed by increasingly obvious systemic flaws, and ultimately to signs of collapse. This is a story about the limits of state control, not its achievements.

I begin in chapter 1 by examining the boundary surveys of the

1850s and 1890s, paying particular attention to how the teams of surveyors wrote about the natural environment. I start here because these were the years during which the border was surveyed, mapped, and demarcated for the first time, and because it was the first moment of confrontation between agents of the state and border land and border water. This is key to understanding the roots of twentieth-century and even twenty-first-century border building projects, since many of the difficulties the surveyors experienced with access, climate, and topography would become long-standing motifs of border construction. The explorers brought with them deep cultural prejudices toward deserts in particular, and often associated those marginal lands with marginal people, including various indigenous groups and Mexicans. This kind of border racism persisted and is still with us. The early boundary surveys did not undertake very much construction on the border, but what they did leave behind is critical to understanding the history of border building. They erected obelisk-shaped structures they called "monuments." The second boundary survey, in particular, carried out in the 1890s, inaugurated the tradition of technological precision that would undergird all future border construction projects. The monuments were emblematic of this.

The Mexican Revolution was a watershed in the history of border construction as well. Like the boundary surveys of the nineteenth century, it predated the biggest and most durable building projects on the line, but it nevertheless helped established core paradigms that laid the foundation for US-side policing in particular. It was during these years that the US government first militarized the line. At the peak of the mobilization, 160,000 soldiers patrolled the border region. The US Army hired Mexican laborers to build parts of its patrol infrastructure during these years, but the military also faced a special new challenge. The 1910s were years in which the US armed forces were converting to mechanized equipment—motor trucks and airplanes. These new vehicles, despite their unreliability, had decided advantages over pack trains and cavalry patrols, and as such required new kinds of transportation infrastructure to accommodate them. Chapter 2 explains these developments and how, as a result, the army built roads throughout the border region to accommodate a hybrid force of animals and machines. These patrol roads, especially in very remote and inhospitable environments, established an important precedent.

The nineteenth-century vision of cartographic and topographic legibility merged with the military vision of geographic coverage, and both were foundational concepts to the history of twentieth- and twenty-first-century border policing and, by extension, police building.

The years between 1924 and 1954 saw the first big construction projects on the border. During this time span, the Border Patrol came into existence and steadily expanded both its enforcement authority and the physical infrastructure of surveillance. During the same decades, the IBWC carried out two major river projects: the straightening of the Rio Grande in the late 1930s and the construction of Falcon Dam in the early 1950s. These were also the years during which the first large-scale border fence was constructed, under the auspices of the IBWC and with the guidance of both the INS and the Bureau of Animal Industry. Chapter 3 explains the physical and ideological overlap between the control of people and the control of the natural environment during this period.

Chapter 4 continues to trace police and waterworks into the 1960s, a time of particularly intense building on the border. In a single decade, the IBWC orchestrated the resolution of a century-long dispute over the Chamizal, a small zone of contested territory between El Paso and Ciudad Juárez. It also built Amistad Dam, the largest concrete structure on the border to date; managed a massive vegetation removal program on the Colorado River; and created drainage infrastructure to desalinate the mouths of both the Colorado and the Rio Grande. Finally, in 1969, the Richard Nixon administration commandeered the ports of entry in an effort to ramp up inspections and stem the flow of illicit psychoactive substances coming into the United States from Mexico. The first three projects were done in close collaboration with Mexican counterparts. The last, called Operation Intercept, was carried out unilaterally, and was hence disastrously unsuccessful. In this chapter, the limitations of the ambition to control both people and nature become particularly obvious. Both environmental management programs and policing initiatives started to show signs that they could not be sustained without collateral damage.

From the 1970s to the present, compensatory building became the dominant mode of border construction. As I explain in chapter 5, building sites on and around border waterways after the 1960s were predominantly geared toward managing the negative effects of previous waterworks. Flooding, silt accumulation, and contamination that resulted from damming, canalization, and border industrialization were met with even more excavation, plant clearing, and damming. Though this type of compensatory building stretches back much earlier in the history of waterworks, riverine construction during this period came to have even more in common with police building, much of which was designed to accommodate incoherent, self-contradictory, and failed policies regarding immigration and banned psychoactive substances. Furthermore, the balance of border construction since the 1970s shifted away from hydraulics and toward a politics of interdiction, exemplified in the barricading megaproject produced by the Secure Fence Act of 2006. This huge addition to policing infrastructure was also accompanied, however, by the most massive expansion of ports and transportation networks since the transcontinental railroads, making it likely that all existing challenges would eventually be magnified.

High-profile people appear throughout this book, including various US and Mexican presidents and other elected officials who helped craft the statutory framework and treaty law that gave shape to the border. Federal agencies, the Border Patrol and IBWC in particular, also occupy central roles in the narrative that follows, as do powerful decision makers in both agencies. The history I tell in this book, however, is not organized around a common set of people or a single bureaucracy, but rather around the spaces of the border itself. Also, because other scholarship has given us such rich portraits of border crossers and border people, it touches only sporadically on the people acted upon by the built world, though whenever possible I have tried to capture the voices of the people who experienced these transformations of border land and border water.[19] More than anything else, this book takes as its common denominator a place—the corridor of the international divide and the border itself—unified not by its environmental or cultural characteristics but by the attention paid to it by builders. To explain the evolution of border building, the long timeline of this history exceeds the life span of any one human being, and indeed, even the life span of most of the federal agencies discussed as well. The built world and its politics tend to persist, in some form at least, across generations.

In that regard, this book also identifies another key feature of the border's built environment: accretion. Very little that has been built has been unbuilt. The railroads laid in the 1880s and 1890s still exist today, as do the dams built in the 1910s, 1950s, and 1960s. And highway systems and surveillance infrastructure have increased in sophistication, but have often been layered on top of previous iterations of roads and watchtowers. This is not unique to the border, but it is important to understanding one of the central ideological premises on which the border is based. Throughout border history, whether one focuses on the activities of various policing organizations, the water management projects of engineers, or the channels of capital, one encounters an aspiration toward permanence and durability. Border builders have often hoped that coercive state power, environmental manipulation, and expanding markets could continue to exist in perpetuity, and that the unforeseen ramifications of policing, hydrological engineering, and long-distance trade could be contained and also managed. These aspirations about the preservation of the nation-state as a political, territorially based form; continued dominance over nature; and perpetual economic growth are embedded in the barriers, dams, and roads of the border region. The history of border construction, however, and in particular the more recent history of compensatory building, prompts us to reconsider the meaning of sustainability in the context of the international divide.

1

THE BORDER ENVIRONMENT IN THE NINETEENTH CENTURY

It took half a century for federal officials from the American and Mexican governments to exhaustively survey the boundary dividing their countries, and even then, disputes about the exact location of the line would persist well into the twentieth century. After the end of the Mexican-American War in 1848, the US and Mexican boundary commission, as well as the United States Geological Survey (USGS), sent men to survey, map, and demarcate the common border. Over the course of fifty years, multiple expeditions set out to subject the land and water of the international divide to the rigors and exactitude of the most advanced mapping technology available at the time. As the technology improved in accuracy, so, too, did the precision of border marking. The first boundary survey, carried out by both the US and Mexican commissions between 1849 and 1856, was chronically underfunded, plagued by incompetence, overwhelmed by the logistics of the task, and limited by inaccurate instrumentation. The main result of the expedition was the production of maps—of both the land border and the river borders. The second bilateral survey, undertaken between 1891 and 1896, focused only on the border west of the Rio Grande, primarily a land border. The major result was the erection of a long line of survey markers. These obelisk-shaped "monuments," made either of stone or cast iron, delineated the western boundary and constituted the first durable built environment of the border line. Though border land had been thoroughly mapped and marked by 1896, it was not until 1899 that Robert T. Hill, a USGS geologist, first surveyed the most remote section of border water, the big bend of the Rio Grande.

In one sense, border rivers—the Colorado and the Rio Grande—were taken for granted as arcifinious frontiers. Neither government built monuments on their banks; the built environment on the land border was meant to make up for the absence of physical features to demarcate an abstractly drawn international divide. But in some ways, waterways presented far greater difficulties than land did. Rivers' uncertain and sometimes dangerous flows made sections of them all but impossible to navigate, and the initial survey of the Rio Grande generated the largest cartographic discrepancies between the American and Mexican commissions. To understand the twentieth- and twenty-first-century history of construction on the international divide, it is first necessary to delve into these nineteenth-century expeditions. These episodes, as well as the reports, survey markers, photographs, and maps they produced, offer a window into the ideological foundations of border building, many of which persist to the present day.

Much has been written about the first boundary survey from 1849 to 1856. This scholarship largely focuses on the tense diplomatic exchanges, controversies, and collaborations between the American and Mexican sections; lurid details of widespread incompetence; precise administrative details of water and treaty law; the legal authority of the boundary commission; and the technical details of nineteenth-century cartography and surveying.[1] Less has been written about the subsequent boundary survey of 1891 to 1896.[2] This chapter focuses largely on that second expedition, not only because it corrected many of the cartographic inaccuracies from the previous survey, thereby fixing much of the border as we know it today, but also because it left much more durable traces on the land. Building on the work of the historian Katherine Morrissey, I focus here on how the surveys left behind human-made constructions.[3] The 1890s survey, in particular, produced the first long-distance, systematic, and semipermanent built environment on the line—258 border monuments. The markers were both a response to and an anticipation of industrial and commercial expansion in the border region. Subsequent development in the following decades would require more construction projects of various sorts, all of which would depend on precisely delineated property lines. From this perspective, the marking of the international divide served two purposes: it established the limits of national territory for both nations, and for some individuals and corporations, it served as just one more property boundary in an increasingly complex network of land use and management throughout the region.

In both governments' original reports of nineteenth-century surveying expeditions along the border line, as well as historical scholarship on their experiences, the theme of environmental hardship is everywhere present; no account fails to point out the extremes of temperature and nearly insurmountable terrain. Put simply, without local knowledge, proper shelter, and sufficient hydration, it was extremely difficult to sustain human life in many parts of the border zone. The greater the distance from transportation infrastructure—established roads and railroads—the greater the risk of bodily system collapse. The hardships of the US and Mexican explorers in the nineteenth century, as well as how they wrote about it and described it, can tell us something not only about the climate, topography, and hydrology they encountered but also about the way they understood the environment itself. Their sense of difficulty was in part informed by cultural prejudices toward "deserts" more generally. Much of the language in both the American and Mexican survey reports is nearly identical in this regard. And, as I explain in the pages that follow, these biases toward ecosystems were also inextricably linked to cultural and racial ideas about indigenous peoples—again, both the American and Mexican commissions agreed on this point. American officials, however, especially in the context of the Hill expedition on the Rio Grande, held similar denigrating ideas about rural Mexicans living in the border region. Drawing on a Euro-American tradition of associating marginal lands with marginal people, Hill cast these Mexican border dwellers as *of the environment* and, as such, fundamentally outside civilization.

Surveys and explorations of border land and border water in the nineteenth century can help us understand not only the agencies, technologies, and methods that were instrumental in establishing the US-Mexico border but also how ideas about the natural world, race, and violence were tightly linked to the border region. Through the border monuments themselves, and through writings, reports, maps, articles, congressional serial sets, and photographs, the surveyors produced data that could be bent to the interests of both state and industry. They also produced *meaning* about the border region. The documents they created—textual, visual, and physical—come together to form a set of foundational arguments on which subsequent border building was based. The dominant claim is that the environment of the border region is extremely difficult to conquer, but it can be conquered. Similarly, the risks presented by border climates and landscapes were interwoven with the dangers associated with border people, particularly indigenous inhabitants and Mexican "bandits." From this perspective, the built environment of border markers was political, despite the monuments' remoteness from population centers, and not simply because they documented a political border on the land and were erected by federal employees of the United States and Mexico. They also embodied a particular ideological position about both nature and border people—that both could be regulated and brought to order through the technological precision of modern cartography.

BORDER LAND

In 1848, the Treaty of Guadalupe Hidalgo ended the Mexican-American War and established a new border between the two countries. Slight modifications would be made afterward, such as those resulting from the Gadsden Purchase five years later, and even in the twentieth century, the resolution of the Chamizal dispute altered the boundary line to a small degree. But aside from these changes, the border that was codified in the Treaty of Guadalupe Hidalgo remains the border of today. It would be several decades, however, before either the governments of the United States or Mexico or capitalists and engineers would begin building substantial constructions on the international divide. In this regard, the treaty created the border politically but not concretely. Nevertheless, the document anticipates building, both of transportation infrastructure and fortification. Article VI looks forward to the railroads, as well as many other corollary and subsequent transport routes, but also to an era of hydraulic engineering inconceivable at the time:

> If, by the examinations which may be made, it should be ascertained to be practicable and advantageous to construct a road, canal or railway, which should, in whole or in part, run upon the river Gila, or upon its right or its left bank, within the space of one marine league from either margin of the river, the Governments

of both Republics will form an agreement regarding its construction, in order that it may serve equally for the use and advantage
of both countries.[4]

And Article XVI, drafted in an era when the dominant armed force in
the border region was neither the United States nor Mexico, but rather
Comanches, Apaches, and other indigenous peoples, established the
right of border fortification: "Each of the contracting parties reserves
to itself the entire right to fortify whatever point within its territory it
may judge proper so to fortify, for its security."[5] Indeed, a constellation of forts and presidios, in various states of upkeep and disrepair,
already existed in the border region. Aside from this, however, Article
XVI anticipates future building around the line and the eventual evolution of what would come to be known as "tactical infrastructure,"
the law enforcement and military term for the border barricades and
fences of the late twentieth and early twenty-first centuries.

Despite the fact that the treaty established a new border between
the United States and Mexico, over a generation would pass before
any durable construction arose on the line itself. Between 1849 and
1856, American and Mexican officials surveyed the border. They built
fifty-two monuments to demarcate the boundary. The average distance between them was about thirteen miles, but some were as close
as one-half mile apart, while others were separated by over eighty-two
miles. Several of them were footed in the wrong place, inaccurately
demarcating the line, and many were made of field stones gathered
from the immediate environs. Of the fifty-two, only fourteen had any
kind of lasting inscription on them.[6] In other words, in keeping with
the lack of funding, poor organization, and weak lines of communication between the American and Mexican survey teams, the initial
border markers did a terrible job of marking the border. In 1882, officials participating in a boundary convention between the two countries came up with the idea of a reconnaissance mission to determine
the condition of the monuments and eventually rebuild the border
survey markers to last. The new boundary survey set out from El
Paso in 1891. But in the time between the two surveys, the border region had transformed in significant ways.

In the intervening years, a wider discourse emerged about environmental degradation. In 1864, between the first and second major

border surveys, George Perkins Marsh published *Man and Nature; or, Physical Geography as Modified by Human Action*. A philologist and diplomat, he is widely considered to be the father of the American conservationist movement, and *Man and Nature* was one of the first major books concerned with environmental destruction caused by activities such as large-scale agriculture and mining. He writes with prescient accuracy, anticipating not only the declensionist narratives of late twentieth-century environmental history writing but also the egregious side effects of the exploitation of natural resources:

> The earth is fast becoming an unfit home for its noblest inhabitant, and another era of equal human crime and human improvidence . . . would reduce it to such a condition of impoverished productiveness, of shattered surface, of climatic excess, as to threaten the depravation, barbarism, and perhaps even extinction of the species.[7]

His dire warning that continued environmental exploitation would lead human society to ruin is particularly compelling to consider in the context of early border exploration and building because it reverses the "barbarism" narrative so often associated with indigenous peoples of the region at the time. For Marsh, unsustainable relationships between humans and the nonhuman world could turn back the clock on civilization itself, revealing the greatest achievements of human societies to be ephemeral manifestations of overexploitation, ending in collapse. For the early border builders, or rather, those who assayed the land and water to assess its suitability for built environment modification, barbarism was instead the obstacle to the continued expansion of market economies and Euro-American political traditions. For them, it was the *absence* of large-scale human intervention, coupled with the presence of border people such as various indigenous groups and rural Mexicans, that constituted barbarity.

They held these ideas of developmental optimism in the face of an already staggering body of evidence that certain kinds of human-nonhuman relationships in arid lands were unsustainable. Between 1885 and 1887, for instance, the cattle industry in the American West collapsed due to overgrazing, and during the 1870s and 1880s in California, hydraulic gold mining washed so much gravel down from the mountains that it buried 39,000 acres of farmland, much of it laced with millions of pounds of mercury.[8] But instead of being downsized or halted, these activities were expanded as Mexican territory became linked to American territory. In addition to ranching and mining on the American side, important connections were made between the United States and the extractivist frontiers of Northern Mexico. In 1877, the Mexican government classified thirty-four roads in Mexico as "federal highways," stretching out over a total of 5,406 miles throughout the country. However, only 330 of these miles led to the border, and many were in terrible condition, passable only by mule train, not wheeled carts.[9] The two countries were unconnected to one another through durable, long-distance transport infrastructure overland, though some trade was carried out via shipping. In the 1880s, this all changed. In 1880, Porfirio Díaz's government awarded two concessions to American businessmen to build railroads from Mexico City to the border.[10] By 1888, two trunk lines snaked northward from Mexico City, the Central Line that connected to El Paso, Texas, and the National Line that ended in Laredo, Texas.[11] These railroads laid the cornerstone of the modern US-Mexico trade relationship. From the 1880s on, market connections deepened, and the interpenetration of the two countries became more complete.[12] From the point of view of American investors and capitalists, Mexico was emerging as a politically stable investment zone and resource frontier. For Mexican technocrats and politicians, the United States was emerging as a valuable source of technological expertise and capital. A new commercial geography was taking shape.

In the words of the historian Paul Vanderwood, the new railroads in Mexico "did not make the country modern, only capitalistic."[13] Huge regions in Mexico remained disconnected from the whole, especially the south and the Pacific coast, as even the northern border states were pulled closer into the American orbit. In part, land surveys laid the groundwork for the new systems of interconnectedness. Building on the Ley sobre Ocupación y Enajenación de Terrenos Baldíos that liberal president Benito Juárez passed in 1863, Presidents Porfirio Díaz and Manuel González oversaw the most massive privatization of land in Mexican history during the 1870s and 1880s.[14] The task of transferring public lands to private ownership fell to the Secretaría de Fomento (Ministry of Development), the same federal bureaucracy responsible for developing the railroads as well as modernizing agriculture and mining. But unlike in the United States, the initial surveys were contracted out to private companies that received one-third of the land they surveyed as compensation. The vast majority of these transfers happened between 1883 and 1893, and much of the surveying took place in the border states of Baja California, Chihuahua, and Sonora.[15] In Sonora, copper mining was revived, and the construction of railroad spurs and increased capitalization made it possible to extract and move the metals long distances for profit.[16] Also by the 1870s and 1880s, herds of cattle in the border region had become enormous, with some individuals' herds topping 17,000 head. By the turn of the century, much of the rangeland west of the Rio Grande was in private hands.[17] As Phelps Dodge and other companies sunk mines and bought up land throughout the border region, and as commercial ranching sprawled, it became more and more important to precisely document property lines.[18] In this sense, the international border of the 1890s was just one more property line in a vast landscape of extractive industries in which some Americans owned land on both sides of the line.[19]

In this context, precision, standardization, and visibility became the watchwords of the second boundary survey, which was the first to include a substantial building program. To the original 52 markers, they added 206 more. Of the final 258 monuments, 238 were cast iron, 36 were masonry, and all were designed to be, in the language of the official report, "permanent construction."[20] To accomplish this building, the boundary commission had to negotiate climates and landscapes in which human life was difficult to sustain.

THE DESERT

For those who participated in the survey of the international boundary in the 1890s, the desert held a very specific set of meanings, nearly all of which carried negative connotations. They saw deserts as distinct from other landscapes along the border, characterized by extreme heat and extreme dryness. Members of the boundary commission were afraid of the drylands, and they associated them with death by exhaustion as well as being killed at the hands of indigenous peoples. Loose sand and long distances between the border line and railroad tracks posed significant challenges for wagon wheels, as well as for the accuracy of their measurements and even their very senses. To them, the desert was an awful place inhabited by awful people, economically worthless and aesthetically hideous.

They referred to the area they surveyed as a "topographic belt" that included not only the international divide itself but also the swath of land immediately adjacent to it in both countries. In all, this strip amounted to 1,810 square miles. Within this zone, they distinguished between six different kinds of topographic features. "Mountains" occupied 360 square miles, "hills" made up 230, and the rest, 1,220 square miles, was filled by "valleys, mesas, and deserts." In this sense, the deserts were defined as the absence of topographic features, places that were "unusually flat and very uniform in slope." This mattered for the visual sightings taken by their survey equipment, since mountains and hills presented logistical challenges to setting up sight lines.[21] Despite these practical hindrances, however, as the historian Dan Flores has pointed out, nineteenth-century Americans were "prepared to see mountains positively," as they had long been considered an aspect of civilization in European cultures.[22] The desert, in this sense, was the absence of mountains, the absence of civilization.

Water, or its scarcity, was another defining feature of the desert. At one point, the author of the American commission report steps outside the scientific tone of the document to directly address readers ignorant of the hazards of arid ecosystems. "To persons unfamiliar with the deserts of the Southwest," he writes, "it will doubtless appear that undue prominence has been given to the question of water in the preceding description of the country along the boundary." He then emphasizes that making sure the expedition had consistent water sources "was *the* problem of the survey, in comparison with which all other obstacles sank into insignificance. To the traveler on the desert the all-important questions are: the distance to the next water, the nature of the supply, and [the] character of the intervening roads [italics in original]."[23] It is also important to note here the connection between water and the built environment of roads. The two-hundred-mile-long road between the Pozo Verde Mountains and the Colorado River, for instance, was particularly infamous for its remoteness. In that whole stretch of desert, there were only five "badly spaced" permanent watering holes, and the long distance from the railroad made rerationing by train difficult or impossible. This was a region they referred to as a "true desert," where almost no one lived or traveled due to the hardships the environment posed.[24]

This part of the desert was the only place on the line that the boundary commissions tolerated a greater than average degree of inaccuracy in their measurements. In order to place each monument, both the American and the Mexican sections calculated the position of each one based on their own tangents or auxiliary lines. If the points differed by less than 2 meters, they calculated a mean distance between them and took that as the "true position." Monument 191, however, in the "true desert" about sixty miles southeast of Yuma, posed a problem. The computations produced by both sections differed by 2.04 meters, slightly outside the margin of what had been agreed was an acceptable differential. Under normal circumstances, the surveyors from both countries would have had to take new measurements. They decided, however, that given the extreme challenges to human life and work in that environment, that would be the one survey marker slightly less accurately sited than all the rest.[25] The official report stated that since this case "occurred on the desert, where water was difficult to obtain, and where remeasurements would have caused serious delay, and as they exceeded the limit but slightly, it was considered best, in the interests of the work, to accept these discrepancies rather than to attempt remeasurements under such adverse conditions."[26]

In addition to the physical hardships posed by the ecosystem, the members of the boundary expedition also did not like the way the desert looked. The boundary commission report describes the Guadalupe Mountains on the triborders of Arizona, New Mexico, and Chihuahua this way: "For the most part bare of trees, they present to the eye a confused mass of peaks, crags, ridges, and cañons."[27] Interestingly, the report uses nearly identical language to characterize the Sierra de los Pajaritos, just west of Nogales: "a confused mass of rocky crags, peaks, flat-topped mountains with vertical sides, enormous trachyte dykes, steep, narrow ridges, and deep cañons, all mingled in startling confusion." The tone of these passages conveys a deep discomfort with the physical forms of the desert. "Confusion" is the dominant theme, as if these physical features were somehow out of order, willfully upending the proper organization of things. On rare occasions, however, the report finds things to admire in the desert. From the top of the Sierra de los Pajaritos, despite their incoherent geology, the commission reported that the "view is beautiful beyond description." But then a couple of lines later, returning to the theme of topographic carnage and the absence of transportation infrastructure, they pointed out that in "this entire region, probably one of the roughest and most cut up in North America, there are no roads and but a few blind trails."[28]

Desert plants, having evolved in unique ways to survive and replicate in arid ecosystems, also elicited both interest and revulsion on the part of the boundary surveyors. Most desert plants stay low to the ground and are relatively small to conserve the little water they take in. This contributed to the typically very long sight lines in drylands. The saguaro cactus, however, native to the Sonoran Desert of Arizona and Sonora, is uncharacteristically massive compared to most desert flora. In the area around the town of Sonoyta, Sonora, the boundary commission reported an especially high concentration of saguaros, some of which were reported to be nearly fifty feet tall. Their numbers and height made the area appear almost like a forest, but since the members of the survey teams' primary cultural and ecological points of reference were deciduous and coniferous woodlands, something seemed very off to them about that many giant cacti. The commission explained that they formed "perfect forests, if the word forest can properly be applied to a collection of the strange, ungainly, helpless-looking objects, which seem at times to stretch out clumsy arms appealing to the traveler, and which one cannot see on its native desert without unconsciously associating it with the uncouth forms of vegetation peculiar to the Carboniferous Era."[29] To their eyes, there was something that recalled the world as it might have been hundreds of millions of years ago, something ancient and primitive in the desert that grated against the image of a proper forest surrounding modern civilization.

The more common association with the desert, however, was nothingness. In some areas, the 1890s survey teams doubted that the original markers from the 1850s had ever even been constructed in the first place. When they departed from El Paso in 1891, the natural landscape challenged them immediately. Their loads were heavy, and the "yielding sands of the desert" made pulling the wagons difficult, compounded by the fact that there was no water for the first fifty miles of the journey.[30] It hardly mattered, they figured, in a place they subsequently described as a "worthless region, where boundary disputes

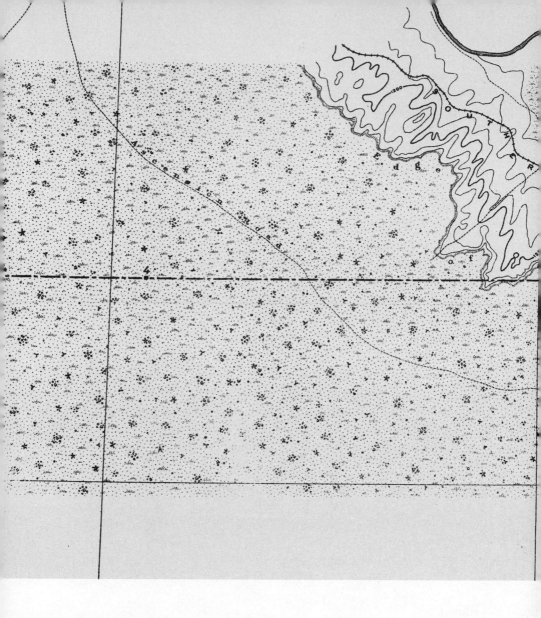

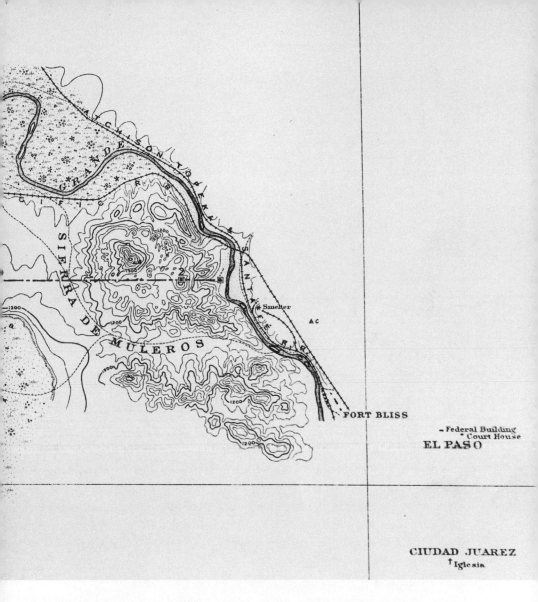

FIGURE 1.1.

Plano El Paso (detail), 1901

The geographic point where the western land border transitions to the Rio Grande river border. The mapmaker ignored the urban plans of El Paso and Ciudad Juárez, focusing instead on the physiography of the New Mexico–Chihuahua border land. Today, people call the Sierra de Muleros depicted here Cristo Rey. *Planos de la línea divisoria entre México y los Estados Unidos del Norte al oeste de El Paso, levantados bajo la dirección por parte de México del Ingeniero Jacobo Blanco, jefe de la comisión mexicana, 1891–1896* (New York: Impr. de J. Polhemus, 1901). Nettie Lee Benson Latin American Collection, University of Texas Libraries, the University of Texas at Austin.

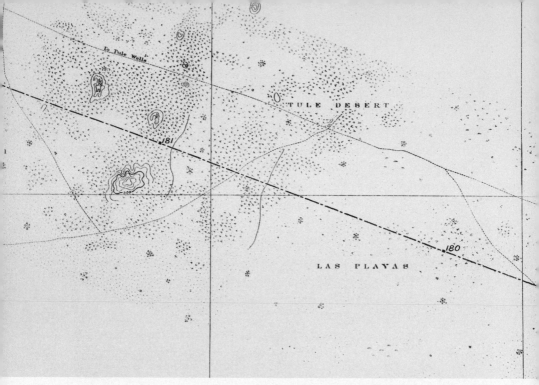

are not likely to occur."[31] They looked for Monuments 3, 4, and 5, ostensibly placed there by the first boundary survey. They could not find them, and concluded that "it is possible they were never erected, as no trace of them exists, and it is hardly presumable that in this part of the desert, where a human being seldom passes, man's agency could have removed them."[32] It was a space conceived as completely outside the human realm, and alongside eighteen others, this area was represented as a topographic map in a large folio-sized atlas of the border west of El Paso–Ciudad Juárez.[33]

The historian Katherine Morrissey has explained how some sections of these maps were produced using general reports, not actual field sketches, and therefore left out some specific details about certain ranches and very local land uses.[34] Nevertheless, the stylistic choices used to represent the desert in topographic maps provide insight into the surveyors' understanding of border ecosystems. A map produced by the boundary commission (figure 1.1) depicts the stretch of land through which it was so hard to pull the wagons and water the animals and men. The topographic map is a uniquely revelatory visual form. It contains, as the art historian Robin Kelsey points out, an "interplay of pictorial and cartographic habits."[35] The contour lines indicate slope.

They are packed most densely around the steepest mountainous areas, offering a sense of the terrain that historically had been the preserve of landscape drawing or painting. Uniform symbols representing scrub brush (in this case mostly creosote) serve as an abstract representation of the kind of vegetation growing there, the sort of detail often found in pictorial representations of landscapes. The outline of the Rio Grande, however, as well as of civic buildings and religious structures in El Paso and Ciudad Juárez, railroads, and the international border itself are cartographic staples within the purview of most maps of the era. Thus, topographic maps could simultaneously convey information on multiple levels about the surface of the earth. Beyond that, the specific details the boundary commission chose to include indicate the kinds of features they thought critical to representing the border region as well as the desert itself.

FIGURE 1.2.

Plano Tule Desert (detail), 1901

Topographic maps are ill-suited to capture the subtleties of desert spaces such as this, since the highly specialized flora of the region do not register from an aerial perspective and are difficult to represent graphically. Though the international divide is marked with the heaviest line, the footpaths and mule trails crisscrossing it would have been far more obvious features in the landscape. *Planos de la línea divisoria entre México y los Estados Unidos del Norte al oeste de El Paso, levantados bajo la dirección por parte de México del Ingeniero Jacobo Blanco, jefe de la comisión mexicana, 1891–1896* (New York: Impr. de J. Polhemus, 1901). Nettie Lee Benson Latin American Collection, University of Texas Libraries, the University of Texas at Austin.

The Rio Grande winds its way in from the north (this section of the river would eventually be channelized and straightened in the twentieth century, completely transforming this serpentine shape) alongside the tracks of the Southern Pacific and Atchison, Topeka and Santa Fe railroads. Adrift in cartographic space, the federal building and the courthouse in El Paso, the church in Ciudad Juárez, and the smelter are also included. The built environments of both capitalism and government take precedence, as well as Fort Bliss in El Paso. The inclusion of the army base is perhaps fitting, since, as Robin Kelsey explains, topographic sketching was central to any nineteenth-century military education.[36] The border monuments are also denoted by number, taking their place on the flat top of the mesa in that "worthless region." In addition to the core topographic, hydrological, and built environment features on the map, a narrow footpath, Ascension Road, breaks off from the base of the mountains and crosses the international boundary. At one point in the top left of the frame, interestingly, it exits the topographic space but remains in cartographic orientation. If one peruses the next few plates in this gigantic atlas, the viewer can follow the path of that small road as it crisscrosses back and forth across the border, ignoring it entirely, further evidence of the abstract imposition of a nation-state boundary in the midst of a single local landscape.

The verbal descriptions in the boundary reports reveal a kenophobia with respect to the desert. The western section of the Arizona-Sonora border region, the area of so many laments by the surveyors, included a place they called the "dreaded Tule Desert," also depicted in a topographic map (figure 1.2). Unlike the pseudo-forests of saguaros nearby, the Tule Desert was "a wide, waterless area dotted with extinct volcanoes and numerous bare, isolated peaks of black or dark-brown igneous rocks, which but add to the loneliness and desolation of the scene." There were mountains, but they were alienating, "composed of a bewildering chaos of trachyte, porphyry, granitic rock, and lava."[37] This area was also isolated from the Southern Pacific railroad running parallel to much of the border line, which forced the men to transport their water 102 miles from Yuma, the first 30 miles in tank cars, the last 72 in water wagons.[38] The language used to describe this desert also translated to graphic representation. The topographic map is almost entirely empty space, signifying the flatness of the land and scarcity of flora.

The desert environment also created optical distortions that interfered with surveying technology and warped bodily senses. The hot, dry air produced what people on the survey referred to as "atmospheric unsteadiness," which included various "peculiarities of atmospheric action," such as "differential refraction," and what they called a "boiling," or "vibration" in the air.[39] This could affect the accuracy of optical equipment, but it also affected the perceptions of the human eye and brain. The report complains that "on the desert the mirage continually mocks the traveler with deceptions apparently so real that it is difficult to persuade him that what he sees is a mere atmospheric freak and has no actual existence."[40] Various "atmospheric freaks" presented themselves, fallaciously of course, to the travelers. "Once a city with all its buildings appeared in a valley many miles to the north," the commission report recalls, "but the morning sun quickly resolved it into a number of large bowlders [*sic*], near the foot of a craggy mountain"—another disappointment in the chaos of desert topography. Desert fauna, too, were subject to phantasmagoric reconfiguration, as "it was also in the heat of the day that distortions of the size and form of animals generally occurred." In one instance, "a band of wild horses was mistaken for a herd of antelope, and followed for several miles as such before the mistake was discovered," and sometimes, "a jackrabbit would loom upon the desert with the apparent size of a cow, while occasionally the legs of animals would be so comically lengthened as to give them the appearance of being mounted on stilts many feet in height."[41]

But despite these incessant motifs of desolation, barrenness, and distortion in the desert, people lived there.

DESERT PEOPLE (INDIGENOUS)

For the members of the boundary surveys, not only was the desert associated with lifelessness and a dearth of recognizable geologic and botanical features; it was also associated with different cultural and racial groups. When the 1890s expedition realized that the previous survey from the 1850s had not measured distances between Monument 9 and El Paso, they weren't surprised, "when the difficulties are considered under which that survey was conducted." The challenge of aridity, a familiar refrain, was here coupled with a reference to the presence of other human beings in the region. The "difficulties," then, were both "the hostility of the Indians and the lack of water and other supplies in this desert region."[42] Certain kinds of people were *of the desert*, and the physical threat they posed to the outsiders of the survey teams were often linked to the threats posed by ecosystems.

On the Arizona-Sonora border, the Mexican section report points out that "this section of desert . . . was always a favorite place for the Apaches in earlier times."[43] These early times were terrible and dangerous for people living in what would become the border region. As the historian Brian DeLay has explained, northern Mexicans in the early nineteenth century wrote about how many places in the north had effectively been transformed into "deserts" due to incessant and overpowering raiding campaigns by various indigenous groups.[44] The numbers DeLay tabulated between the years 1831 and 1848 are grim. In that span of time, just before the first border survey after the Mexican-American War, at least 702 Comanches and Kiowas had been killed by Mexican forces and militias, and 32 had been captured. Though a staggering body count on its own, it was significantly overshadowed by the damage indigenous peoples themselves did. In the same period, 2,649 Mexicans were killed by Comanches and Kiowas, and another 272 were captured.[45] DeLay calls this multidecadal mismatched battle the "war of a thousand deserts," a term meant to capture the extent to which indigenous raiding had depopulated once-thriving Mexican settlements in the north.

It was in this context that the first boundary commission of the 1850s arrived on the newly conceived border line. According to the nineteenth-century Mexican historian Manuel Orozco y Berra, who wrote widely about Mexican geography, the Mexican section engineers had to contend with all manner of struggle during the 1850s expedition. In keeping with the well-established rhetorical tradition, common to both Americans and elite Mexicans alike, he linked indigenous peoples to arid ecosystems. "They lost their horses and mules to an assault by barbarous Indians," which he explains by pointing out that "the scarcity of resources hampered the small security escorts that were at risk in the desert."[46] He goes on to itemize their tribulations: they were forced to hunt for food sometimes; travel long distances on foot; withstand the intense cold of the winter months and the intolerable heat of the summer; try to avoid both fatigue and heatstroke; and contend with hunger, thirst, and sickness, as well as poisonous reptiles and ferocious beasts. Orozco y Berra wrote with an ardent nationalism, proud that the Mexican section of the commission had withstood these travails "for the national honor and scientific reputation of Mexico." The scene for this hardship was the indigenous desert; "our engineers had to struggle throughout their scientific endeavors against all the dangers of an immense country, a desert without water, occupied only by rough and wild tribes."[47]

In the years between the boundary survey of the 1850s and the survey of the 1890s, the United States and Mexico took measures to supersede indigenous power in the border region. Between 1877 and 1879, US Minister to Mexico John Foster tried to negotiate with Secretario de Relaciones Exteriores Ignacio Vallarta to allow American troops to cross the border at will if they were chasing indigenous peoples.[48] These negotiations went on for two years, during which time Vallarta protested that border patrols like this would ignite "old hatreds" among people living in the border region, and would devalue the "territorial rights of Mexico."[49] American officials were driven by an urgency to fully conquer the border region, and they were convinced that they had enough justification to cross the border whenever they wanted, regardless of Mexican protests.[50] Eventually, in 1882, the Mexican envoy extraordinaire and minister plenipotentiary, Matías Romero, and Frederick T. Frelinghuysen, the US secretary of state, signed a treaty that authorized reciprocal troop movements across the border. As the historian Rachel St. John points out, however, these military crossings were confined to areas considered to be unpopulated deserts.[51]

Lines of communication were also established between American and Mexican officials, such as between the governor of Sonora Luis E. Torres and the army general Miles Willard in Arizona. Due to the military border patrols of both countries, the ability of indigenous peoples to move freely, raid, and fight was significantly handicapped and in many cases eradicated.[52] But when the second boundary survey headed west from El Paso in 1891, the native inhabitants of the region were still classified as a threat. The US War Department provided a military escort for the team, including twenty enlisted men of the Tenth Cavalry and thirty enlisted men of the Twenty-Fourth Infantry, whose job it was to "accompany the expedition as a protection against Indians or other marauders."[53]

Part of the association between native peoples and desert ecosystems had to do with a perceived similarity between the sparseness of the landscape and the ability of indigenous groups to accommodate themselves to it. For instance, many of the arid lands in the Arizona-Sonora border region were home to people who called themselves Tohono O'odham, or "desert people," who had lived there as long as any of them could remember.[54] In stark contrast to indigenous viewpoints, the American and Mexican commission reports, though filled with hundreds of pages of scientific measurements, were at best full of wild and inaccurate guesses, loaded with cultural prejudices, about the deeper meaning of the O'odham homeland. It was a place the American section described as "a region probably as little traveled and as little known by white men as any in our country," which was accurate. The report continues: "This entire region is a hopeless desert, in which none but these hardy Indians could find subsistence."[55] The bodies of the survey teams were susceptible to the heat and dependent on proximity to railroads, and they imagined themselves traversing an alien, prehistoric, and awful world. The O'odham, in stark contrast, were *of the landscape* in a different way, somehow inscrutably part of the "hopeless desert."

From the point of view of the O'odham, they had indeed invented methods of sustaining themselves in the drylands. They developed specific ways of talking about rain, always hedging against saying anything would happen for sure, for rainfall in the desert is always a rare and unpredictable occurrence. And though it often appeared as an empty space to outsiders, the arid environment they inhabited was nevertheless stocked with mesquite trees, cacti, agave plants, and yuccas, as well as a range of animals that included bighorn sheep as well as jackrabbits. The O'odham used these flora and fauna as sustenance for hundreds of years, though they sometimes incorporated other resources, such as wheat, cattle, and horses from Jesuit and Franciscan missions as early as the seventeenth century.[56]

Amid these corporal challenges and cultural discomforts, the primary objective of the 1890s boundary survey was to build physical structures on the line. Unlike the border markers from the 1850s that had been fewer and farther between, sometimes inaccurately sited, and sometimes, seemingly, never built at all, the updated border monuments were meant to embody the regularity, accuracy, and industrial precision befitting a border region that was fast coming to occupy a critical role in a continental system of capitalist exchange. Visibility was paramount. They were never footed more than five miles apart and were positioned in conspicuous locations so that any one of them could be seen from the one adjacent to it. They were prefabricated from cast iron, serialized, and standardized.[57] Both the American and Mexican commission reports include a photograph that foregrounds a sample border monument (figure 1.3).[58] Behind it, lined up neatly, stand over a dozen more identical to it, all next to the El Paso foundry that fabricated them. The image seems meant to demonstrate to

FIGURE 1.3.

Monument Model, 1899

A line of prefabricated, obelisk-shaped border "monuments,"
waiting to be hauled out into the desert and placed in the ground.
The point at the top of each one would mark the exact location
of the international boundary; the monuments were footed half
in Mexico, half in the United States. *Report of the Boundary Commission upon the Survey and Re-Marking of the Boundary between
the United States and Mexico West of the Rio Grande, 1891–1896,*
Part II. Nettie Lee Benson Latin American Collection, University
of Texas Libraries, the University of Texas at Austin.

the viewer the survey's ability to achieve maximum uniformity, an interpretation supported by the fact that the photograph appears in both countries' reports. Each monument weighed 710 pounds and came with exact specifications for how to ensure it was securely erected. The composition of the earth mattered. In areas with soft dirt or sand, workers were instructed to mix exactly eighteen cubic feet of concrete to hold the markers in place, and where necessary, the monuments were bolted directly into the "natural rock."[59]

Getting this heavy material into regions far from transport infrastructure was very difficult. Again, we return to the Arizona-Sonora border region. The American commission report complained extensively about this area, which it identified as the deadliest part of the international divide. "It is hard to imagine a more desolate or depressing ride," the commission reported about the road between Sonoyta and Yuma. They had heard that during times when the road was more

FIGURE 1.4.
Monument 201, 1899

Shovels, one of the most basic tools of construction. Not pictured are the complex instruments required to figure out exactly where to dig the hole and insert the survey marker. *Report of the Boundary Commission upon the Survey and Re-Marking of the Boundary between the United States and Mexico West of the Rio Grande, 1891–1896*, Part II. Nettie Lee Benson Latin American Collection, University of Texas Libraries, the University of Texas at Austin.

traveled, over four hundred people had died of dehydration while trying to make the journey. In this landscape, there was "little to distract the eye from the awful surrounding dreariness and desolation except the bleaching skeletons of horses and the painfully frequent crosses which mark the graves of those who perished from thirst." In a single day's ride, the expedition counted sixty-five graves on the side of the road. This scared them, "a record probably without a parallel in North America."[60] Daniel R. Payne, the photographer for the American section of the expedition, took photographs of monuments placed in this region that offer more insight into the relationship between the desert border and border building (figures 1.4 and 1.5).[61]

FIGURE 1.5.
Monument 197, 1899

Hoofprints and wagon ruts in the sand attest to the flurry of activity surrounding the erection of Monument 197. Wind erosion would soon erase these signs, leaving only the obelisk and surrounding scrub. *Report of the Boundary Commission upon the Survey and Re-Marking of the Boundary between the United States and Mexico West of the Rio Grande, 1891–1896*, Part II. Nettie Lee Benson Latin American Collection, University of Texas Libraries, the University of Texas at Austin.

If government archives are, as Robin Kelsey suggests, partly self-promotional, designed to "glorify and reassure" the state itself of its efficacy, legitimacy, and perhaps even perpetuity, then both the survey

monuments themselves and the photographic album produced to accompany them are testaments to that position.[62] In the photograph identified as the "Yuma Desert" (figure 1.4), we see one of the few scenes included in the album that depict the actual construction process. Three men are gathered around the monument in the center of the frame, shovels in hand, sand displaced from digging. Deep wagon tracks in the soft earth in the foreground point to the interplay between moving heavy equipment and successfully completing the task of erecting survey markers meant to be permanent. Interestingly, the wagon tracks appear in several of the photographs taken of monuments in the Yuma Desert (see also figure 1.5) even when the builders are not present. Though these ruts in the sand were ephemeral marks in the desert at the time, no doubt soon to be blown away and disappear entirely, their inclusion in the official government photographic album gives them a second life within the visual production of the state. The tracks in the photograph serve as a semipermanent index, a trace of the construction process itself and the challenges the builders faced in desert environments in particular.

Sand was one challenge, rock another. The most extreme building site was Monument 153, in the desert of O'odham country. The survey marker was placed on top of a rocky outcropping called Pico de la Lezna, ostensibly for its resemblance to the pointed tip of an awl. Another photograph (figure 1.6) captures the process of hoisting the monument to the top. It required a technical ascent by a climber who carried a rope to the summit, anchored it, and then hoisted both men and materials up the nearly sheer face. The exact location on which they planned to fix the monument was occupied by a "knife-edge" crest, which they blasted off to make room. They bolted down the obelisk, five hundred feet above the desert floor nearby. It took them four days of "excessive labor" to

FIGURE 1.6.
Monument 153, 1899

Perched on top of a nearly vertical rock formation, this survey marker was nearly inaccessible to anyone without technical climbing skills. It was important to the survey team to produce a photographic record that could speak to their ability to conquer any topographic feature. *Report of the Boundary Commission upon the Survey and Re-Marking of the Boundary between the United States and Mexico West of the Rio Grande, 1891–1896*, Part II. Nettie Lee Benson Latin American Collection, University of Texas Libraries, the University of Texas at Austin.

accomplish the task.[63] Insofar as their objective was the maximum visibility of the monuments, this was a natural choice for a construction site. The metanarrative advanced by the boundary reports, however, suggests another, complementary reading. The continued horrified descriptions of the hazards of the desert are important not only because they reveal the cultural presuppositions of the expedition teams with respect to the natural environment of the border region but also because they help establish a story of environmental conquest. The border becomes fixed not only in maps but also on land, and the difficulties presented by the landscape itself serve to reinforce the capacity of the nation-states that overcame them.

Yet another purpose of the border monuments was to delineate space arbitrarily and rectilinearly across uneven topography according to the logic of the territorially bounded modern nation-state. As Robin Kelsey points out, "long, straight international boundaries were a rarity" in the mid-nineteenth century, a fact made clear by the oddity of bolting a 710-pound iron object to the top of Pico de la Lezna.[64] The more traditional approach to establishing borders was to use the contours of nature itself to serve as guides. The Colorado and Rio Grande Rivers acted as such, but border water brought with it a different set of frustrations, as well as similar ideas about deserts and the people who lived there.

BORDER WATER

The drafters of the Treaty of Guadalupe Hidalgo understood that the two border rivers were not necessarily fixed in the earth, but rather had the potential to shift course and, in places, run along multiple channels. Article V of the treaty offered a legal solution to these uncertainties by specifying that the international divide should follow the "deepest channel" of the riverbed. The document was silent, however, on what should happen if a border river changed course, thereby ceding territory to one country or another. For over three decades after the war, when indigenous peoples still controlled much of the area in the border region, and before capital-intensive, cross-border market connections had been fully established, the movement of the river borders was not a great concern. The 1890s boundary commission report, for instance, notes that "extensive projects for irrigating and cultivating the fertile lands of the Colorado River Valley and vicinity are now being promoted, but up to the present time practically none of this land is cultivated, except by Indians."[65]

The problem of shifting rivers became increasingly salient as the nineteenth century drew to a close. The boundary convention of 1884 between the United States and Mexico, incidentally held in Washington the same year the first cross-border railroad connection was finished at El Paso–Ciudad Juárez, established more specific protocols for what to do with unstable border rivers. It held that if a river's path changed slowly, "through the slow and gradual erosion and deposit of alluvium," then the international boundary would follow, but if it suddenly abandoned its old bed and opened a new one "by the force of the current," the border would remain where it had been, but on dry land.[66] In 1889, the International Boundary Commission and its Mexican counterpart, the Comisión Internacional de Límites, were established to adjudicate claims related to the river borders shifting, in addition to the task of resurveying and building monuments on the land boundary. Between 1889 and the early 1930s, when the boundary commissions began undertaking major construction projects on border rivers, their primary function was to resolve boundary disputes. During that span of time, over six hundred cases were brought to them, all of which revolved around questions of border hydrology. Most of the claims were relatively small, no more than a few hundred acres, but in total, the commissions' resolutions involved over 30,000 acres of land along border rivers.[67] As subsequent chapters explain, some particularly dramatic controversies, such as the Chamizal dispute in El Paso–Ciudad Juárez, resulted in massive construction projects. Even lesser known is the fact that the cartographic fine-tuning of remote parts of the Rio Grande continued until the 1970s.

By the 1970s, border mapping and building was assisted by extraterrestrial satellites and the full force of modern engineering expertise and materials science. In the second half of the nineteenth century, however, the process of delineating the US-Mexico boundary according to the paths of the Colorado and Rio Grande Rivers was an overwhelming confrontation with an environment that was in some ways even more intractable than the deserts. And despite the insistence on and commitment to technological precision and accuracy in

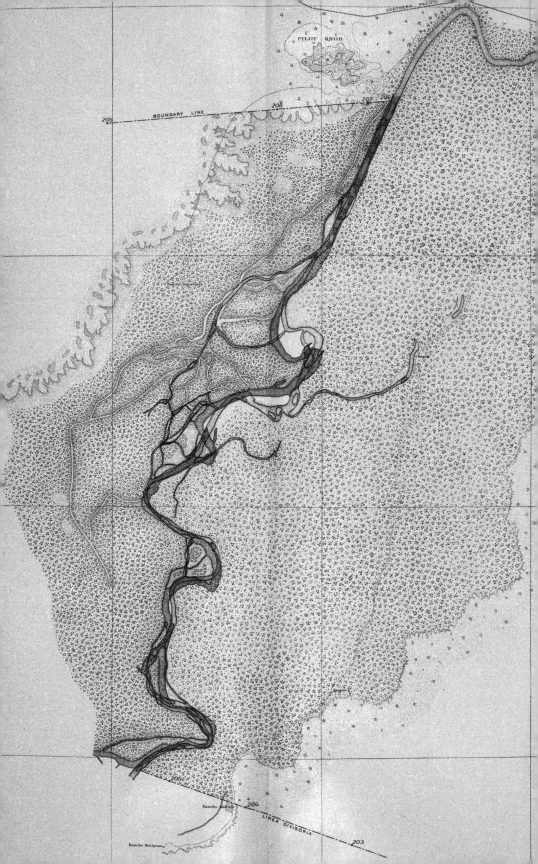

situating the border monuments in locations that corresponded precisely to maps, huge sections of border rivers were left cartographically indeterminate. The only color plate in the topographic map series
produced by the survey commission visually represents this concession to inaccuracy (figure 1.7). The historian Katherine Morrissey
explains that the American section based its drawings on fieldwork
carried out in March 1893, while the Mexican representation of the
river was based on the explorations of the engineers José González
Moreno and Manuel Alvarado in the following year. A consensus on
the exact location of the river could not be reached, so the map was
represented in color to distinguish between the conflicting versions.[68]
But unlike on the land border, where discrepancies could be solved by
remeasurement, the capillary forms representing multiple riverbeds
and arroyos testify not only to discrepancies in fieldwork but also to
the nature of an unfixed river.

FIGURE 1.7.

Plano Colorado River (detail), 1901

Before commercial agricultural
interests on both sides of the
border developed infrastructure to
control it, the Colorado River did
not follow a single path. Here, near
its mouth and at the tetra-borders
of California, Arizona, Baja California, and Sonora, the US and
Mexican survey teams could not
agree on the location of its channel,
so they made this map depicting
both versions overlapped. *Planos
de la línea divisoria entre México
y los Estados Unidos del Norte al
oeste de El Paso, levantados bajo la
dirección por parte de México del
Ingeniero Jacobo Blanco, jefe de la
comisión mexicana, 1891–1896*
(New York: Impr. de J. Polhemus,
1901). Nettie Lee Benson Latin
American Collection, University of
Texas Libraries, the University of
Texas at Austin.

The description of the earth around
the lower Colorado River as "fertile"
stood in stark contrast to the visual
representation of the area. To the
east lay the Yuma and Tule Deserts,
the most feared and loathed sections
of the journey. Indeed, the mouth of
the Colorado flowed through arid
lands covered in only the sparsest
vegetation. This is clear from the topographic detail—regular, nearly uniform stippling indicating mostly sand
and low-lying scrub. Nevertheless, the
boundary report's comments anticipated correctly that, with the 1902
Reclamation Act that opened the door
to the large-scale irrigation of the arid
West in the United States, as well as
the Mexican government's development of the area as a massive cotton-
producing zone, the region would
shortly be transformed beyond recognition.[69] In this way, the desert meant

something different to the boundary teams when the drylands were adjacent to major waterways. The inherent "worthlessness" of deserts could be mitigated, or even negated entirely, so the thinking went, by harnessing and diverting river water. This premise would drive border construction into the twentieth century, as well as the reconfiguration and commercialization of many parts of the American West and the Mexican North.

THE DESERT

The Colorado River border would also eventually generate much controversy between the United States and Mexico because so much of the massive discharge of that great waterway was diverted and consumed in the United States. The Rio Grande, on the other hand, was for much of its length an international river, forming around twelve hundred miles of the international boundary. The fact that it was a long border river brought with it many problems, some of which are explored in subsequent chapters. The first of them, however, was the survey of the river itself in the late nineteenth century. The river's big bend region in particular posed a far more significant practical problem for surveyors than any other area on the divide. Not only is that area a desert, but through much of it the river flows through deep canyons. The first boundary survey in the 1850s, which was chronically underfunded, mismanaged, and poorly executed by both governments, tolerated the most inconsistencies in the Rio Grande mapping.[70] The American section surveyed the entire river but did so mainly by traversing the adjacent land, not by navigating the waters themselves.[71] Much of their expedition traveled in Mexican territory, whereas the Mexican section of the commission surveyed only sections of the river.[72] The two commissions coordinated and collaborated even less on the Rio Grande surveys than they had on the land boundary, and their results were often mismatched.[73] The maps were accepted anyway, and the second boundary survey in the 1890s did not attempt to deal with the Rio Grande at all; instead it was preoccupied with fixing the mistakes of the first commission on the land border.

The first government-sponsored expedition through the canyons of the Rio Grande did not come until 1899 and was not part of the binational commission. Robert T. Hill, working for the United States Geological Survey, successfully surveyed 350 miles of the most impenetrable part of the border region by navigating the waters themselves.[74] In 1901, he published an article in the popular *Century Magazine* detailing the expedition.[75] In a marked departure and tone from his other published academic geological studies, the short piece is hyperbolic and melodramatic, which effectively gives a clearer window into popular prejudices of the day about both desert ecosystems and rural Mexicans alike. In his word choice and tone, he was intentionally playing, I think, on the presumption that his eastern readers thought deserts were exotic, God-forsaken places.[76] Though he spent much of his professional career studying the geology of the border region, and in this way was an advocate for the intrinsic scientific value of the land of the American Southwest, he nevertheless talked about the deserts as if he found them deeply repulsive, just as the authors of the boundary commission report did.

In awe of John Wesley Powell's storied surveys of the great canyons of the Colorado River, Hill tried to imagine himself as the Powell of the border. And in keeping with the narrative form of adventure writing, he made sure he itemized the difficulties involved in mounting the expedition in the first place. Pointing out to his readers that the stretch of river he was attempting to navigate had been pronounced impassable by the boundary commission, he detailed some of the logistics involved in building and transporting the three flat-bottomed boats he took down the Rio Grande. They procured the lumber in San Antonio, shipped it 150 miles by rail to Del Rio, a small town on the border, and there they constructed the boats. They put the finished watercrafts back on the train, this time headed west to Marfa, where they were placed on hay wagons that pulled them 75 miles "across the desert to the river at Presidio del Norte."[77]

For Hill, it was most important to convey that nearly everything about the desert environment existed completely outside the realm of civilization. "Every other aspect of the Big Bend country—landscape, configuration, rocks, and vegetation—is weird and strange and of a type unfamiliar to the inhabitants of civilized lands," he wrote. "There is no natural feature that can be described in familiar words."[78] If the assumed point of reference for the civilized world was a forested terrain, temperate climate, and largely rain-fed agricultural systems, the Big Bend country was indeed a world apart. Hill approached the topography of desert washes with particular aggression, saying that these "great arroyos are mocking travesties, which suggests that nature became tired of making this country before turning on the water."[79] This was not simply a different landscape he was describing; it was also somehow unfinished, raw and bare, but without hope of ever evolving into a more advanced state of being. The very hot climate helped fuel this pessimism. Hill wrote that "these great extremes of temperature shatter even the very rocks into fragments."[80] It was an environment destroying itself. Some plants were able to survive, however. He referred to these as the "spiteful, repulsive vegetation" of the desert, or the "mocking desert flora."[81] Hill was quick to note that "there are no true forests except upon the tips of the highest peaks," and that outside the canyons the men were surrounded by "merciless, waterless wastes of thorn," or the "horrible ocotillo deserts."[82]

In contrast to this wasteland narrative, as Hill and his team drifted day after day through the "weird desert," multiple federal agencies, led by Hill's own Geological Survey, were at work figuring out how to convert the arid lands of the border region into productive agricultural zones, effectively replacing the "spiteful, repulsive vegetation" with cash crops.[83] Already in 1888, before the second boundary survey had even convened, the USGS had begun building gauging stations along the Rio Grande as part of an irrigation survey.[84] They monitored rainfall, mapped watersheds, and measured discharge at various points in the river. By the turn of the century, nine stations had been established along the international river itself, managed by both the American and Mexican sections of the boundary commission.[85] Another seventy-six were placed at strategic locations on US rivers, however. These were monitored by American agencies, though there was an intense interest in discharge from the major Mexican rivers as well, especially since the Rio Grande delta, an area that would soon become a high-intensity agricultural zone, was supplied with 70 percent of its water from Mexican tributaries.[86] This work is represented in a map of the border river zone that is conceived not as a political boundary but as a set of drainage basins that could potentially be reorganized according to the interests of irrigated commercial agriculture (figure 1.8).

This was, in effect, the civilization narrative in a different form, insofar as society according to Euro-American models was synonymous

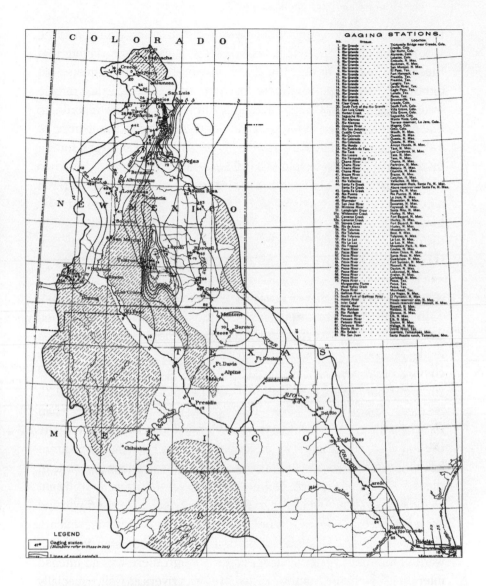

FIGURE 1.8.

Rio Grande Basin, 1915

This map of the river border was produced in the context of a US government document detailing water resources. This cartographic vision is uninterested in the political division between the United States and Mexico, focusing instead on rainfall measurement, closed basins, and the location of gauging stations that measured water flow at various points along the rivers in the watershed. Follansbee and Dean, *Water Resources of the Rio Grande Basin,* front matter.

with the exploitation of natural resources. But the environment itself was not the only impediment to realizing this vision for development. The people who lived there, too, imagined as *of the desert*, were also antithetical to civilizational ideals. Not many people lived in the remote areas along the Rio Grande. Excluding the more densely populated cities of El Paso and far south Texas, for most of the Texas border region the population density hovered just above 1.3 people per square mile by 1910.[87] The people who did live in remote areas, however, were often thought of by government officials as outsiders to both the American and Mexican polities.

DESERT PEOPLE (INDIGENOUS AND MEXICAN)

For the first boundary survey in the 1850s, Apaches, Comanches, and other indigenous peoples were the primary concern of expedition members. As part of that survey, in 1852, Second Lieutenant Duff C. Green and his men attempted to navigate the Rio Grande through the Big Bend area on boats, but they failed and had to cross overland through Coahuila instead, joining the river again at Eagle Pass–Piedras Negras. Though officially there to shepherd M. T. W. Chandler, a civilian magnetic and meteorological recorder whose task it was to survey the canyons, the group was effectively a military detachment organized around the expectation that a violent confrontation might take place.[88] Green was concerned not only about the immediate threat to his life posed by Indians but also about the economic and political threats the border posed to southern slave society. During his bypass through Coahuila, he stumbled upon a camp around Santa Rosa that was led by "Wild Cat," or Coacoochee, a Seminole elite born in Florida. Hampered by notoriously weak frontier defense in those years, the Mexican government had signed an accord with Coacoochee, as well as Mascogo and Kickapoo chiefs, to assist in fighting Comanches and others. What particularly concerned Green was the presence of so many "Negroes" at the camp. He complained that such a settlement was "very injurious to the slave interests of Texas, as runaways will always find a safe home."[89] For Green, the ever-present threat of "hostile" Indians, along with this gathering of refugees from chattel slavery and Native displacement in the United States, themselves convened to assist the Mexican government in its own wars of subjugation, interrupted both the mapping projects of the state and the economic project of forced labor. Indeed, as the historians Sarah Cornell and James Nichols have demonstrated, fugitive slaves from the United States sought refuge across the border when they could, even though the lives they encountered in Mexico were often fraught in new and different ways. Even in the early years of border history, we can see how mobility across the international divide unsettled social relations and disturbed elites.[90]

In a note at the end of Green's letter detailing his experiences on and near the Rio Grande, he flatly states: "I send a map which of course cannot be correct as I had no compass."[91] This is likely due to the destruction from floodwaters of most of his belongings at the beginning of the expedition. A "severe storm" caught the team by surprise, the water rose fast from runoff in the mountains, as it does in the desert, and they almost lost everything, "while the roaring of the water prevented any commands from being heard."[92] Robert T. Hill was determined to avoid problems like this. And by his time at the close of the century, the threat of indigenous peoples had largely vanished. At one point on his expedition he pointed out a small settlement near the San Carlos Mountains, "the remnant of a once famous, desperate tribe from which the creek and the mountains take their names."[93] Nevertheless, Hill worried about Mexicans. Like the reports of the boundary commission that associate marginal lands with marginal people, in part he establishes the wildness and barbarity of the expedition by casting Mexicans as bloodthirsty predators.

He set the stage for his readers by reminding them that the Big Bend area was "sometimes called Bloody Bend," and was known as a "'hard country.'" The river merely separated "this hard portion of Texas from a similar and still harder portion of Mexico." He reported that he had heard from locals that just below Presidio "there were murderers, thieves, and bandits, who would destroy any one invading their domain by shooting volleys at night into sleeping camps."[94] To him, the border region was a place of mindless violence, driven by motives as inscrutable as the desert itself. And the purported randomness of Mexican violence was met with extreme prejudice from Americans. At one point, Hill discovered that the local guides he had hired to accompany him had not joined the expedition for "scientific purposes" but rather to lynch a man named Alvarado they believed to be a bandit who lived along border waters.[95] The danger posed by border people was underscored by the nature of their built environment, too. They lived in "miserable adobe houses" made of "dirty adobe soil . . . made no less repulsive by the filthy pigs, burros, chickens, and other inhabitants."[96] Hill saw a lack of proper order here, just as he had seen in the desert, as well as an association between the human world, animals, and the desert earth that was far too intermingled to pass for civilization.

THE BORDER LAND AND WATER SURVEYS OF THE SECOND HALF of the nineteenth century were important diplomatic and technological milestones in the history of the international divide. They were also major confrontations with all aspects of the natural environment. The climate, topography, and hydrology of the area were all key factors for the movements and survival of the survey expeditions, as well as for the accuracy of their measurements. And aside from their hardships, they also brought with them specific culturally grounded ideas about the flora, fauna, and human beings who occupied the deserts. They did not like what they found, and they inaugurated a long tradition of not only physical construction on the line but also skepticism, dismissiveness, and revulsion about desert environments and people. In the survey markers themselves—the monuments—we can read the political and scientific projections of modern nation-states, as well as industry and agriculture, that sought to convert the region into a zone of government control and profit. New kinds of police bureaucracies emerged in the 1920s that sought to build surveillance infrastructure and fencing on the border, and new engineering expertise made it possible to control the movement of surface water on the border like never before. In the interim, however, the outbreak of the Mexican Revolution in 1910 threatened to undo the economic and political groundwork laid down between the United States and Mexico. Drawing on many of the same assumptions about border environments and border people, the US Army militarized the border, and in so doing further expanded the built environment of the international divide.

2

THE BORDER AND
THE MEXICAN REVOLUTION

B etween 1910 and 1920, a revolution unfolded in Mexico. The conflict was driven by multiple factors, from elite political dissatis-
faction to uprisings from below.[1] Scholars estimate that as many as
1 million people died in the fighting. In addition to the great loss of
life, this was also a time of rapidly increased movement across the
US-Mexico border in both directions. Many of those who weren't
caught up in the fighting fled to the United States as refugees, just as
some Americans in border towns rushed to sell armaments to various
factions in Mexico. Amid this violence and confusion, Presidents
William Howard Taft and Woodrow Wilson militarized the border.
By 1917, there were 160,000 American troops on the line, the largest
domestic military mobilization since the Civil War. The purpose of the
troops was varied. At first, the soldiers' job was to enforce neutrality
laws, which meant policing American arms dealers who were profiteer-
ing from unauthorized weapons shipments south. As the decade wore
on, the Wilson administration chose a favorite in Venustiano Carranza.
Carranza was a former governor of Coahuila and military leader who
became head of state in 1914, was recognized by the United States in
1915, then presided over the Constitutional Convention in 1917. He
subsequently served as president until 1920. His ascendance to power
fractured his alliance with Pancho Villa, which led to what the historian Friedrich Katz calls Villa's "savage and bloody guerilla struggle in
Chihuahua."[2] As border towns became more violent, caught up in the
internecine struggle, the US military on the line shifted its focus away
from American arms dealers and worked to prevent incursions, raids,
and other cross-border activity they often called "banditry."

Much has been written about the Mexican Revolution, and scholars still debate the extent to which it was a popular uprising or a struggle among elites, as well as what kind of a legacy it left for twentieth-century Mexican politics and society.[3] The purpose of this chapter, however, is neither to rehash a narrative of the conflict nor to offer an interpretation of it. Rather, my aim is to explain how the revolution related to the built environment of the border region and to the American military deployment there. It was a time of reciprocal destruction and building in the border region. In the northern Mexican border states, various factions of combatants destroyed many hundreds of railroad bridges, and though private industry and government entities worked tirelessly to rebuild them, they were quickly destroyed again as the fighting continued throughout the decade. Meanwhile, on the American side, the US Army built, expanded, or repurposed hundreds of miles of patrol roads to move equipment and men to remote regions along the line. Both the demolition and construction were part of similar dynamics tied to American foreign investment and capital in Mexico. The railroad destruction and repair, alongside road building, also demonstrate the extent to which transport infrastructure was linked to both market integration and militarism in the border region.

The political complexities and geographies of the Mexican Revolution are legion. In the pages that follow, two key facts are especially pertinent to the analysis. The first has to do with leadership. The schism between Carranza and Villa led the latter to attack Columbus, New Mexico, in 1916. Villa hoped this would provoke a US military intervention in Mexico that would destabilize Carranza's government. The United States did in fact invade: General John Pershing led seven thousand men on a "Punitive Expedition" into Mexican territory. This produced great tension between Wilson's and Carranza's governments but did not ultimately lead to outright war between the two countries. It also failed to achieve its stated goal; they never found Villa. Nevertheless, from the perspective of the US Army, it provided a valuable proving ground for the troops to learn how to operate newly invented mechanized vehicles and build ephemeral infrastructure in remote arid regions. So even though the expedition never met its official objective, the experience of moving men and equipment through Mexican hinterlands proved a valuable exercise that enhanced the overall military capacity in the border region.

The second key fact, related to the first, is that much of the military activity during the revolution took place in the border region. Chihuahua, in particular, was the epicenter of the violence.[4] In that huge state, Pancho Villa built an army, the División del Norte, composed of the men who had once worked on the railroads, on the ranches, and in the mines of Chihuahua and neighboring regions. At its height, the Northern Division counted 50,000 professional soldiers, most likely the largest revolutionary force Latin America has ever seen.[5] The Pershing expedition, too, spent most of its time in Chihuahua. On the US side, military border patrols worked in very close proximity to the international boundary throughout the revolution. They fanned out from various bases, achieving remarkable geographic coverage in regions distant from established transportation infrastructure.

I argue that it was during these years, before the advent of the US Border Patrol, that the border region was first converted into a modern militarized police zone. As in chapter 1, where I examine the second half of the nineteenth century to explain how government officials from both countries confronted and imagined arid landscapes and border people in anticipation of future development, this chapter also provides a foundation for understanding the origins of large-scale twentieth-century building projects. The prejudice and distrust US state institutions often held toward border environments and desert dwellers was amplified during the Mexican Revolution. The Chihuahuan Desert, in particular, was both a site of conflict in the revolution and a patrol landscape for American troops on the border. American officers and soldiers focused on the difficult access, climatic extremes, and aridity of this region, and often associated the hardships of their duty with the unpredictability of the Mexican conflict and even Mexicans themselves. The desert was also cast as a useful training ground that could help the US military better prepare for future wars abroad. And though the major building projects of the twentieth century had yet to begin, the mechanized reconnaissance missions the US Army developed during the conflict, alongside remote patrolling maneuvers and aerial surveillance, all established templates for how to engage militaristically with the border region. Variations on these tactics persist to the present day, accompanied by a more durable built environment of policing.

MILITARIZATION

The Mexican Revolution brought an abrupt end to the Porfiriato, the three and a half decades between 1876 and 1911 when one man, Porfirio Díaz, dominated the Mexican government and economy.[6] He had been instrumental in bringing about political stability, at least compared to the tumultuous half century since Mexican independence. He invited significant foreign investment into Mexico to expand markets. Much of this development was propelled by the United States, Germany, and Great Britain.[7] During his multiple administrations, a heavily capitalized landscape emerged in the border region and beyond, largely oriented around railroads and mining. When the fighting started in Mexico, 61.7 percent of American investments in Mexico were in railroads, totaling $644,300,000, and 23.9 percent were in mines, valued at $249,500,000.[8] And as the historian Richard White argues in his study of North American railroads, the trunk lines of both Western Canada and Northern Mexico cannot be "unhooked" from the American transcontinentals; they formed a single, cross-border network that spanned the continent.[9] This connectivity, in turn, facilitated a massive extension and expansion of the resource frontier of the American West.

Even in remote areas far from official railroad ports, capitalists and entrepreneurs built cross-border infrastructure. The Boquillas cable line is a good example. Used before and during the Mexican Revolution, it was a conduit that connected the Puerto Rico Mine in the far north of Coahuila to American transportation infrastructure in the Big Bend region. A series of high wooden trestles supported almost eight miles of metal cable, three miles of which were in Mexican territory and five in Texas. W. D. Smithers, a photographer obsessed with documenting nearly every aspect of the border region between Texas, Chihuahua, and Coahuila, took thousands of photographs in this area during the first half of the twentieth century. Several of them figure prominently in this chapter, as they offer an invaluable vision of the border region that often reveals a level of nuance and detail difficult to find in textual records. In one of his early photographs, he is standing atop one of the trestles as the cable line stretched across the Chihuahuan Desert scrubland (figure 2.1). In the center of the frame, a large bucket used to haul zinc, silver, and lead ore is hoisted over a

desert floor sparsely dotted with creosote bushes. Once the material reached the American side, it was loaded onto pack mules and carried about eighty miles to Marathon, Texas, which took about two days. From there it was loaded onto train cars on the Southern Pacific line and moved west to the El Paso smelter.[10] At first blush, this might appear to some viewers as a remote desert

FIGURE 2.1.
Boquillas Cable, ca. 1928

The mine ceased operations in 1919, twenty-five years before Big Bend National Park was established in 1944. The ruins of many of the trestles are still there today, as are many of the cables and buckets, all of which are too heavy to have moved very far from the original path of the tramway. W. D. Smithers Collection of Photographs, Harry Ransom Center, the University of Texas at Austin.

curiosity. Indeed, it was the geographic isolation of this mine from major transportation infrastructure that necessitated the laborious construction of a pulley system in this area. Nevertheless, I argue that it is precisely the remoteness of this cable operation that testifies to the scope of foreign-controlled extractivism in Mexico that had been greatly accelerated and expanded by Porfirian policies.

For instance, in 1884, the year the first cross-border railroad lines were completed at El Paso–Ciudad Juárez, American businessmen had interests in 40 mining sites throughout Mexico. In eight years that number had grown to 2,383, and by the beginning of the Mexican Revolution, 81 percent of the capital in the Mexican mining industry was American capital, and Americans owned seventeen of the thirty-one largest operations in the country.[11] This investment and ownership created an economic system that depended on a massive overland cross-border movement of goods, especially from enclave economies like the Cananea Copper Mine in Sonora.[12] By 1910, thirty-one American companies owned almost 16 million acres in Chihuahua alone, or around one-quarter of the largest state in Mexico.[13] When the fighting broke out, Mexico was transformed from a predictable destination for American and other foreign investment to one of the most volatile and unstable nations in the hemisphere.

The value and extent of American interests in Mexico, a geographically contiguous country, led both the Taft and Wilson administrations to militarize the two-thousand-mile-long border. The number of troops sent to the border fluctuated dramatically, as did their posts and patrols. The logic that governed their purpose along the international divide shifted three times over the course of the revolution. In the first years, from late 1911 to early 1915, the US armed forces patrolled the border in large part to enforce US neutrality.[14] In this period, the army acted as a *posse comitatus*; it supported and cooperated with civilian law enforcement agencies and was largely preoccupied with domestic policing. From 1915 to early 1917, the military shifted toward a defense paradigm in response to increased violence along the border. This included Pershing's intervention in Chihuahua and Durango.[15] The increase in raiding is most directly traceable to the breakdown of the alliance between Venustiano Carranza and Pancho Villa, Carranza's former ally turned guerrilla fighter. And from 1917 to 1920, the United States maintained troops along the border, but by then Carranza had achieved relative stability and drafted a new constitution, and the United States had joined the Great War.[16]

In 1910, in the first days of the revolution, there were 11,401 US soldiers stationed in the Army Departments of California, Colorado, and Texas.[17] None of them were tasked with patrolling the US-Mexico border. The boundary of the Army Department of California did not even extend down to the international divide, and its forces were nearly all oriented toward the insular possessions and territories of the Philippines and Hawai'i. The Department of Colorado, with its forts in northern New Mexico and Arizona, was still preoccupied with the activities of indigenous peoples. By 1911, however, the secretary of war declared that "the most noteworthy military activity of the year was the mobilization of troops in Texas." By summer, these infantry, artillery, and cavalry units had fanned out along the entire border, and their numbers had swelled to over 20,000.[18]

This land mobilization was matched at sea. On March 6, 1911, the warships and support vessels of the US Navy were scattered up and down the coasts of California, the mid-Atlantic, and Central America. The Pacific fleet had ships docked in the San Francisco Bay, as well as in Los Angeles. The Atlantic fleet's vessels were stationed at various points along the coasts of the Northeast, from Brooklyn to Boston, as well as Pensacola, Florida, and Puerto Cortés, Honduras. Most were sitting at naval bases, going about business as usual. It had been over ten years since many of them had been called upon to fight in the Spanish-American War. Most, however, were freshly laid down, never field-tested. The next day, on March 7, these far-flung shipyards sprang to life as thousands of marines and seamen scrambled along the docks preparing to converge on two major points: San Diego, California, and Guantánamo Bay, Cuba. That was the day over twenty commanding officers of as many ships received urgent, confidential telegrams from Assistant Secretary of the Navy Beekman Winthrop. Every message began the same way: "Trouble with Mexico is probable."[19]

The largest armored cruisers, such as the USS *Tennessee* and the USS *California*, each with complements of over 800 officers and enlisted men, mobilized overnight. These two flagships were supported by at least eighteen other auxiliary cruisers, dreadnought battleships, destroyer tenders, light and protected cruisers, gunboats, stores ships, and hospital ships that carried a total of more than 7,300 men. This arsenal was intended, according to Winthrop, more as an insurance policy than anything else. In a confidential telegram to the commanding officer of the USS *California*, he declared that a "general insurrection in Mexico is probable. It will be necessary to protect American interests, to prevent importation of arms and ammunition and possibly to land force."[20]

The US military on the land border, in conjunction with customs agents and immigration inspectors, constantly monitored Mexican troop movements, their numbers, and the kinds of weapons they used. Almost daily telegraphs clicked out messages from nearly every major border port of entry back to Washington, detailing the unfolding events on the Mexican side. American forces reorganized themselves according to the changing geography of violence, constantly varying their numbers along the line to correspond to the most unstable regions in Northern Mexico. This was mostly precautionary, however, in the early years of the revolution; the vast majority of the American troops' energy was spent on coordinated support and cooperation with civilian law enforcement officials.

The US government and military also collaborated closely with Francisco Madero, the first leader of the Mexican government during the revolution. In 1911, Madero asked the United States to enforce its neutrality laws in an effort to stem the flow of arms to his onetime ally Pascual Orozco.[21] In March of 1912, Congress enacted a joint resolution to amend the existing neutrality laws. That same year, a subcommittee of the Committee on Foreign Relations in the Senate was already interviewing businessmen along the border to try to figure out how well US neutrality was actually being practiced. Six senators, chaired by William Alden Smith of Michigan, traveled to El Paso, Texas, in September 1912. They spent just over four months in El Paso; Washington, DC; and New Orleans questioning 147 witnesses, all of whom had deep interests in Mexico, especially in mining operations, cattle ranching, and oil. The subcommittee's question was always the same: "Have you any information that will help the committee in determining whether any persons, associations, or corporations, domiciled in or owing allegiance to the United States, have heretofore been or are now engaged in fomenting, inciting, encouraging, or financing rebellion, insurrection, or other flagrant disorder in Mexico against the lawful, organized government of that country?"[22]

The two biggest arms dealers in El Paso were the Krakauer, Zork and Moye Hardware Company and Shelton Payne Arms Company. Representatives from both these firms testified at the hearing, and they were all cagey in their responses, careful not to admit to willful violation of the neutrality laws. Adolph Krakauer, the owner of Krakauer, Zork and Moye, was an unapologetic "Díaz man," and seemed chagrined to think that his guns, ammunition, and dynamite ended up in the hands of Madero's revolutionary troops. Nevertheless, he answered with the same "it's none of my business" argument border arms dealers would also make during the twenty-first-century drug wars. He said, "For all I know, some of these cartridges that were bought may have been for the Madero government. I do not know. I was not supposed to know. It was not my business to know. I took very good care not to know; but our business is supplying arms and ammunition, it has been for the last 25 years, and I do not propose on account of this revolution to stop it." His son Robert was even more vague and obfuscating: "We made a great many sales of arms and ammunition in the course of our business to individuals who came in and paid their money for it. Where they eventually went we do not know and did not inquire."[23]

Before the arms embargo, D. M. Payne of Shelton Payne Arms had made nearly $150,000 selling .30-30 Winchester rifles, cartridges, machine guns, pistols, rifle and pistol scabbards, belts, saddles, cartridge bags, and Mannlicher rifles to Madero's government via the consul in El Paso, though he also sold guns to Pascual Orozco's anti-Madero front.[24] When the committee adjourned on January 9, 1913, Francisco Madero had only a few weeks left to live before his eventual assassination. The senators often referred to the "lawful, organized government of that country," which referred to Madero's new government, and throughout the hearings, they often spoke of "two" revolutions: Madero's initial overthrow of Porfirio Díaz and the counterrevolutions that challenged Madero's legitimacy. Satisfied with Madero as the Mexican head of state and interested above all in the stability of the country, they were interested in who, if anyone, was running guns and money to counterrevolutionaries.[25]

On the border, an onslaught of weapons seizures had begun. Customs agents in the spring of 1911 seized twenty-four Mausers at nearly the same time as Secret Service agents confiscated fifty-six rifles and 250,000 cartridges in Presidio, Texas.[26] The following summer the Fourth Cavalry stopped a shipment of 50,000 cartridges at Columbus, New Mexico, and customs officers at Eagle Pass, Texas, seized more rifles and 4,000 rounds.[27] In the winter of 1913, the army stopped another 8,000 rounds from going south at Presidio, Texas.[28] Collaboration between civil law enforcement and the military was the rule, a fact that a US attorney in Texas praised: "The military and Texas Rangers act in harmonious conjunction with quite a degree of efficiency, finding quantities of Mauser rifle ammunition and military equipment."[29]

The soldiers' task, first and foremost, was to assist civil authorities in the enforcement of neutrality laws.[30] This meant preventing guns and ammunition from moving south.[31] In other words, the army was on the border in large part to police the activities of American citizens, especially gunrunners.[32] This support role is also evident in the hugely increased workload of the Department of Justice. On March 14, 1912, Taft prohibited the export of coal or any material used in war, arms, and munitions of war into Mexico, and newly elected President Woodrow Wilson said in a speech to both houses of Congress on September 27, 1913, that he would "follow the best practice of nations in the matter of neutrality by forbidding the exportation of arms or munitions of war of any kind from the United States to any part of the Republic of Mexico."[33] As a result, the attorney general assumed, in his own words, a "very large amount of work along the border between that country [Mexico] and the states of Texas, Arizona, and New Mexico."[34] The year 1913, in particular, brought a "large number of criminal prosecutions."[35] The early border militarization was in large part a law enforcement initiative.

Some troops even came directly from the Philippines to Fort Bliss in El Paso. From there they were ordered to various locations in Arizona and Texas to help enforce the neutrality laws as well as prevent raids on ranches. After Madero assumed the presidency, the US military presence on the border was drawn down to only 6,754 in anticipation of increased political stability.[36] When Madero's government was overthrown in February of 1913, however, more unrest erupted in the Mexican border towns. Many of the wounded were brought to the American side and treated in both civil hospitals and the medical service of the army. Also, many of the American border towns were filled to the brim with refugees fleeing the violence in Mexico. Troop numbers surged again as various factions fought for control of the Mexican border towns; around 11,450 officers and enlisted men patrolled sixteen hundred miles between Sasabe, Arizona, and the Rio Grande delta.[37] By 1914, a considerable number of military personnel were involved in one way or another with the Mexican Revolution. US gunboats that had been sent to Veracruz were withdrawn to Galveston and Texas City, though the number of soldiers in the border region had significantly increased. A total of 741 officers and 19,944 enlisted men were on border patrols.[38]

After Villa's attack on Columbus in 1916, however, border militarization increased even more rapidly and shifted away from a domestic policing initiative toward combat readiness, and Pershing's column entered Mexican territory in military formation. The secretary of war lamented that up until then, "our country has been singularly free from international boundary difficulty which required more force than could be found in the organizations of the Regular Army within the country. The sort of duty presented by the Mexican difficulty, therefore, is unusual and may well have been unanticipated." He lauded the troops, however, saying that "duty in Mexico and on the border has been of the most trying kind which soldiers can be called on to perform."[39] Wilson federalized the National Guard through the National Defense Act of 1916, and within a year, the number of men under arms posted along the international divide skyrocketed from around 20,000 to 160,000.[40] In the following section, I explain the environmental factors that made this kind of military duty particularly "trying." Also, this was the period during which the built environment of remote patrols mattered the most, a topic taken up in more detail in the last section of this chapter.

Matters were complicated further in the South Texas border region by the outbreak of a rebellion led by Mexican Americans in 1915. Rising in protest against dispossession, repression, marginalization, and economic exploitation, the rebels were met with brutal and often indiscriminate counterattacks not only by government organizations like the Texas Rangers but also by lynch mobs. Accounts from local newspapers offer grisly details of episodes in which Mexican Americans were shot by posses after being taken prisoner; how they were broken out of jails by masked men, then shot or hanged; and how one body was found, left to rot, with seventeen bullet holes in it.[41] Scholars have estimated that the death toll was probably somewhere between five hundred and five thousand dead. The historian Benjamin Johnson believes a number in the "low thousands" is most probable, but in any event, such a wild discrepancy in these numbers further testifies to the lack of accountability, transparency, and due process in South Texas at the time, as well as the extreme legal vulnerability and invisibility of Mexican Americans.[42]

Apart from the rebels who actively fought back, many others developed ways to counteract the violence. According to the border

photographer W. D. Smithers, some Mexican Americans during those years became *avisadores*, or signalers. They used mirror flashes, or *avisos*, to communicate over long distances to one another about the movements of US cavalry units and Texas Rangers. Smithers believed it was "almost as good as radar," a

form of guerrilla communication to help people stay safe and clear of the path of armed agents of the state. Or, as he put it, speaking to the indiscriminate nature of border policing during those years, "not one Mexican was guilty of any offense to fear the patrol, but all wanted the information about it."[43] Decades later, in 1966, Smithers took a series of photographs of a man named Ben Cobos near Marathon, Texas, which he claimed were the first pictures ever produced of an *avisador* (see figures 2.2 and 2.3). In the early days, for obvious reasons, no one who knew how to send signals would consent to be photographed.

Cobos and Smithers met as old men in the desert of the Big Bend

region to take these photographs. They were almost the same age, seventy-two and seventy-one, respectively, and each of them had spent their formative years in the border region. Smithers was born in Mexico, in San Luis Potosí. His father was a bookkeeper for the American Mining and Smelting Company. He spoke Spanish, worked as a teamster for an army mule train during the Mexican Revolution, and later worked in the Army Signal Corps after enlisting in the cavalry in 1917, around the time he photographed the Boquillas mining tramway. He was also one of the most prolific photographers of the border region during those years, producing many thousands of images of a wide variety subjects in both the United States and

FIGURE 2.3.
Ben Cobos with Mirror Flash, 1966

Ben Cobos, a curandero and freighter, spent his whole life in the desert around Marathon, Texas. In these two photographs, he is demonstrating how Mexican Americans in the region used to signal each other over long distances to avoid potentially lethal interactions with the US Army. W. D. Smithers Collection of Photographs, Harry Ransom Center, the University of Texas at Austin.

Mexico. Cobos, on the other hand, had spent his entire life in the desert of the Big Bend. He worked as a freighter, charged with a nine-mule wagon hauling loads of mercury from the mines in Terlingua to Alpine, Texas. Each round trip took over two weeks; years of his life were spent camping out in the remote desert with the animals. Smithers described him as a *curandero*, or folk healer, and, given Smithers's own background in army logistics and communications, he was sympathetic to and fascinated by the history of *avisadores*.[44]

In the first image, Cobos stands on a flat plain holding a four-inch round mirror that appears as a ball of light in his hands. In the second image, a flash, a blinding halation completely obscures his body. Smithers points out in his notes on the photographs that the *avisos* were meant to be seen from one to forty miles away, not fifty feet.[45] "Sunlight from a mirror is a powerful element," he wrote, "a genius is needed to harness and control it."[46] The code of long-range flashes that *avisadores* sent in the border region might have been a critical form of self-protection and may have even saved lives during the chaotic years of the Mexican Revolution and even beyond. It is also important to note that they depended in part on the characteristics of certain border ecosystems, the desert in particular. Not only was sunlight in plentiful supply in such arid regions, but the scarce, low-lying vegetation made it possible to see across great distances unobstructed. The environment in which Cobos stood to pose for these pictures mattered during the years of the revolution in other ways, too, and in part helped define the nature not only of fighting in Mexico but also of US building in the border region.

THE BORDER ENVIRONMENT

Military history is intrinsically linked to environmental history. From the point of view of officers and soldiers, questions about topography, hydrology, and climate are of constant concern not only for combat but for supply trains, communication, and patrolling.[47] Arid environments in particular pose specific challenges such as dehydration and heatstroke for any kind of human movement through them. Military activities in deserts are even more complicated, however. Noncohesive sand is problematic on a variety of levels. Blowing dust can decrease visibility, both of the landscape and through glass windows. It can become lodged in rotor and turbine blades or any other exposed mechanical part, as well as in lubricants, which can in turn impair motor performance. Vehicles with either wheels or tracked treads, both of which are typically extremely heavy, have difficulty negotiating sand and often compensate by operating in low gears, which in turn can lead to engine overheating. Bunkers and fox-holes are always at risk of collapsing in sand, if it is even possible to build them in the first place. Aside from all this, the heat can at times create anomalies that can distort radio and other electronic transmissions, and it can produce mirages, another distortion of vis-ibility that can lead to misconceptions or miscommunications.[48] These concerns, among others, became especially pertinent in the context of the Mexican Revolution, though some of them had already been experienced by the nineteenth-century boundary surveyors.

Even among civilians, the revolution raised a broader interest in Mexico's natural landscapes. By 1914, after four years of hostilities in Mexico and increasing US military response to the conflict, members of the American Geographical Society had become curious about the role the environment played in the violence of the Mexican Revolution. Mark Jefferson, a professor of geography at Michigan State Normal College, wrote a brief article that year for the *Bulletin of the American Geographic Society of New York* describing the relationship between the fighting and the "Mexican Plateau." He was interested in the topography of Mexico, which he described as a "curiously 'upstairs' country." Most people, he explained, were congregated in cities in the central highlands, over five thousand feet above sea level, though much of the territory held by revolutionary troops was in the low-lying country of the north. "The *area* held by the rebels is very large," he wrote, "perhaps a third of Mexican territory, but a great deal of it is uninhabited."[49] In other words, the land held by the revolutionaries was desert, the low-altitude arid country of the border region, far re-moved from the seat of political power in Mexico as well as the urban centers of the country. In those years, before large-scale surface water diversion and groundwater pumping, population centers in the dry-lands had to be scattered and sparse; that was the only way not to overdraw the limited and far-flung water sources throughout the re-gion. And, of course, this was also the landscape patrolled by the US Army throughout much of the decade.

Jefferson's views represented the dominant environmental thinking at the time. Two years after he wrote about the revolution, he was elected president of the American Association of Geographers. And in 1919, he served as the chief cartographer of the American delegation to the Paris Peace Conference. But before that, in 1917, his ideas about the environment of the revolution helped inspire another article focused on similar themes published by the American Geographical Society. The anonymous author of that article immediately sets aside the fighting in Morelos, the stronghold of Emiliano Zapata's forces just south of Mexico City, focusing instead on the "long, desert, frontier region of the north" and its relationship to American army patrols. The role of the nonhuman world was central: "features of the relief, climate, and vegetation of the frontier" were all, according to the article, "involved in one form or another in the problems of military control."[50]

From his perspective, the deserts of the border region posed two significant problems for armed maneuvers: the scarcity of water made it very difficult for the "beasts," and loose, sandy ground made transportation challenging. Motor vehicles had yet to fully supplant animal power in the activities of the armed forces, and heavy artillery and supplies were particularly difficult to pull through sand. Desert plants were, with few exceptions, "dull and dusty," and in some sections of the border region, the author reported no vegetation whatsoever. The theme of emptiness, so common in discourse about deserts, both then and now, was thus revisited. Also, the language used to describe hydraulic features paralleled the vocabulary used to describe Mexico's conflict. "The Rio Grande is a storm-water stream, subject to great and sudden floods. The rainfall occurs principally in the form of violent showers or cloudbursts." The dangerousness and extreme character of the natural world of the desert were in sync with the unpredictability and bloodshed of the revolution.[51]

It was not only the climate and the terrain that interested geographers, however. They were also concerned with the built environment, particularly railroads. The obvious function of railroads was to facilitate the movement of supplies and troops, though the geography of rail lines also powerfully influenced the character of combat. In remote regions, far from railroads, much of the fighting took place in open country. Trench warfare, which depended on maintaining and continuously resupplying a stronghold, was typically impossible. This meant exposed, scattered combat in intense and potentially lethal climates. Or, put in early twentieth-century geographic terms, the "power of concentration in a desert is limited even on the part of a rich nation. Northern Mexico has always been desert and it is now destitute."[52] The desert, already an uncertain and precarious space, was made more so through the violence of the revolution.

Finally, at the conclusion of the article, the author quotes several paragraphs from Mark Jefferson, who had been invited to offer updated thoughts on the environment and the revolution. He pointed out that the "scene of action" remained the same, the "thinly settled, desertic, and arid north." Returning to the common association between deserts and nothingness, he argued that even "a strong government would have trouble maintaining order in a region so poor in food and water, where the only thing that abounds is empty space." The void of the desert posed a particular tactical problem in his view. Picking up on another common refrain—the association of marginal landscapes with marginal people—he flatly stated, "American troops may be trained to ride like Mexicans, to find their way and fight in the desert like them, but they cannot hope to match them in *doing without*, an art in which the Mexican has a lifelong training, and the American none."[53] In this way, the violence of the revolution matched the ecosystem; Mexicans were cast as *of the environment* in ways that Americans weren't, and the harshness of that climate was a testament to the intractability of the border region—again, echoes of the nineteenth-century boundary survey reports.

Yearly reports from the War Department to Presidents Taft and Wilson also emphasized specific characteristics of the arid terrain of the border region. Major General W. W. Wotherspoon, for instance, the chief of staff of the army in 1914, wrote that the US troops on the border "had the task of patrolling and guarding the very long line, much of which is desert, all of it exceedingly hot."[54] Similarly, Newton D. Baker, the secretary of war in 1916, described the border as "a long and irregular boundary line, passing in places through cities and towns, but for great stretches running through sparsely settled regions and through a wild and difficult country."[55]

The hot climates of the border region did provide some military benefits, however. The mobilization to the border was a nationwide project that drew soldiers from far-flung locales, many of them in the freezing north, such as Fort D. A. Russell in Wyoming and Fort Snelling in Minnesota.[56] This was a useful training opportunity for horse operations according to Henry L. Stimson, the secretary of war in 1911. For him, the border region was "a country admirably suited for Cavalry work and training at all seasons of the year. The necessity imposed upon our Cavalry for patrolling the Mexican border has incidentally brought out the advantageous character of our three southwestern states—Texas, New Mexico, and Arizona—for Cavalry training and drill."[57] Here the value of the arid border region was expressed in terms of military preparedness and training. Horses could be taught and drilled on how to operate in military contexts, unimpeded by heavy snow and ice, and in turn, the cavalry units of the US Army would be better fit for combat missions around the globe. Horses were also well equipped, given the proper provisions, to penetrate the remote regions of the border landscape, much of which was still far removed from transportation infrastructure. Stimson underlined this point: "I deem it proper to call attention to the fact that the brunt of this entire work fell upon and was performed by Cavalry, and that during any continuance of unsettled conditions on that long and sparsely settled frontier, such patrol work must be continued by that arm of the service."[58]

In the context of sustained and far-reaching border patrols, the best way to access remote sections of the border region was on horseback. "Remoteness" as a concept, however, is meaningful only in terms of the broader human-built world. Difficult access to certain regions or terrains effectively translated to how far those places were from transportation infrastructure. Again, the railroads were a critical factor in how military leadership thought about the border region. "The railroads of the United States have been built in response to commercial and industrial needs," wrote Secretary of War Lindley M. Garrison in 1916, but he emphasized that the United States lacked "strategic railroads" and that "our frontiers have been neglected as possible scenes of military operations." During the Mexican Revolution, however, the commercial railroad system of the United States was partially converted to serve military interests, particularly to transport tens of thousands of soldiers and heavy equipment. Pancho Villa's attack in New Mexico proved to be a critical watershed, not only politically but also in terms of transport infrastructure and US military movements. Garrison continued, "the disturbed condition on the Mexican border and consequence of the Columbus raid gave us an actual experiment in the use of our railroads."[59]

Villa's attack also coincided very nearly to the introduction of motor trucks for military use. Border patrols were mechanized extremely quickly after the advent of trucks of various sorts. Pershing brought a staggering number of machines into Mexico. A landscape that had been dominated for centuries by horsemanship was fast converted to a space of internal combustion. To pursue Villa through Chihuahua and Durango, Pershing and his men used 588 trucks; fifty-seven motor tank trucks that were there to haul water, oil, and gasoline; ten motor machine-shop trucks to make repairs as necessary to all the engines; six motor wrecking trucks; seventy-five automobiles; and sixty-one motor-cycles. Most roads in Northern Mexico or the US Southwest, however, had not been built to accommodate this new kind of traffic, so they also brought with them eight tractors to repair the roads themselves, as well as other kinds of road machinery. In all, their motor vehicle budget totaled just over $2.1 million.[60] For their nearly eleven months in Mexican territory, the expedition received supplies steadily; where the railroad left off, motorized vehicles took over. The kind of spatial coverage that had been so recently the exclusive purview of horses had become, at least partially, mechanized. Or, in the words of Garrison, "The development of the motor truck in the past few years has produced a vehicle which is able to traverse wild, unbroken country."[61] For him, the hardships posed by the natural environment could be overcome by technology, even though initial attempts were plagued by malfunctions, logistical problems, and either bad or nonexistent roads.

The "wild, unbroken country" of Northern Mexico, however, had in fact already undergone significant alteration by mining and timber operations, as well as railroad construction. The internecine conflict in Mexico brought with it much destruction as various factions tried to cut off one another's supply lines and sabotage the property of foreign capitalists.

DESTRUCTION

At the end of the summer of 1913, Major P. D. Lockridge of the Thirteenth Cavalry submitted a report to his commanding general. Lockridge was stationed in El Paso, one of the key positions on the border during the revolution. In his summation of the "military situation" across the border in Mexico, he detailed activities ranging geographically from the Colorado River to points southeast of El Paso, toward the Big Bend area, and across the deserts of the border region. He meticulously itemized the number of combatants; their location in specific cities and towns across Sonora and Chihuahua; for whom they fought; and the number and type of their weapons, ranging from machine guns to machetes. By this time, Francisco Madero had just been killed by his onetime ally Victoriano Huerta, who had then taken the presidency for himself. Huerta's usurpation of power was widely perceived as illegitimate, and a broad coalition known as "constitutionalists," led by Álvaro Obregón in Sonora, Pancho Villa in Chihuahua, and Venustiano Carranza in Coahuila, continued fighting against his "federal" troops. The federals were mainly foot troops, whereas the fighters in the north usually rode horses into battle. Lockridge learned most of what he knew about military activities in Mexico from miners, merchants, engineers, and railroad men who had fled the country. As such, his report also offered a detailed account of transportation infrastructure and railroad destruction.[62]

Huerta's federal army used the railroad trunk lines to move men and supplies north, so the fighters in the north tried to destroy them whenever possible. The railroads in Sonora were left largely functional, but the Ferrocarril Central Mexicano (incorporated into the Ferrocarriles Nacionales de México after 1909) that connected Mexico City to Ciudad Juárez was in terrible condition by 1913.[63] Throughout this railroad's central northern corridor, rebel troops had burned ninety-two bridges supporting the tracks, and in some cases removed the rails themselves, then bent and twisted them. Some of this damage was monumental. One bridge, for instance, was 1,500 feet long, requiring a large amount of labor and materials to reconstruct. Though federal troops constantly shipped supplies and men north to make temporary repairs, the destruction was constant, and the railroad was consistently passable only south of Aguascalientes.[64]

It was not only the long-distance trunk lines that came under attack, however. Regional railroads, too, were heavily damaged. The Madera Lumber Company in Chihuahua was perhaps the best example of not only the destruction in the north but also the extent to which the railroad infrastructure itself was linked to foreign resource extraction. The timber lands it owned in the mountains were part of its larger network that included two large sawmills in Chihuahua; the El Paso

Milling Company in Texas; and a series of five short railways to connect them, four of which the company bought and one of which they built to move lumber out of Mexican forests and into far-flung US markets. The company produced a map in a time of optimism before the revolution crippled their operations. It was a vision of foreign occupation and extraction in Northern Mexico they thought would last longer than it did (figure 2.4).[65] Between 1909 and 1918, the company invested $30 million in building out their infrastructure, and this map indicates that had it not been for the fighting, they had plans to build even more.[66] In the center of the map sits a gargantuan tract of 2,600 square miles in the Sierra Tarahumara, all owned and leased by the Madera Company, British owned and incorporated in Canada.[67] The Ferrocarril Noroeste de México runs along its eastern edge as it bulges west from the central trunk line of the Ferrocarril Nacional. More spurs were planned, though. The dotted lines to the west indicate that the company had designs to build new lines to both the coast and to Douglas, Arizona, an important port of entry in the copper mining country of the Arizona-Sonora border region. In fact, much railroad building did occur on the Ferrocarril Noroeste during the years of the revolution, but it was not new construction, it was repair.

In 1919, a beleaguered L. R. Home, the president of the railroad, wrote from Toronto to a company lawyer in El Paso, comparing their troubles over the course of the decade to "St. Paul's narration of his imprisonments, floggings, stonings, shipwrecks, and other incidents of his career."[68] The landscape of Chihuahua was uneven, certainly in the mountains where pine and oak trees grew so plentifully but also in the desert lowlands, cut with innumerable arroyos. This meant that the path of the Ferrocarril Noroeste was supported by hundreds of bridges, which were the most vulnerable points of sabotage for retreating factions. According to an internal company report, 714 bridges had already been burned by 1913. They were not left to smolder and rot, however. The company was intensely interested in maintaining the steady operation of its sawmills and export business, so they constantly sent out labor teams to repair, crib, or shoo-fly (temporary reroute) incinerated bridges. They managed to maintain operations for years despite the intensity of the fighting in Chihuahua, though often as soon as they rebuilt the bridges, they were burned down again.[69] This cycle of destruction and repair became a new way

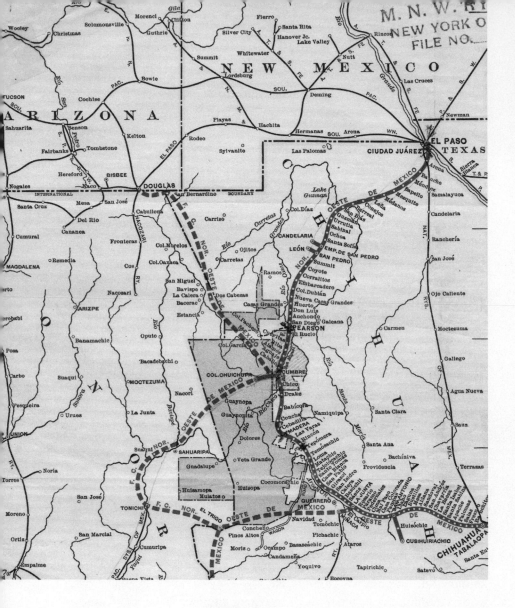

FIGURE 2.4.

Ferrocarril Noroeste de México (detail), ca. 1919

A section of the border region as envisioned by a British-owned lumber company operating in Chihuahua. In the center is the timber country of the Sierra Madre Occidental. The dotted lines represented railroad spurs they wanted to build, but the only one already built led to El Paso, Texas, and the sawmill there. Records of the Ferrocarril Noroeste de México, 1910–1919, Nettie Lee Benson Latin American Collection, University of Texas Libraries, the University of Texas at Austin.

of life, conditioned by the pressure of return on investment. On the American side, however, a new landscape of patrol infrastructure was emerging that would only continue to expand.

BUILDING

A ttacks on railroads also happened on the American side, often accompanied by widespread lynching of Mexican Americans. Outside Harlingen, in South Texas, Mexican American rebels burned a seventy-five-foot trestle in 1915, rendering it impossible for trains to cross, and cut telegraph lines, crippling communications. They burned four more trestles outside Brownsville and derailed a train carrying agricultural commodities.[70] The broader history of the US border region during the 1910s was not rooted in destruction, however, but rather in building. The logistics of the military deployments to the border, unprecedented in both size and scope, were staggering. This effort was compounded by the fact that the patrols were expected to operate in remote areas along the line, far from preexisting transportation infrastructure in most cases. Matters were further complicated by the transition from animal power to machine power. Recently invented motor vehicles and airplanes were incorporated into the armed forces during the Mexican Revolution, and though the transition was rapid, they did not entirely replace mule trains and cavalry units. Instead, a hybrid border patrol emerged in which beasts of burden and war worked in tandem with mechanized equipment. All of this translated into the construction and expansion of paths, trails, and roads to carry equipment, supplies, and men into areas along the border that were extremely difficult to access.

Like nearly every other border organization, the army had a multifaceted relationship with Mexicans. On one hand, the US military's presence on the border was oriented in part toward national defense, rooted in ideas of territorial sovereignty and martial preparedness that overdiagnosed the problem of "banditry" and its association with people of Mexican origin. On the other hand, however, the army was just another contractor of Mexican labor. On three occasions between the summer of 1918 and the spring of 1919, the War Department hired Mexican-born workers to help build military infrastructure along the border. For these and other activities during the Great War, the secretary of labor waived the more stringent provisions of the Immigration Act of 1917, including the literacy, head tax, and contract labor mandates, to allow for the relatively unencumbered importation of workers. Mexicans built army buildings along the border in all four border states, they cut firewood for military outposts in the Southern Department of War, and they molded adobe bricks and built structures at ten cavalry posts in the Big Bend area of West Texas. Then, when their contracts expired, the War Department sent them back to Mexico.[71] Much of the army's focus was on less obvious parts of the border's built environment, however. Commanding officers, horsemen, infantrymen, teamsters, and even US presidents were all interested in how to gain access to remote parts of the border region, not just in where to muster troops.

The Big Bend region of the West Texas deserts was the ultimate challenge. Scarcity of water; long distances from railroads; and the most rugged, mountainous topography of the entire border region converged to present serious logistical difficulties for those who wanted to patrol the line. In these spaces, animals were critical. Smithers took a photo in 1917 that testifies to this (figure 2.5). The image depicts a typical mule train winding single file along a path locals called the Comedor Trail, a mile outside Candelaria, Texas, a tiny settlement directly on the international divide.[72] What mattered most for Smithers in this photo were the mules; he took this picture to demonstrate how they moved through remote regions.

Fifty mules in all were destined for Evetts Ranch, private property that had been partially converted into an outpost for the Eighth Cavalry.[73] The epicenter of cavalry patrols in the area was in Marfa, Texas. From there, various squadrons of the regiment fanned out along the border, rotating every few months. Each regiment contained twelve rifle troops that were stationed anywhere between 54 and 160 miles from the Marfa headquarters.[74] To sustain these formations of men and their horses, their outposts at Evetts Ranch, Indio, Ruidosa, and Candelaria had to be constantly supplied with provisions by mule train, including hay, oats, and other necessities. All fifty pack animals carried a net cargo of 9,600 pounds, or about 192 pounds per animal, but with the added weight of the canvas and ropes, the gross load was around 250 pounds atop each beast of burden.[75]

The mules themselves were a type of infrastructure. They were monetized and standardized, and packers that worked with them knew the details of their bodies' component parts and how they fit together with *aparejos* (a type of packsaddle) and other cargo equipment. The animals usually weighed one thousand pounds, stood fifteen hands high, and cost an average of $140, except for larger mules, which cost $184, that pulled wagon trains. W. D. Smithers included very few nonphotographic materials in his massive collection of border pictures. However, having worked as a teamster himself during the Mexican Revolution, he felt it important to include a line drawing of a mule's body (figure 2.6). The

FIGURE 2.5.

Pack Train and River, 1917

Just outside Candelaria, Texas. The Rio Grande appears in the left of the frame, and the center is dominated by a small agricultural plot and irrigation ditch. W. D. Smithers Collection of Photographs, Harry Ransom Center, the University of Texas at Austin.

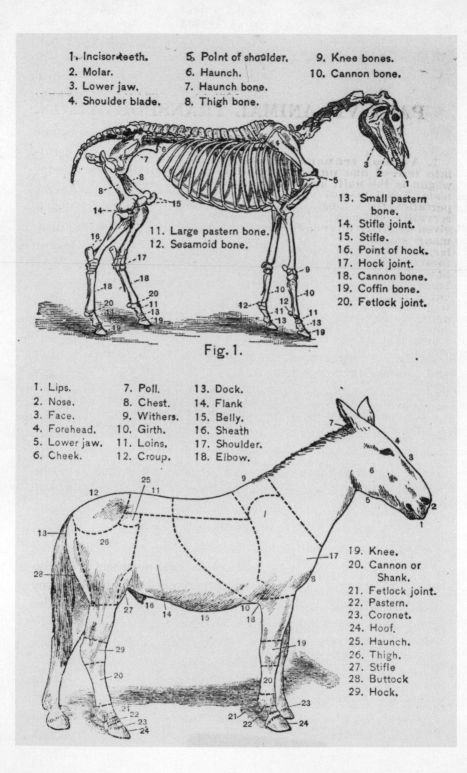

1. Incisor teeth.
2. Molar.
3. Lower jaw.
4. Shoulder blade.
5. Point of shoulder.
6. Haunch.
7. Haunch bone.
8. Thigh bone.
9. Knee bones.
10. Cannon bone.

11. Large pastern bone.
12. Sesamoid bone.

13. Small pastern bone.
14. Stifle joint.
15. Stifle.
16. Point of hock.
17. Hock joint.
18. Cannon bone.
19. Coffin bone.
20. Fetlock joint.

Fig. 1.

1. Lips.
2. Nose.
3. Face.
4. Forehead.
5. Lower jaw.
6. Cheek.
7. Poll.
8. Chest.
9. Withers.
10. Girth.
11. Loins.
12. Croup.
13. Dock.
14. Flank
15. Belly.
16. Sheath
17. Shoulder.
18. Elbow.

19. Knee.
20. Cannon or Shank.
21. Fetlock joint.
22. Pastern.
23. Coronet.
24. Hoof.
25. Haunch.
26. Thigh.
27. Stifle
28. Buttock
29. Hock.

"important bones and joints" are all labeled, as are the body parts. In his inscription on the back, he assures the viewer that anyone who worked with these animals on the border patrols would have known all the "working parts" and how to properly balance the cargo and forgo any "malpractices."[76]

This anatomical expertise was matched and accompanied by new forms of technological knowledge during those years. At the start of the Mexican Revolution, the United States had recently become the greatest industrial power in the world. In 1890, the United States produced more pig iron and steel than Great Britain for the first time in history, and by 1910, US steel, coal, and industrial production was many times greater than that of all the European powers.[77] The Mexican Revolution also coincided with a profound transformation within the US armed forces, fueled in large part by the US industrial boom. Elihu Root, the US secretary of war during the eleven years that preceded the Mexican Revolution, had already begun moving the War Department toward a paradigm that privileged the mobilization of matériel over soldiers. For instance, in 1903, the US Army traded their nineteenth-century Krag-Jørgensen rifles for the new Springfields, which were faster-loading, clip-fed, bolt-action rifles with a higher muzzle velocity and longer range than the Krags. US soldiers carried Springfields for nearly half a century afterward, but an even larger techno-military transformation came not with arms but with motor vehicles. In 1911, three years after Henry Ford's men assembled the first Model T, the inspector general of the United States began to contemplate its military applications. The first trucks ever driven by US soldiers were driven to the Mexican border, and when Pershing's column entered Mexico in 1916 in pursuit of Pancho Villa, they relied on a truck convoy for supplies and maneuvering for the first time in the history of the army.[78]

Soon after Villa's attack, the Quartermaster Truck Company set out from Ft. Bliss in El Paso to Columbus, New Mexico, to offer reinforcements. The convoy illustrated both the chronic malfunctions

FIGURE 2.6.

The Mule, date unknown

During the transition to mechanized operations in the armed forces, for a time, such as during the Mexican Revolution, machines operated alongside animals. Detailed technical expertise in the constituent parts of a mule was required by their handlers. W. D. Smithers Collection of Photographs, Harry Ransom Center, the University of Texas at Austin.

of the new technology and the paucity of transport infrastructure to carry it. El Paso and Columbus were only 105 miles apart, and despite the fact that the convoy took the best roads available, it still took them twenty-four hours to arrive. Nearly every truck had mechanical problems, and nearly all the drivers of the White half-ton trucks and Jeffery Quads had learned how to drive only days earlier. This was the convoy that drove into Mexico during the Punitive Expedition in pursuit of Pancho Villa.[79]

Infantry and cavalry regiments led the way into Mexico, marching down dirt paths, making them wider in the process and digging deep ruts into the earth. They were followed by a steamroller with a name plate on the side that read "Good Roads." Its job was to smooth out the ground in preparation for the truck convoy that followed. This heavy machine ultimately helped partially improve 125 miles of road in Chihuahua.[80] The truck convoy was primarily designed to carry supplies that ordinarily were tasked to horse- and big mule-drawn wagon trains. Perhaps the most important vehicle was the Avery tractor, an enormous machine with enormous power. Its rear wheels were six feet tall and made of steel; it essentially operated as a locomotive without tracks, pulling a long string of wagons behind it.[81] Two of the heavy machines Pershing brought into Mexico were the Holt and the Caterpillar. Both vehicles had a combination of tractor treads and untracked wheels. They pulled road graders, but in many instances, they found the ground was not solid enough to establish a solid road bed, and when it rained, the water "obliterated" their improvements. The best they could hope for was to make a passable corridor, and in the face of complaints that President Carranza prohibited use of the Ferrocarril Noroeste to resupply, the expedition was dependent on this semi-ephemeral road network.[82]

With respect to Pershing's Punitive Expedition, Secretary of War Newton D. Baker wrote to President Wilson the following year, saying that "the expedition was in no sense punitive, but rather defensive. Its objective, of course, was the capture of Villa if that could be accomplished, but its real purpose was an extension of the power of the United States into a country disturbed beyond control of the constituted authorities of the Republic of Mexico, as a means of controlling lawless aggregations of bandits and preventing attacks by them across the international frontier. This purpose it fully and finally accomplished."[83]

This "extension of power," such as it was, was achieved through the ability to overcome not only hostile forces but also a hostile environment and a paucity of transport infrastructure.

W. D. Smithers was fascinated by the logistics of Pershing's expedition, and he drew a map to illustrate the troop movements in Chihuahua (see figure 2.7).[84] His sense of the interaction of the region's topography with the built environment is particularly instructive, offering a glimpse into how those involved in border patrols and building might have imagined their surroundings. He notes two points of entry, one down in the Bootheel of New Mexico near High Lonesome Wells and Culberson's Ranch, and the other at the site of the attack, Columbus. Cavalry, infantry, and pack trains made their way southward, converging on Colonia Dublán, originally a Mormon settlement and a satellite town of the Canadian and American lumber expatriates in Madera and Pearson.

Smithers was careful to include three other notable features as well. He notes the route of the Ferrocarril Noroeste, the railroad linking the timber lands of the Sierra Tarahumara to the El Paso sawmill and beyond, as well as the Southern Pacific line and its spurs running parallel to the border in the United States. No map I have been able to find that was produced by state agents omits the railroads, critical to every aspect of market integration as well as militarization. The topography also mattered. It is not very detailed in this map, but it is almost perfectly accurate in terms of location. The troop movements were confined, as much as possible, to the lowland valleys, winding in between the often jagged and steep desert mountains, depicted in the map simply as dark spots. Finally, and of particular interest in the context of this book, Smithers noted the number and location of the obelisk-shaped survey markers erected by the 1890s boundary survey. This all adds up to an excellent example of how the built and natural environments of the border region constantly refer to one another, helping to orient and link tactical possibilities and transportation connectivity.

Meanwhile, on the US side, the border patrols that had been dominated by cavalry units were being partially converted to accommodate motorized vehicles. A young Dwight Eisenhower became involved, having just graduated from West Point in 1915, the year before Villa attacked Columbus. President Taft had already begun sending troops

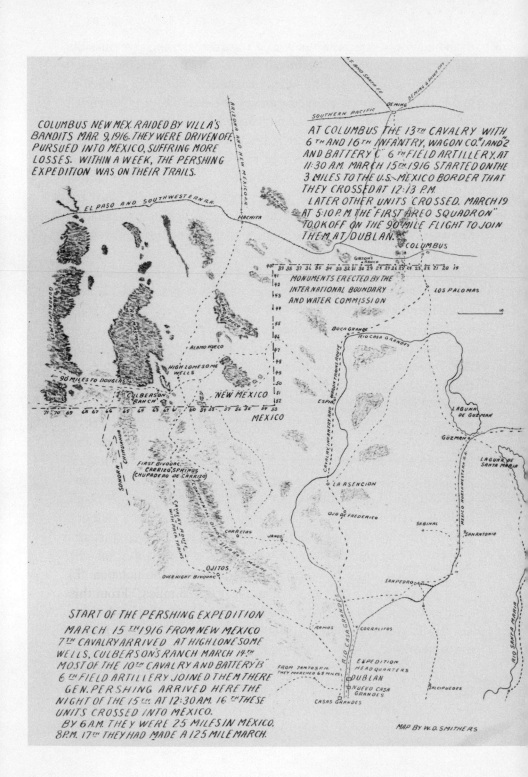

COLUMBUS NEW MEX. RAIDED BY VILLA'S BANDITS MAR. 9, 1916. THEY WERE DRIVEN OFF, PURSUED INTO MEXICO, SUFFERING MORE LOSSES. WITHIN A WEEK, THE PERSHING EXPEDITION WAS ON THEIR TRAILS.

AT COLUMBUS THE 13TH CAVALRY WITH 6TH AND 16TH INFANTRY, WAGON CO. 1 AND 2 AND BATTERY "C" 6TH FIELD ARTILLERY, AT 11:30 A.M. MARCH 15TH 1916 STARTED ON THE 3 MILES TO THE U.S. MEXICO BORDER THAT THEY CROSSED AT 12:13 P.M. LATER OTHER UNITS CROSSED. MARCH 19 AT 5:10 P.M. THE "FIRST AREO SQUADRON" TOOK OFF ON THE 90 MILE FLIGHT TO JOIN THEM AT DUBLAN.

MONUMENTS ERECTED BY THE INTERNATIONAL BOUNDARY AND WATER COMMISSION

DEMING & SILVER CITY
SOUTHERN PACIFIC
DEMING
A.T. AND SANTA FE
COLUMBUS
GIBSON'S RANCH
LOS PALOMAS
10

EL PASO AND SOUTHWESTERN R.R.
ARIZONA AND NEW MEXICO
HACHITA
GUADALUPES
90 MILES TO DOUGLAS
HIGH LOMESOME WELLS
CULBERSON RANCH
ALAMO HUECO
NEW MEXICO
MEXICO

BOCA GRANDE
RIO CASA GRANDES
ESPIA
LAGUNA DE GUZMAN
GUZMAN

SONORA CHIHUAHUA
FIRST BIVOUAC CARRIZO SPRINGS (CHUPADERO DE CARRIZO)
CAVALRY ROUTE WITH PACK TRAINS
CONTINENTAL DIVIDE
SIERRA MADRE
CARRETAS
JANOS
OJITOS
OVERNIGHT BIVOUAC

CAVALRY, INFANTRY AND WAGON TRAINS ROUTE

LA ASENCION
OJO DE FREDERICO
SABINAL
SAN ANTONIO
LAGUNA DE SANTA MARIA
MEXICO NORTHWESTERN R.R.

RAMOS
CORRALITOS
SAN PEDRO
RIO SANTA MARIA

START OF THE PERSHING EXPEDITION
MARCH 15TH 1916 FROM NEW MEXICO 7TH CAVALRY ARRIVED AT HIGH LONESOME WELLS, CULBERSON'S RANCH MARCH 14TH MOST OF THE 10TH CAVALRY AND BATTERY "B" 6TH FIELD ARTILLERY JOINED THEM THERE GEN. PERSHING ARRIVED HERE THE NIGHT OF THE 15TH. AT 12:30 A.M. 16TH THESE UNITS CROSSED INTO MEXICO.
BY 6 A.M. THEY WERE 25 MILES IN MEXICO. 8 P.M. 17TH THEY HAD MADE A 125 MILE MARCH.

FROM 7AM TO 8 P.M. THEY MARCHED 68 MILES
EXPEDITION HEADQUARTERS
DUBLAN
NUEVO CASA GRANDES
CASAS GRANDES
RIO CASA GRANDES
SALCIPUEDES

MAP BY W.D. SMITHERS

to the border, a duty that was widely regarded as the worst possible assignment, even more arduous than deployment to the Philippines.[85] Eisenhower was eager to move into a combat role, so he applied to join Pershing's expedition, but he was not selected. Instead, he ended up in San Antonio, Texas, training national guardsmen for border duty, most of whom he believed were barely competent to patrol the border and completely unprepared to fight in a foreign war.[86] This incompetence was compounded, Eisenhower believed, by the difficulties presented by too few roads to transport men and equipment. This skepticism was reflected in the difficulties the Pershing expedition had with engine breakdowns and bad or nonexistent roads between El Paso and Columbus, and into Chihuahua and Durango. But in the Big Bend region, a hybrid patrol network of both animals and machines achieved remarkable geographic coverage.

Another map drawn by W. D. Smithers illustrates this. It also shows a militaristic understanding of geography in which territory is categorized according to national boundaries and soldiers' access (figure 2.8). He drew a set of dotted lines, representing transport and patrol routes. They converge on the army camp at Marfa from various points along the Rio Grande.[87] On the Mexican side, the village of Pilares is identified as a harbor for "some of the worst outlaws." The impassibly steep escarpments of the Candelaria Rim, the Vieja Mountains, and the Chinati Mountains are represented in black, and the Southern Pacific railroad line passes through the upper-right quadrant of the image along with the notation "El Paso–Marfa 196 miles." From this map we also learn that aside from the Rio Grande, the troops had no access to natural water sources. Eighteen water stops are listed on the left, each one of which would have been crucial to supporting the number of animals that both the cavalry units and the supply trains

FIGURE 2.7.

Pershing Map, date unknown

This map of the Pershing expedition between New Mexico and Chihuahua incorporates railroads, border markers listed by number, accurate locations of topographic impediments, and surface water. In other words, the accumulated work of building transportation infrastructure, mapping, surveying, and demarcating the border region was all brought to bear in the context of a military invasion, as it would continue to be in the context of US federal border policing during the twentieth century and into the twenty-first. W. D. Smithers Collection of Photographs, Harry Ransom Center, the University of Texas at Austin.

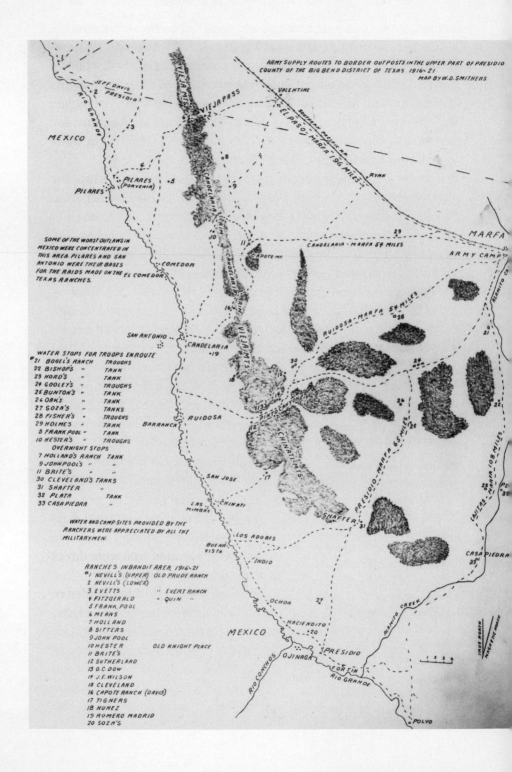

needed. Every single one of them is listed as either a tank or a trough, artificial reservoirs ranchers built to supply their livestock with predictable water sources. This also indicates the extent to which border patrolling in this region was a joint production of both armed agents of the state and private individuals. Ranchers, many of whom had had their own confrontations with people from the Mexican side, provided an invaluable support network for the army that included both water supply and, at times, places to muster.

Most of the paths were manageable only by animals. Only two, the Pinto Canyon route between Marfa and Ruidosa and another from Marfa to the border town of Presidio, were wide and flat enough to accommodate mechanized transport. This fascinated Smithers, and in addition to taking several photographs of vehicles having accidentally burst into flames or broken down, he also documented their successful operations. In one such photograph, two tractor wagon trains crawl up a dirt road between craggy outcroppings of rock and nearly vertical slopes (figure 2.9). The advent of motor trucks did not immediately translate to an entirely mechanized fleet of patrol vehicles. Instead, a hybrid form emerged. In this image, Holt tractors have taken the place of mule power, but the chain of covered wagons maintained its traditional form. The wagons were unsteady and often fell over. They moved very slowly, never more than fifteen miles per hour, and very likely traveled at barely more than a crawl through the mountains. They progressed so slowly, in fact, that men on foot could walk next to them, as did the two men in front of the train in the foreground who were directing the driver through a sharp turn.[88]

FIGURE 2.8.
West Texas Patrols,
date unknown

Remarkable geographic coverage of one of the earliest remote border patrols between 1916 and 1921. The movements of the troops were contained on the eastern banks of the Rio Grande and confined to narrow canyons, passes, and sometimes steep descents as they negotiated the rough topography of West Texas. W. D. Smithers Collection of Photographs, Harry Ransom Center, the University of Texas at Austin.

Despite the remoteness of the border region, the US military in the 1910s achieved what was perhaps the most extensive geographic coverage of any policing agency in border history. The paths that could not support machines they traversed with wagon trains led by animal power. Candelaria Rim Road was the worst, a 1,700-foot descent. In

a photograph Smithers took looking south, the Rio Grande lies somewhere nearby, just out of the frame on the right (figure 2.10). The ridgeline imposed an impossible obstacle for transit, except for the space through which the dirt road winds in the foreground. It was one-way only. The grade was too steep to pull even empty wagons up it, and descending was a dangerous proposition. There are twenty-eight wagons in this picture, and they had to be taken down two at a time along the most precarious sections. The wagon master, three assistants, and two blacksmiths dismounted, used bolster chains to lock the rear wheels of each wagon, and directed them down in a controlled slide; their brakes were useless

at that angle.[89] Perhaps no other part of the border region resisted both technological advancement and attempts to achieve geographic patrol coverage more than there. Nevertheless, the attempts to conquer it in the 1910s, however difficult and ineffectual, represented a turning point in the history of border policing insofar as they affirmed a new commitment to extremely remote border patrolling, as well as new commitments to mechanized means of border surveillance.

Other attempts were made to gain military control over preexisting cross-border transportation routes by blurring military and civil policing activity. In September of 1915, for instance, Major General Funsten, the commanding officer in the south Rio Grande area, wrote to the director of immigration at El Paso, saying that the "situation on [the] lower Rio Grande between Laredo and [the] gulf has become so serious that I desire to absolutely control all intercourse across [the] river both at international bridges[,] licensed ferries[,] as well as places where crossings are not authorized."[90] Meanwhile, the civilian immigration inspector in Brownsville was convinced that he and his inspectors on the bridges were marked for assassination in Mexico, and they all stopped crossing to the Mexican side for any reason. By then, four thousand troops occupied the Rio Grande valley in South Texas, and they all started to make a point of pushing all traffic, licit or otherwise, through the official ports of entry.[91] The greatest technological innovations were not deployed to monitor the ports of entry, however. The largest outlay of military equipment was in the hinterland.

The extraordinary geographic coverage of the border militarization in the 1910s was also achieved by testing another newly developed military technology in the border region. In 1919, the US War Department established an armed aerial surveillance and reconnaissance patrol to aid the cavalry and infantry units on the ground. They called it the US Army Border Air Patrol, and though the program was shuttered in 1921, its very existence fueled the growing consensus within various branches of the US federal government that the border needed to be policed. Stacy C. Hinkle, one of the pilots of the air patrol who later wrote an autobiographical history of the aerial guard, described the purpose of the airborne squadron the way nearly all border policing initiatives have been described: he cited the Mexican government's inability to cope with its own problems and understood the American armed presence on the border as the only reasonable response to violence in Mexico. When US Army border planes were grounded in 1921, Hinkle proudly declared that the mission had been successful, that their activities had helped stamp out raiding and vandalism, and that they had brought to an end an "81-year reign of terror" in the border region.[92] This assertion, and others like it, completely ignored the influence of American capital in the Mexican countryside and the social inequalities it produced, another crucial impetus for such a large US military response on the border.

The Border Air Patrol was manned by thirty officers and seventy-one enlisted men who flew twelve DH-4 British-designed De Havillands out of eleven airfields scattered from the Pacific Ocean to the Gulf of Mexico. This required an infrastructure of its own, including hangars and ground transport. Gas and oil, for instance, were difficult to come by in Marfa, Texas, one of the air bases, and what fuel they had often had dirt and water in it. Emergency landing fields were hard to find. As was the case with nearly all the army patrols on the border, the men at Marfa lived in tents, ephemeral colonies of improvised shelter. Communications infrastructure was still in a primitive phase. The pilots' instructions were to look for groups of armed men on the border, assumed to be working at the behest of Pancho Villa, but they had no radios in the open-air biplanes they flew. They navigated mainly by landmark, following roads, rivers, and rails by sight—again, a link between border policing and border environments. If they saw anyone on the border, they dropped the location to the nearest cavalry unit from the plane.[93] One of Smithers's photographs captured a De Havilland—the men called them "river flyers"—dropping a message to cavalry riders below (figure 2.11).[94] The information was placed into a small pouch with a lead weight in it and a cloth streamer to help the men on the ground find where it landed. This photograph was also taken in the Big Bend region. The aerial surveillance system the planes provided operated in concert with an increasingly complex amalgam of mules, horses, trucks, tractors, and the roads and ephemeral camps that supported them. All of the military outlay took into account both the geography of conflict in Mexico and the physical geography of the border region.

By February of 1917, however, there were no more American troops in Mexico, and a great many of the border guards were repurposing themselves to fight in the European war. In April, two months after the Pershing expedition had abandoned its search for Pancho Villa and decamped from the mountains and deserts of Northern Mexico, the United States committed itself to the Great War, and the border was all but forgotten.[95] By November of 1918, the United States had assembled the largest fighting force in its history, numbering just over 3.5 million soldiers.[96] The federal government maintained a force along the US-Mexico border of just over 30,000, still larger than the Border Patrol of today.[97] In the context of the World War, however, these men along the border represented just under 1 percent of all active duty military. In his 1917 report, the secretary of war did not even bother to offer specifics on the Mexican border, saying only that

the border operations had done a good job of training them for the war in Europe.[98]

The troops on the border still played a defensive role, as they had since 1915, though they carried out their duties in the border region in relative obscurity. Their orders were to prevent "bandits" from crossing the international line, to prevent cross-border raiding and depredations, to guard the railroad bridges, to intern Mexican forces driven across the line, and to try to enforce the most recent arms embargo of October 9, 1915, though the War Department deemed it "not practicable" anymore to keep up the continuous patrol of the entire border line.[99] The only policy change that accompanied the demobilization of troops along the border was that they were now encouraged to direct all traffic, not just that involved in the Mexican Revolution, through the official ports

FIGURE 2.11.
Plane and Cavalry, 1920

Machines and animals worked together to patrol and surveil the border. W. D. Smithers Collection of Photographs, Harry Ransom Center, the University of Texas at Austin.

of entry and prevent unauthorized crossings "in light" of the war with Germany.[100] In other words, the military activity in the border region during the 1910s helped create a new paradigm for border policing that made sharper distinctions between official ports of entry and unauthorized crossings through the rivers or over land. Based on its experiences during the revolution, the US Army also advocated for a civilian border patrol to step in in their absence.

In October of 1918, as the Hundred Days Offensive was nearing a close in Europe, Acting Secretary of War Benedict Crowell wrote a letter to the secretary of labor about the Mexican border. In it he explicitly advocated the creation of a civilian border patrol. He suggested, quite simply, that plans for "an increase in the force available for Patrol duty under the Bureau of Immigration should be carried into effect," an opinion formed by the army's experience along the line. Crowell said that an internal "study of the conditions along the Mexican border" had convinced the War Department that such a force was necessary. He pressed the secretary of labor, claiming that an "increased force of Immigration Inspectors would perform a most useful function in the more adequate guarding of the Mexican border, the necessity for which has long been felt."[101] By the time the Department of Labor received these letters from the War Department, the idea of creating a federal police force along the Mexican border had already been circulating through the offices of the federal immigration agency for several months. In the summer of 1918, the bureau drafted a plan, "Proposal to Establish an Immigration Patrol Service on the Land Boundaries," but the secretary of labor quashed it, saying that he had not seen enough interest in such a patrol by other government departments. The War Department took the opportunity to make its views clear, and by November their lobby (along with the Departments of State, Navy, Justice, and Labor) had convinced Immigration that, in the words of the commissioner general of labor, "the establishment of a patrol on the border is essential to thorough and efficient enforcement of the law."[102]

Historians have often framed the advent of the US Border Patrol in 1924 in the larger context of the 1920s, an era of increased immigration restrictions, US military and economic supremacy, and an intensified nationalist preoccupation with territorial sovereignty. From this point of view, the Border Patrol emerges amid a cacophony of "nativists," including "eugenicists, xenophobes, scholars, Klan members, labor organizers, and others" whose policies were guided by fantasies of racial purity and fears of societal contamination.[103] In this decade, according to the historian Mae Ngai, "immigration policy rearticulated the US-Mexico border as a cultural and racial boundary."[104] While the American victory in the Great War and the Immigration Act of 1924 were both watershed moments in American history, and though nativism already had a long history in US politics, these larger developments were not the only factors that reshaped the border in the 1920s. The idea of border policing had already been firmly established within the War Department thanks to its border operations during the Mexican Revolution, and the landscape of coercive force had already been thoroughly articulated in the built world of the border region. The paradigm developed in the 1910s by the US military based on technological innovation, aerial surveillance, geographic coverage, and the requisite construction projects to support these outlays of equipment and manpower while navigating extreme climates and topography remained the most durable features of border policing even into the twenty-first century.

AFTER HIS TIME IN SAN ANTONIO PREPARING SOLDIERS TO patrol the Mexican border, the young Eisenhower went back to Washington, DC, where he joined the first cross-country truck convoy in 1919. They departed from "Zero Milestone" just south of the White House and set out in motor vehicles that constantly malfunctioned in a trip across the country in which roads were "average to non existent." During the first three days, they averaged just over five miles per hour, and their excruciating slowness was compounded by the fact that sometimes the heaviest trucks broke through the surfaces of the rare roads that were in fact paved.[105] His sense that military superiority was linked to roadbuilding stayed with him throughout his career in the army and into his presidency. This also translated into a vision for effective policing and surveillance, as well as other kinds of large state-led construction projects. As president from 1953 to 1961, Dwight Eisenhower oversaw the construction of Falcon Dam on the Rio Grande; the execution of Operation Wetback, a massive deportation drive run by his old West Point classmate Joseph Swing, whom he had appointed as INS commissioner; and the passage of the

National Interstate and Defense Highways Act that inaugurated the interstate highway system. Each of these developments reverberated in the border region, one as a bilateral water management project, another as an immigration enforcement policy, and the latter as an expansion of the transport routes to and from the international divide.

For Eisenhower, as well as for many others involved in the militarization of the border during the 1910s, the troops' activities around the international divide and in Northern Mexico were formative experiences that established the border region as a modern militarized police zone. The army border patrols made use of the most sophisticated technology for both access to hinterlands as well as surveillance, they balanced diplomatic concerns with the interests of international capitalism, and they helped carve out a physical landscape of remote border policing that would be used and reused in generations to come.

3

POLICE AND
WATERWORKS ON
THE BORDER

ASPIRATIONS TO CONTROL
THROUGH BUILDING

The three decades between 1924 and 1954 were critical for the development of federal border policing and for the development of waterworks on the international divide. Within that span of time, the US Border Patrol grew from a fledgling organization with uncertain enforcement authority and only the bare minimum of resources to a much more powerful organization run by Joseph Swing, a battle-hardened former army general who orchestrated Operation Wetback, one of the largest single deportation drives in American history.[1] Similarly, the International Boundary Commission (IBC), renamed the International Boundary and Water Commission (IBWC) in 1944, transformed from a bureaucracy dedicated primarily to small land claims arbitration along the border rivers to an engineering agency that executed massive reconfigurations of the physical shape and flow capacity of the Rio Grande and beyond. This chapter explains why these two seemingly unlike histories are in fact intimately connected, and how they developed the built environment of the border region with the hope of gaining control over both people and the natural world.

In the pages that follow, I argue that the history of policing and the history of hydraulic engineering during those years were united in multiple ways on the international divide. Both organizations were border builders. The Border Patrol advocated for fences and lookout towers, the IBC/IBWC straightened the river and dammed it. Both agencies were also united by a common aspiration: control. Where the border police wanted to gain control over the passage of people, animals, and contraband across the line, the water engineers sought to dominate nature itself. The extent to which they succeeded in

achieving this objective, however, was varied, but in both cases officials often looked to physical construction as a solution to a wide array
of perceived problems. Also, the two organizations worked with one
another hand in glove; since the IBC/IBWC was charged with managing the land around the international divide, the construction of
police infrastructure often had to be negotiated with the IBC/IBWC,
despite the fact that the boundary commission had no official role
in policing. This is all the more provocative because the IBC/IBWC
was a binational agency.[2] The Mexican section, called the Comisión
Internacional de Límites (CIL), renamed the Comisión Internacional
de Límites y Aguas (CILA) in 1944, shared joint responsibility for all
projects on the Rio Grande.[3] However, the first long-distance land
border fence, built by the IBWC's US section mainly between 1948
and 1951, was a construction project exclusively on US soil.[4]

It is also important to recognize the extent to which hydraulic engineering during those years, both in a broader context outside the
border region as well as near the line, was linked to large-scale labor
migration from Mexico. Beginning in the first decades of the twentieth
century, groundwater pumping technology and surface water diversion infrastructure helped capitalist agriculture flourish in places like
the San Joaquin and Imperial Valleys of California, South Texas, the
Salt River Valley in Arizona, and elsewhere.[5] These expansions, in turn,
created a sustained demand for migrant labor. The Bracero Program,
a guest worker arrangement between the United States and Mexico
started in 1942 to fill wartime agricultural labor shortages but continued until 1964, accelerated this trend. The Bracero Program alone
facilitated over 4.5 million contracts for workers, though many others
crossed the border to work in the fields without the required paperwork. The Border Patrol and the IBC/IBWC were embedded in these
larger systems of movement, exchange, and development.[6] Though
there was much controversy at the time about the proper role of border
policing in the context of the guest worker program, and though much
of the border fence building after 1947 was tied to the outbreak of foot-
and-mouth disease in central Mexico, the Border Patrol nevertheless
advocated for changes in the built world of the border to assist them
with both surveillance and apprehension of people.[7] And though not
all the projects undertaken by the IBC/IBWC were directly linked to
commercial agriculture, the agency borrowed expertise about hydraulic engineering from the Bureau of Reclamation and the Army Corps

of Engineers, both of which were instrumental to the irrigation of arid lands in the American West.[8]

To demonstrate these connections, I first explain how water management set the stage for commercial agriculture in many arid sections of the border region. This, in turn, helped spur the cross-border movement of Mexican laborers, often the targets of the Border Patrol. Other water engineering projects were also linked to border policing. I focus here on two, the straightening of the Rio Grande around El Paso–Ciudad Juárez in the late 1930s, and the construction of Falcon Dam in the early 1950s, both of which were connected, though in different ways, to surveillance and policing. Meanwhile, in the interim, the IBWC, in large part at the INS's behest, oversaw construction of the largest border fencing project to date on the western land border. Finally, I explain the extent to which a new era of border policing and deportation in the 1950s, exemplified by Operation Wetback in 1954, relied on the built environment of the border region for its tactical capacity. The overall picture that emerges is not only one of rapid transformation and expansion of federal bureaucracies but also of a radical reconstruction of the border's built world, on both land and water.

COMMERCIAL AGRICULTURE

The advent of the Border Patrol in 1924 coincided with the rise of what the environmental historian Donald Worster calls the "hydraulic society" of the American West. He borrows the term from the German Marxist scholar Karl Wittfogel to describe the massive conversion of arid lands into fertile sites for large-scale agriculture. In Worster's view, the consolidation of a system of dams and irrigation works throughout the western states created a society in which those who dominated water dominated people. The expansion of irrigation infrastructure between 1890 and 1909 was remarkable, paralleling the expansions in new railroad tracks during the same period. In 1890, there were only 1.5 million irrigated acres throughout the giant states of California, Nevada, Utah, and Arizona, but in little less than a generation this number had swelled to 14 million acres throughout the Southwest.[9] Worster saw this new hydraulic landscape of the American West, including the US-Mexico border region, as "a land of authority and restraint" and as a "coercive, monolithic, and hierarchical system, ruled by a power elite based on the ownership of capital and expertise."[10]

Though this characterization meshes well with the infamous megalomania of people like Floyd Dominy, the commissioner of the US Bureau of Reclamation from 1959 to 1969 who oversaw some of the largest and most controversial dam projects in the western states, Worster has been taken to task for presenting the West so monolithically, ignoring the nuances of cultural contact, competing ideas of governance, and the voices of the masses.[11] The historian Eric Meeks, for example, has shown how Tohono O'odham people in Arizona recalibrated regional migration practices to accommodate new large-scale cotton agriculture. As desert dwellers, they had long been accustomed to moving sporadically throughout their homeland to adjust to the delicate balance of resources available to them. They then adapted these subsistence strategies to wage labor in the context of commercial agriculture.[12]

Not all groups had the same opportunities to adapt, however. The idea that power is produced through technical expertise, bureaucratization, and the capture of resources meshes well with what we know about the ways in which the first large migrations of Mexican farm laborers to the Southwest met with hard exploitation.[13] From this perspective, resonances between the objectives of capitalist agriculture and a new era of federal policing can be seen in a shared impulse toward social engineering, the creation of hierarchies, and the institutionalization of systems of control. Worster also points to the hubris embedded in the design of major waterworks projects, dams in particular. In his view, hydraulic technology was based on "the illusion that it could bring natural forces under absolute, tight, efficient control, but in truth it multiplied the ways it could work its own demise.... There was more to go wrong, and it did go wrong, on a scale commensurate with the technology involved."[14] With the benefit of hindsight, we can imagine a similar appraisal being taken of the border policing apparatus that has never succeeded in its often-stated goal of bringing "control" to the border.

Water projects linked to commercial agriculture produced demand for workers from Mexico. In the 1910s, the US Congress tightened immigration laws, but it carved out exceptions for Mexicans because the maintenance of the US-Mexico economy was more important to US policymakers than placating racial and nativist anxieties about Mexicans coming to the United States. Railroad, mining, agriculture, and cattle lobbies that sought open access to Mexican workers won out over overt racists, patriotic societies, and the American Federation of Labor, who sought Mexican exclusion.[15] By the late 1910s, large-scale growers in the Southwest had become desperate for Mexican labor. The US Congress introduced a series of immigration restrictions in the winter of 1917, including an $8 head tax and a new list of people who were "excluded from admission to the United States." These inadmissible aliens included, among many others, contract laborers.[16] Mexico was quickly becoming a source of contract laborers, however, and neither they nor their employers wanted to pay head taxes. So nearly instantly the secretary of labor made special exceptions for the United States' southern neighbor, and within two and a half years nearly 27,000 Mexican laborers had been admitted outside the parameters of the 1917 immigration act. The majority of these workers went to work in fields and on railroads.[17]

But that was not enough. In 1918, growers in Arizona sowed 70,000 acres of cotton, and the very next year they ratcheted up their planting by just over one-third, bringing the total acreage up to 92,000. Texas's crops ballooned, too, as did Texas oil fields. Dormant mines roared back to life in Arizona, and sugar beet farmers in California, Colorado, Utah, and Idaho all siphoned as much labor as they could. In Arizona, a construction and roadbuilding boom absorbed the usual labor pools from Texas, Oklahoma, and local indigenous populations. Mexican fieldworkers had typically constituted just under half of the workforce, but the growers and builders wanted more for their crews. The governor of Arizona wrote directly to the secretary of labor in that time of "industrial distress," beseeching him to keep making exceptions for Mexico, claiming that "Mexican labor is an absolute necessity."[18] And the costs of losing it were huge. In Arizona alone, in the early summer of 1919, growers claimed that they stood to lose two-thirds of their crops, unpicked and abandoned, at a value of $10 million.[19] The governor of Texas wrote to the secretary of labor, too, with his own urgent request for more workers from Mexico. In certain Texas counties, he argued, growers faced a possible loss of half their crops.[20] Massive irrigation projects had transformed the arid border regions into productive agricultural zones, and noncitizen labor was seen as a crucial tool to maintain the scale of commercial agriculture and construction booms.[21]

For those people of Mexican descent living in the United States as citizens, their land often came under threat through various mechanisms by big agricultural interests. Ultimately, much of their land was lost, sold off piece by piece out of economic necessity, abandoned after lengthy court battles, ceded due to unvarnished threats, or foreclosed due to tax delinquency.[22] This dispossession was directly linked to irrigation development that hiked land values and lent itself to large-scale production over family farms. For Mexican-origin people of any citizenship status, the new landscape of the border region had become Worster's "coercive, monolithic, and hierarchical system, ruled by a power elite based on the ownership of capital and expertise," and their new place in it was often as wage laborers.

On the Mexican side, too, even on a small scale, irrigation policies brought tension to the border. In El Paso–Ciudad Juárez, for instance, the two largest and oldest settlements on the border and the site where the Rio Grande becomes the international divide, people had diverted the waters of the river for irrigation for centuries using loose rock dams. During much of the nineteenth century, four main ditches split off from the river and channeled water toward crops in and around El Paso: the El Paso town acequia, which was abandoned in 1898; the Isleta and Socorro acequias, both abandoned in 1901; and the San Elizario acequia, which stayed in use into the 1900s. These were small, local, and most likely earthwork projects. Building on the momentum of the Reclamation Act of 1902, however, the statute that established the Reclamation Service (later to be renamed the Bureau of Reclamation) and provided funds to build irrigation infrastructure in the arid West, the El Paso Valley Water Users Association formed a corporation in 1905, alongside the Franklin Canal Company, to divert as much water as they could from the Rio Grande in collaboration with the publicly funded Reclamation Service.[23]

In 1908, upon learning of this plan from a newspaper article published in the *El Paso Herald*, the city council of Ciudad Juárez, backed by the Mexican embassy in Washington, DC, protested against the construction of the Franklin Canal, a modern irrigation project that had the capacity to siphon more water from the river than the old acequias could.[24] According to both local and federal officials in Mexico, it would "undoubtedly harm the preferential secular rights to the calm waters of the Rio Grande" that were afforded to growers on the Mexican side.[25] Just two years earlier, Chihuahua governor Enrique Creel; the geographer Antonio García Cubas, appointed by the Secretaría de Relaciones Exteriores (Ministry of Foreign Relations); and Joaquín D. Casasús,

Mexican ambassador to the United States, had organized an effort to guarantee the water rights of Mexicans living along the international river border. They succeeded, albeit controversially, and the treaty of 1906 authorized the annual delivery of 60,000 acre-feet of water to the Juárez Valley, even though this provided for nearly six times as much irrigated land in New Mexico and Texas as in Chihuahua.[26]

In the end, despite protests from Mexico, public and private interests in the United States succeeded in building the Franklin Canal. As a concession, the US Department of State offered to convene a special committee to study the equitable distribution of water between the two countries, to which the Mexican government agreed, lacking any other recourse. They sent Fernando Beltrán y Puga, an engineer and the head of the Mexican section of the boundary commission, to represent Mexico.[27] As I discuss in the next chapter, the story of the Franklin Canal did not end there. It would take on multiple new meanings as the built environment of the border evolved, each new iteration revealing different aspects of embedded inequality in the border region.

The new large farms, produced by real estate consolidation as well as the water infrastructure that made them possible, had, through their scale, efficiency, and management, created a new political landscape in the border region. State governors had become advocates for large-scale growers, and a new laboring class was emerging, subordinated by citizenship status, disinheritance, social exclusion, and its role as a primary object of police contact.[28] But commercial irrigation was not the only manifestation of hydraulic engineering in the early twentieth century. Water managers, armed with new technological expertise, building materials, and machines, also sought to control as many aspects of rivers as they possibly could. They were particularly concerned with flood control, and they leveraged their powers to change the shape, course, and locations of rivers themselves.

THE STRAIGHTENING OF THE RIO GRANDE

Despite the 1924 advent of the Border Patrol—the agency that would eventually grow to be the biggest builder on the international divide—the first major construction project on the line was carried out by the IBC. It was called the Rio Grande Rectification Project. The career of Joseph Friedkin offers a valuable window on border construction during these years, as well as on the development of the US section of the boundary commission. He was the epitome of a border builder, involved in nearly every major border construction project of the twentieth century. He worked for the IBC/IBWC for fifty-two years, though he first trained as a mining engineer. President John F. Kennedy appointed him commissioner of the agency in 1962, President Lyndon B. Johnson gave him the rank of ambassador in 1968, and upon his retirement in 1986 he received the US Department of State Distinguished Honor Award for his role in the settlement of the Chamizal dispute. He had local ties, having grown up in El Paso, though as a federal employee and part of a binational bureaucracy, the border construction projects he oversaw were wide-ranging both in type and geography.

He was born in Brooklyn in 1909 to a Russian immigrant father and an Irish mother. His father worked in show business, moving the family from place to place, following the theater, performing mainly in quasi-vaudeville acts. When Joseph was six, however, his father decided the family should have deeper roots, and they settled in El Paso.[29] Joseph went to high school in El Paso and eventually attended university at the local school, the College of Mines and Metallurgy of the University of Texas (later renamed the University of Texas at El Paso). He graduated as a mining engineer in 1932 and hoped to put his skills to use in Arizona. But he entered the job market in the depths of the Great Depression. Many of the mines in Arizona had closed down, and Mexico restricted passports on foreigners coming in, dashing his hopes of joining a long line of American technical experts working in extractivist industries in Mexico.[30]

For a year and a half, he taught chemistry and physics at El Paso High School, his alma mater. In 1934, however, eager to plot a new course for his life and see concrete results from his education in engineering, he got a job as a surveyor with the IBC and left the classroom. It just so happened that he was hired right at the beginning of the first major border river engineering project, the straightening of the Rio Grande, there in his adopted hometown of El Paso.[31] At that time, the governments of the United States and Mexico permitted the river to "meander" through the alluvial flats of the border region. The waterway had dozens of bends and twists that would be completely unrecognizable to anyone familiar with the border today.

The Rio Grande's winding, wayward route posed two problems for urban settlement and agricultural production. Its shifting course created uncertainty as to the exact location of the international divide, and perhaps more importantly to the residents of both El Paso and Ciudad Juárez, it had a tendency to flood. The flooding was exacerbated by the construction of Elephant Butte Dam in 1916, about 120 miles north of the international divide. The dam was built by the Bureau of Reclamation and designed to support agriculture in the Mesilla Valley in New Mexico, just north of El Paso. This meant that the maximum discharge of the river was artificially shifted from late spring to late fall to accommodate growing cycles. Because of this interruption, more and more silt collected in the river at faster than normal rates, causing it to overflow during heavy rains and flood neighboring communities on both sides of the border. These were all seen as problems for hydraulic engineers to solve, despite the fact that, in part, they had been created by other hydraulic engineering projects.

The rectification plan was also designed to protect irrigated agriculture. By 1930, 70,000 acres were already under cultivation on the American side of the border, served by irrigation and drainage works as well as top-quality roads. The Mexican side had about half that amount under cultivation with far less developed supporting infrastructure for irrigation and transport.[32] This commercial imbalance was taken into consideration when assessing the overall cost of the project; upon its completion in 1938, the United States had paid $5,080,573 and Mexico only $692,805.[33] In this border construction project, though the work was supervised by a binational commission, the United States nevertheless exerted disproportionate influence.

Even though work did not begin until 1933, the rectification had been a topic of discussion for several years. In 1927, commissioners from both countries had begun to formulate plans for the straightening and stabilizing of the river that would also include building levees, flood control reservoirs, and another dam (Caballo Dam) just south of Elephant Butte, as well as increasing the gradient of the river itself to accelerate its flow. The rectification required not only an elaborate legal framework to codify the complexities of manipulating a river that also served as an international border but also an unprecedented kind of construction on the divide.

The rectification was mainly an earthwork project. It was carried out by machines—draglines with hundred-foot booms equipped with buckets between two and three cubic yards in capacity. The idea was to cut out the bends in the riverbed. By the end of the project, workers had actually shortened the length of the river. In the construction zone—the stretch of river between Cordova Island in El Paso and Fort Quitman—sixty-seven miles of river were simply removed. In fact, it is important to note, the urban centers of the two border towns had problems with flooding as well, but a disputed piece of land known as the Chamizal, of which Cordova Island was a part, made river rectification there politically impossible. Another thirty years would pass before that section of the river was touched by IBWC construction equipment.

Setting aside this several-mile stretch in the urban areas, construction machines had plenty to do downriver. The long-boom dragline excavators moved over 6 million cubic yards of material, reducing 155 miles of winding, silt-carrying water to 88. As a result, the Rio Grande became a slightly shorter river. IBC surveyors, of whom a young Friedkin was most likely one, mapped the entire area under construction to ensure that no change occurred in the amount of territory possessed by either the United States or Mexico. The areas in the bends that were cut off during the rectification were called "parcels." Of 178 such parcels, 85 were ceded to the United States, 69 to Mexico, and 24 remained in the floodway channel. In the final calculation, 5,121 acres had been ceded back and forth, exactly measured, between the two countries. A once-winding river now cut a straighter path through the El Paso–Ciudad Juárez border region.[34]

The rectification project also produced corollary border building sites. Canals leading away from the river for irrigation underwent major modifications, and new concrete grade-control structures were placed at four locations along the river. Also important, however, was how the river work prompted the need for both elongated bridges connecting the United States and Mexico and brand-new ports of entry. By 1938, not only had the Rio Grande been straightened, but three new bridges had been built across it that connected the two nations.[35]

Looking back many years later, Friedkin fondly remembered the straightening of the Rio Grande. "We call this one of the most peaceful land boundary settlements," he stated proudly. It was carried out because people in the area "needed the protection," a bilateral project that was able to "provide a service, provide a benefit, for both countries."[36]

However, Pedro Martínez, the president of the Jesús Carranza ejido, as well as his fellow ejidatarios, did not see it this way. The ejido, or communally held agricultural land, was a key component of land reform after the revolution. In early August of 1933, as news circulated about the rectification project, the inhabitants of Jesús Carranza, located on the outskirts of Ciudad Juárez, became nervous. They wrote a letter to the Secretaría de Agricultura y Fomento (Ministry of Agriculture and Development) asking for more information. "They told us it was a project of defense," the petition explains, "but . . . we don't understand what it is that's being defended against." From their perspective, the straightening of the Rio Grande cut away parts of their cotton fields, compromising their livelihood. They declared, to no avail, "We do not comply with this work because we have not had any say-so."[37]

For their part, officials in Mexico City such as Enrique Jiménez D. in the Secretaría de Relaciones Exteriores and Luis Garibay Jr. in Ciudad Juárez, an engineer for Agricultura y Fomento, set about clarifying the legal authority for expropriation of ejidal lands in the Juárez Valley. This included not only the settlement of Jesús Carranza but also another ejido called San Isidro de Río Grande, which had to be reshaped to accommodate the Acequia Madre de Juárez so it could feed the San Agustín and Guadalupe canals. They established that the Comisión Nacional de Irrigación (National Commission on Irrigation) considered these communal lands "indispensable" for the continuation of the rectification project and mandated that those affected be compensated and compelled to move. National ejido policy dictated that when communal lands were expropriated for the public good, an equal amount of land had to be made available to those who lived there, though for the residents of the Ejido de Jesús Carranza, this likely did not feel like the agency they sought over the matter.[38]

As the Mexican government fine-tuned its expropriation policies for border dwellers, the leadership of the US Border Patrol was trying to figure out ways to expand its enforcement authority. These were also the years during which both the American and Mexican governments worked together to deport hundreds of thousands of Mexicans living in the United States during the Depression, also on an unprecedented scale.[39] As the capacity of border construction—both physically and legally—increased, so did the capacity of border policing. These developments intersected with one another.

In 1937, as the rectification project was nearing completion, the magazine *Scientific American* took an interest in the engineering feat it required. L. M. Lawson, the American commissioner of the IBC, wrote an article for them. He described for popular science readers the nature of the site, the ingenuity of the engineers who masterminded the straightening of the river, and the general goodwill between the United States and Mexico during the project. He also enumerated the benefits of the rectification. Chief among them was the elimination of the flooding threat that had plagued the region for decades. From a diplomatic point of view, he explained how the river project would prevent future channel changes, thereby defusing potential controversy over the exact location of the border (despite the fact that the Chamizal dispute still lingered). And finally, crucially, he pointed out that the rectification would lead to "more satisfactory enforcement of the immigration and customs laws of both countries."[40] A straightened river produced a new landscape that was easier to patrol and surveil. There was less territory to guard, and due to the extirpation of vegetation along the river banks to make way for the straightening and new floodplains and levees, it was easier to see for longer distances. For Lawson, border policing and hydraulic engineering were thus linked concretely, though the most robust collaboration between the IBC/IBWC and the INS took place not on the river but on the western land border.

WESTERN LAND BOUNDARY FENCE PROJECT

B etween 1939 and 1951, notwithstanding a suspension of construction during World War II, the IBC/IBWC completed 237 miles of border fences across 674 miles of land between the Pacific coast and El Paso–Ciudad Juárez where the river becomes the border. Most of this construction took place after 1948, however, propelled by concerns about a foot-and-mouth disease outbreak in Mexico in 1947. To build it, the IBC/IBWC collaborated with the INS and the Bureau of Animal Industry, as well as the National Park Service and at least six private contractors. Called the Western Land Boundary Fence Project, this border building endeavor was the first major construction project on the line geared explicitly toward the regulation of both human and animal movement. In that regard, the different agencies that advocated for border fencing in those years were driven by different conceptions of geography. The INS and the Border Patrol, on one hand, primarily advocated for fencing around ports of entry. To them, the border was a constellation of ports, discrete points within a larger landscape where immigration and contraband inspection could take place. The Bureau of Animal Industry, on the other hand, understood the border in terms of the sprawling, remote spaces in between the ports of entry. Bolstered by the massive quarantine measures taken after the foot-and-mouth disease epizootic, BAI officials lobbied for fencing in the outlying grazing country where potentially infected animals could wander.

The legal authorization to build fencing along the western border was codified in the Act of August 19, 1935, 49 Stat. 660, which itself was linked to a 1924 statute that authorized US-Mexico cooperation in assessing the equitable use of the waters of the Rio Grande. Here again, policing and building were linked to seemingly unrelated hydraulic projects. The 1935 amendment permitted the IBC to "construct and maintain fences, monuments and other demarcations of the boundary line between [the] United States and Mexico, and sewer systems, water systems, and electric light, power and gas systems crossing the international border."[41]

The US section of the boundary commission built two general types of fences: "ranch" fences and chain-link fences. Ranch fencing constituted the overwhelming majority of fence construction during these years. As the name suggests, this type of barrier was primarily designed to keep animals from moving back and forth across the border. This was particularly important to the Bureau of Animal Industry, the agency tasked with enforcing the foot-and-mouth disease quarantine at the border. This particular type of fencing has the longest history in the border region. Rachel St. John has traced its origins back to 1909 in Southern California. In that instance, the BAI was also the principal agency promoting fence construction, though then it was primarily concerned with Texas fever ticks.[42] In both cases, however, remotely located fencing initiatives were primarily the purview of federal agencies interested in managing rangeland and protecting capitalist husbandry.[43]

Chain-link fences, on the other hand, were divided into two types and were primarily intended to thwart the movement of human beings. "Class 2" was designed for areas just outside of towns but near ports of entry. These fences were eight feet high and made of 2" × 2" mesh of No. 9 gauge wire. On top were three strands of barbed wire on overhanging arms, adding an extra foot to the total fence height. They were set in concrete and held up by steel line posts. They were meant to be both difficult and dangerous to climb.

"Class 1," on the other hand, was the most robust antihuman barrier system yet to exist on the border. These fences were meant for densely populated areas immediately surrounding ports of entry. They were ten feet tall, with the same 2" × 2" mesh, though of No. 6 gauge wire, which was harder to cut through with shears. Again, three strands of barbed wire were strung atop the fence on overhanging arms, designed to cut, maim, or otherwise entangle human flesh. The concrete curb into which the fence was sunk extended eighteen inches underground to guard against tunneling. Perhaps the most significant distinction between Class 1 and Class 2 chain-link fencing, however, was the fact that Class 1 fencing was artificially illuminated. Running alongside the steel line posts that supported the mesh were a series of wooden poles that carried a three-phase 2,300-volt primary circuit and a 6.6 ampere series lighting circuit. Lights and reflectors were mounted on the same poles and placed about 150 to 200 feet apart.[44]

The Immigration and Naturalization Service was the biggest proponent of chain-link fencing, partially to address a long-standing anxiety for some about the remote areas of the border region. For instance, in one of the first congressional hearings dedicated to the newly created Border Patrol in 1926, Henry St. George Tucker of Virginia framed his concerns about border policing in terms of both security and infrastructure. He complained, "A port of entry is the last place in the world that a smuggler or an alien trying to get into the country would go through; he would go through across a ford somewhere on the Rio Grande, somewhere out in the wastes."[45] Nevertheless, Border Patrol officers between 1924 and 1954 were often focused on the built environment of roads and ports as the backbones of their policing activities rather than on "the wastes." That was the purview of the Bureau of Animal Industry.

By the late 1940s, Border Patrol officers and immigration officials had become thoroughly dissatisfied with the condition of the existing fencing around the ports of entry. Complaints about flimsy or nonexistent fencing echoed through the major western border towns. For instance, W. A. Carmichael, the district director for the INS in Los Angeles, was a strong proponent of police building on the border, especially around Calexico, the gateway to the mega agricultural growing region of the Imperial Valley. For him, the kind of construction that was best for police involved a constellation of features that included not only fencing but lighting systems, patrol roads, and watchtowers as well. All this was designed to enhance the tactical advantage of police by increasing visibility. A crucial component of this was not only the built environment but the way that the built environment interacted with local flora. In a memo to the commissioner of the INS, Carmichael made sure to point out that "no vegetation or other obstruction should be permitted between the road and the fence."[46] These ideas were similar to those of IBC Commissioner Lawson when he pointed out why the straightening of the Rio Grande would be a boon to law enforcement.

The artificial illumination of the line was important to border police. Outside the port of entry near El Centro, California, patrol officers felt that they were at a disadvantage at night. They wanted electric lights on the border, complete with tamperproof wire circuits embedded in conduits encased in concrete, heavy glass shields over the bulbs to deflect rocks thrown at them, and even reflective paint on the fence itself. As one officer put it, waxing almost poetic, "As I visualize such a completed fence, it would appear at night as a ribbon of light, on which any dark object such as a man would stand out conspicuously."[47]

In Southern California, both the natural environment and waterworks factored into designs for police building on the border. In some cases, such as the All-American Canal, water infrastructure was enlisted into the service of policing. The canal is an eighty-mile-long aqueduct that runs parallel and very close to the international divide. It was built by the Bureau of Reclamation in the 1930s as one of the largest irrigation canals in the world. It diverts water from the Colorado River to the arid Imperial Valley and was therefore instrumental to the staggering rise of both commercial agriculture in the region as well as cross-border agricultural labor migration. In an official memorandum from 1948, a patrol inspector in Southern California pointed out how such a body of water could be incorporated into the built environment of policing. He

speculated that when the border fence was constructed, it would divert "prospective line jumpers" around it. "Fortunately," he wrote, "we have the All-American Canal to assist us at the point where the fence ends." Pointing out that the channel was a minimum of two hundred feet wide with a one-hundred-foot waterway, he concluded that it was a "very satisfactory barrier." However, to

ensure that it was not traversed at night, he also advocated mounting searchlights on watchtowers in the vicinity.[48] The idea of enlisting hydraulic infrastructure in the project of border policing fits well within the context of commercial agriculture in this area, which, as the historian Benny Andrés Jr. has shown, was already dependent on racial stratification among Mexicans, Japanese, South Asians, and Filipinos.[49]

FIGURE 3.2.
Nogales Fence, 1947

In Arizona, too, border
police took pictures
of existing sections
of border fencing
to demonstrate its
inefficacy. Records of
the Immigration and
Naturalization Service,
Record Group 85.

The Calexico office of the INS even took photographs to demonstrate what they saw as the deplorable condition of existing border fencing in 1948. In one of the pictures, three men sit on top of a crumpled fence, seemingly unconcerned by the fact that a federal official was photographing them (figure 3.1). Another man looks directly at the camera while two others are caught midstep. This picture is only one of a series that the INS took as evidence that, to their minds, more durable barriers were necessary on the line.[50]

INS officers in Arizona took a similar set of photographs around the same time. Immigration officials there bemoaned the fact that people could dig under the existing fence. In one image, a Border Patrol officer is shown intentionally prying apart strands of barbed wire to demonstrate the inability of such fencing to disrupt unauthorized crossings (figure 3.2). On the back of the photograph is a handwritten

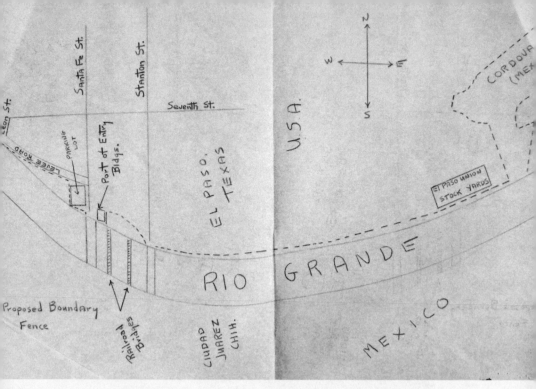

Santa Fe St.

Stanton St.

Leon St.

Seventh St.

LEVEE ROAD

PARKING LOT

Port of Entry Bldgs.

EL PASO, TEXAS

N
W ← → E
S

U.S.A.

CORDOVA (MEX

EL PASO UNION STOCK YARDS

RIO GRANDE

Proposed Boundary Fence

Railroad Bridges

CIUDAD JUAREZ CHIH.

MEXICO

FIGURE 3.3.
Proposed Fence in
El Paso, 1947

Map of El Paso, Texas, hand-
drawn by an INS official. It
was meant to show where
border police wanted to
construct a boundary fence.
Records of the Immigration
and Naturalization Service,
Record Group 85.

note: "fence full of holes." Arizona INS
officials advocated for the "chain-link set
in concrete" design to prevent this. H. D.
Nice, the officer in charge in Nogales, specifically referenced the heavy-gauge woven
mesh fence manufactured by the Cyclone
Fence Company and the Continental Steel
Corporation. He found their products
attractive for border fencing because they
had previously been used to guard industrial plants.[51]

One INS official in Texas even produced a hand-drawn map of El
Paso to show where the agency believed border fencing was necessary (figure 3.3). The features of the city's urban plan that the amateur
draftsman chose to include are noteworthy; they reveal the features of
both the built and natural worlds that border police considered to be
particularly important. Four cross-border road bridges and two other
railroad bridges hold special prominence. Also included is the area
called Cordova Island, just east of central El Paso. This 385-acre piece
of land was not actually an island at all but rather part of Mexican

territory that existed north of the river. This was a disputed zone, and because this area did not conform to the river-based geography of the border, it offered attractive opportunities for smugglers and posed a tactical challenge for border police. It was the bane of the Border Patrol's existence in El Paso.

G. J. McBee, the chief patrol inspector in El Paso in 1947, wrote that "aliens operating in this section are not the common 'wetback' encountered along other parts of the border; but are predominantly of the criminal classes, engaged in the smuggling of aliens and contraband to enter for the purpose of theft and depredation." To his mind, a solution to this problem could be found in construction. He found the lack of "obstruction" on the border an egregious omission, and like his counterparts on the western border, he disliked the night. They had no powerful lights to illuminate the border and were rendered weaker for it. So McBee advocated for a constellation of building projects in El Paso to help him and his men take control of movement across the line.[52] All of these proposals by various federal policing officials along the border were taken seriously by the IBWC, and nearly all aspects of their plans were executed as part of the Western Land Boundary Fence Project.

Chain-link fence construction around the ports of entry was vastly more expensive then the ranch-type fencing in remote areas. On average, chain-link fencing cost $26,647 per mile to build, whereas ranch fencing cost an average of $2,773 per mile. What this meant is that in the most intense phase of building, the three-year span of construction between 1948 and 1950, the total cost of chain-link fencing around the ports of entry actually exceeded the total cost of ranch fencing, despite the fact that ranch fencing stretched just over 115 miles through the border region and chain-link occupied a mere 13 miles, split between six different ports—Naco, Lochiel, Douglas, and Nogales in Arizona, Calexico in California, and Columbus in New Mexico. Of these, Calexico won the lion's share, with 5.62 miles surrounding the port, the gateway to the Imperial Valley. When the final costs were tabulated for that three-year period, the US federal government spent $320,446 on ranch fencing and $348,366 on chain-link. Much of this discrepancy in price had to do with the fact the chain-link fencing systems required more materials and a more elaborate installation process.[53]

The relative difficulty involved in accessing the construction sites also mattered for border fence builders. In 1948, the IBWC organized a series of flights over the western land border. The planes crisscrossed back and forth over the line, at times veering into Mexican airspace, most likely authorized to do so by virtue of their affiliation with the commission and its bilateral authority. These were low-altitude reconnaissance missions. The planes flew only about one thousand feet above the ground in order to take oblique-angle photographs from the air. The purpose was to survey the landscape to ascertain how difficult it would be to construct fencing in remote areas. In this way, the photographs themselves also constitute a critical part of border construction.

FIGURE 3.4.
Nogales, Arizona;
Nogales, Sonora, 1948

Nogales, Arizona, and Nogales, Sonora, press against one another in this desert valley. They are joined by cultural connections and a railroad but divided by a fence. Records of the International Boundary and Water Commission, Record Group 76.

In one photo, two towns, both named Nogales, one in Arizona, the other in Sonora, are nestled in a Sonoran Desert valley (figure 3.4).[54] In the background, the Patagonia Mountains of Arizona nearly fill the frame. This photograph was taken from the Mexican side of the border looking east. The two towns are nearly indistinguishable;

the starkest feature of the built environment is the cross-border railroad
running through the center of both
Nogaleses, designed as connective
tissue between the two countries to
facilitate long-distance trade, particularly in metals. The border is visible,
however. What could be mistaken
from a distance as a wide boulevard
in the middle of the frame is actually
two streets, one in the United States,
one in Mexico, bisected by the inter-

FIGURE 3.5.
Columbus, New Mexico; Palomas,
Chihuahua, ca. 1948

Once the site of Pancho Villa's raid
that triggered the Pershing expedition, Columbus, New Mexico, takes
on a different meaning when photographed from the air by the boundary
commission in anticipation of border
fence construction. Records of the
International Boundary and Water
Commission, Record Group 76.

national divide. In the foreground, a spindly border fence climbs out of
the valley, over the first hill, and down into the wash outside of town.

In contrast to the wrinkled and uneven topography of the Sonoran
Desert surrounding the two towns named Nogales, Columbus, New
Mexico, and Palomas, Chihuahua, lie somewhat separated in a yawn-
ing flatland of the Chihuahuan Desert. There, the IBWC also took aerial photographs. The view in the one reproduced here is looking south
(figure 3.5). Columbus, the small town that Pancho Villa attacked in
1916 that set into motion the brief American military invasion into

Northern Mexico, occupies the center of the frame.[55] In the distance, the even smaller town of Palomas sits in apparent isolation in the arid expanse. Again, the definitive features in the built environment visible from the air are transport routes—the railroad and roads. A now-defunct railway line passes through Columbus, once an important corridor for moving metal extracted in Arizona and Sonora to the smelter in El Paso. That was part of the heyday of Sonoran Desert mining that a young Friedkin had hoped to join but couldn't. Perpendicular to the tracks, a road passes through town and extends off into the vanishing point, running through Palomas along the way. Somewhere in between the two towns lies the international border, imperceptible from this vantage.

Based on these photographic series, as well as reports from field engineers on the ground, the IBWC generated a classification system that described how easy or hard it would be to build border fences. They took four factors into consideration: topography, the characteristics of the ground itself, proximity to railroads, and proximity to roads, in keeping with a long-standing history of connections between the natural and built environments of the border region. The easiest places to build were on level areas within twenty miles of a railroad and on ground of neither rock nor deep sand. The trains were critical to moving building materials. Pliable—but not too pliable—earth made driving posts easier, with no rock breaking, blasting, or woozy construction in sand needed. Worksites located twenty to fifty miles from railroads were that much harder to build on, and some sections of the boundary fence were located over fifty miles from the nearest track. Rolling ground was typical, though semimountainous and mountainous areas posed serious challenges due to more rocky soil and numerous arroyos. In the best cases, good roads led to worksites, facilitating the movement of laborers out into the field. In other cases, there were only bad roads. Sometimes there were no roads at all, but the construction sites could be reached by all-terrain trucks. In the worst cases—even in the late 1940s, several years after a fully mechanized war and squarely within the nuclear age—workers still had to use pack trains to get to federal border fence construction zones.[56]

In 1951, Congress halted appropriations for fence building. They said that no additional barriers were necessary, especially with respect

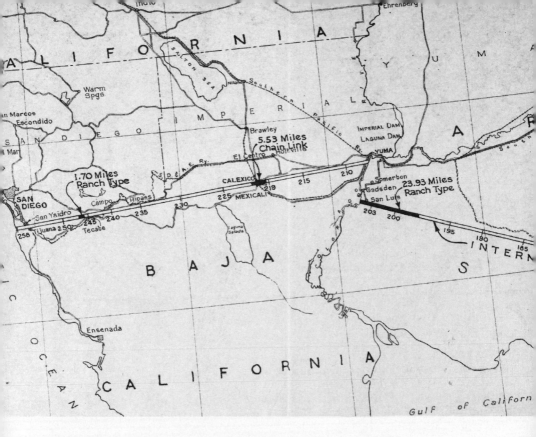

to ranch fencing, because foot-and-mouth had been contained. As a capstone project, the IBWC produced a map in 1953 to document the total extent of fencing on the western boundary at the time (see details in figures 3.6–3.8). Officials were careful to indicate the larger landscape of the built environment of the border, especially major and minor roads, railroads, and ports of entry. From this vantage, the correlation between the diverse built environment of fencing, the landscape of transport infrastructure, and the distinct objectives of immigration policing versus animal management becomes clear.

FIGURE 3.6.
Western Land Boundary Fence Project, California (detail), 1953

Pedestrian fencing, especially around Calexico, the gateway to the Imperial Valley, was paramount in California. Records of the International Boundary and Water Commission, Record Group 76.

Yet despite the extent to which this fencing project was orchestrated by government agencies, the overwhelming majority of construction was carried out by private contractors. They were also often pegged to specific localities. For instance, of the six private

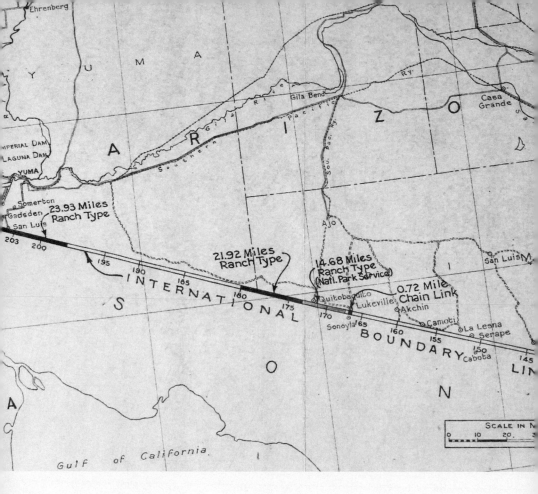

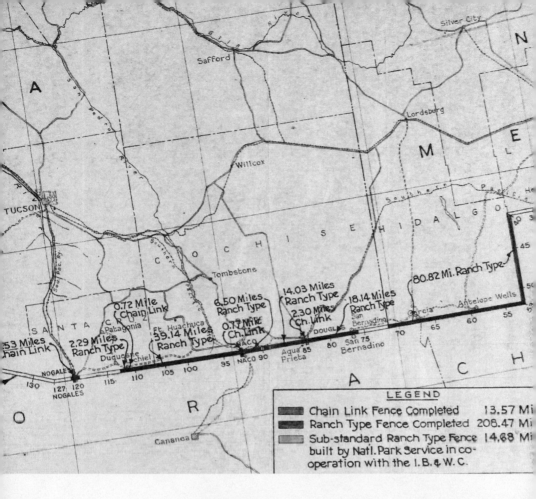

FIGURE 3.7.

Western Land Boundary Fence Project, Arizona (detail), 1953

Unlike in California, fencing in Arizona was dominated
by "ranch-style" barbed wire. Records of the International
Boundary and Water Commission, Record Group 76.

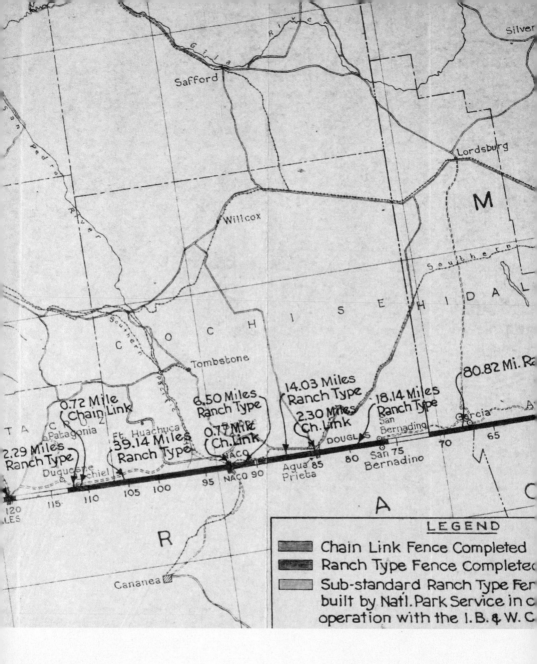

Gila River

Safford

Silver

Lordsburg

M

Willcox

Southern

San Pedro River

Santa Cruz River

C O C H I S E   H I D A L

C

Southern Pacific

Tombstone

80.82 Mi. Ra

14.03 Miles
Ranch Type

2.30 Miles
Ch.Link

18.14 Miles
Ranch Type

Garcia

6.50 Miles
Ranch Type

0.72 Mile
Chain Link

0.77 Mile
Ch.Link

San
Bernadino

70   65

DOUGLAS

39.14 Miles
Ranch Type

2.29 Miles
Ranch Type

Ft. Huachuca

Patagonia

Duquesne

chiel

NACO

95   NACO 90

Agua 85
Prieta

80   San 75
Bernadino

A

120
LES

115   110   105   100

T A   C R U Z

R

Cananea

LEGEND

Chain Link Fence Completed
Ranch Type Fence Completed
Sub-standard Ranch Type Fer
built by Natl. Park Service in c
operation with the I. B. & W. C

FIGURE 3.8.

Western Land Boundary Fence Project, New Mexico
(detail), 1953

With the exception of the Bootheel, the southern border of New
Mexico was left largely unfenced. No fences were constructed along
the Rio Grande river border, so the map ends at El Paso. Records of
the International Boundary and Water Commission, Record Group 76.

fence-building companies the IBWC hired to construct the western boundary fence, only two, R. E. Trappman and W. F. Anderson, built both ranch-style and chain-link fence on sites in more than one state. The former constructed border fencing in all three western border states, while the latter worked only in Arizona and New Mexico. The other four companies worked more locally. San Xavier Rock and Sand Co. built only chain-link fence only in Arizona, Amidon Fence Co. built only ranch-style fence in California, and King-Hoover Construction Co. and A. V. Fralie constructed only ranch fence in New Mexico. In fact, the only government agency directly tasked with building border fencing was the National Park Service, but its construction, too, was also quite local, building 14.58 miles of ranch fencing within Organ Pipe Cactus National Monument.[57]

In a 1947 letter between L. M. Lawson, the commissioner of the IBWC and overseer of the Rio Grande Rectification Project, and T. B. Shoemaker, the acting director of the INS, Lawson makes the material connections between the IBWC and other federal bureaucracies clear. He wrote plainly that the fence building section of the International Boundary and Water Commission functioned "primarily as the construction and maintenance agency for the other agencies of the government interested in the fence projects as an aid in the performance of their respective functions." He pointed out the extent to which the plans for the fence had been adapted to serve the needs of the Department of Agriculture in response to the foot-and-mouth quarantine, and expressed his sympathy and attentiveness to the desires of the Border Patrol for chain-link fencing around the ports of entry. To that end, he suggested another avenue for potential collaboration: he gladly offered to make use of surplus fencing at the Crystal City internment camp by giving it a second life on the border.[58]

BORDER PATROL TOWERS

Fences were not the only type of construction that border police used to deter unauthorized crossing. As the IBWC was building fences at the Border Patrol's behest on the western boundary, the Border Patrol was also constructing and operating a string of watchtowers at strategic points along the international border. A photograph tucked within the internal memoranda and interagency correspondence of the INS depicts a typical design (figure 3.9). This image was meant to be seen by agency employees to help them understand the technical specifications of the towers.[59] On the photograph itself, the exact dimensions of the concrete footing and angle iron necessary for construction are noted. High-powered lights seem to be mounted to the roof of the observation tower, and a wooden utility pole is intentionally included in the frame of the photograph, likely to demonstrate the connectivity between the surveillance and communications infrastructures.

Oral histories give us a good sense of how these towers were used. Edwin Reeves joined the Border Patrol in 1925, a year after its creation. He was born in Beaumont, Texas, and was posted at various stages in his thirty-year career in all the major border towns along the Rio Grande: Brownsville, Laredo, and El Paso. Before that, he worked for the railroad in Texas during the Mexican Revolution, went to France and Belgium to work with naval aviation units there, then came back to the railroads until he became a border guard.[60] In the very early years, there was almost nothing concrete to show for being a Border Patrol officer. No badges, uniforms, or even, at the very beginning, lodging; some early patrolmen reported sleeping in the county jail in Bracketville, Texas.[61]

Reeves seemed to relish thinking back to the cat-and-mouse games between border police and alcohol smugglers during Prohibition, especially on and around Cordova Island. "They'd come over at the neck, a little outfit, and after they got in there they could just spread everywhere," he said. Lookout towers helped. He fondly recalled the tactical advantage they provided. One man posted on top with binoculars could look down and see anyone trying to enter the "island." Fellow border police gathered at the base of the tower, and the man with the binoculars relayed down to them the positions of the unauthorized crossers. The law enforcement officers gathered at the base, hidden a few blocks back from the line, were invisible to people on the Mexican side. In the early days, they had no electric lighting; the system worked only in daylight and by the light of the moon.[62]

Arthur Adams got a job with the Border Patrol in 1949. He had spent six years in the navy during the war, and afterward worked the graveyard shift at General Motors testing diesel locomotive engines

Reinforced Platform

"x3"x1/4" angle iron

2½" x 2½" x 3/16" angle i

2'x12'x8" concrete

18" x 18" x 24" concrete pads .

in his native Chicago. His nocturnal work with heavy machines cost him his hearing; fifteen engines roaring through the night on the test floor damaged his inner ears. He saw a Civil Service advertisement for Border Patrol jobs, and at $3,051 a year, it paid better than anything else he could find. He applied, interviewed, got in, and was posted to El Paso. He headed to the border from the industrial north and took up work that privileged sight over sound.[63]

Adams spent a lot of time in lookout towers on the line. When he arrived on the border, there were at least five of these structures punctuating the low-rise skyline of El Paso. Three were down in the satellite villages of San Elizario and Fabens, several miles east down the river from the center of the city. This was the region where most of the agriculture was, just outside of town. The fields were irrigated by water diverted from the newly straightened Rio Grande. The presence of the towers attested to the already well-established relationship between commercial agriculture and unauthorized Mexican labor.

The other two towers were centrally located near downtown El Paso. They would have been familiar and unmistakable features of the urban fabric from the point of view of people living on both sides of the border. One tower sat atop the Border Patrol headquarters at the time, located by the Santa Fe Bridge, the primary conduit between the plaza in Ciudad Juárez and the plaza in El Paso. The other was on Paisano Drive, a road that ran parallel to the river, right next to Cordova Island. Despite his time in the armed forces, and his intimate familiarity with massive internal combustion engines, sometimes Adams got nervous climbing up the tall ladders to reach the top of the border lookout towers. "It was a fair piece up that ladder," he said. He sat up there for hours, looking down on the border and on the roads on both sides of the line. Again, he worked at night. At dusk, he ascended to the perch. He could see buses in Mexico, packed full of workers brought in bunches to work menial jobs in El Paso and the surrounding fields. The towers served to enhance the ability of a single person to surveil a broad landscape and heightened that observer's ability to anticipate where an unauthorized crossing might take place. Then the police lookout would climb down, and as he put

FIGURE 3.9.
Border Patrol Tower,
ca. 1949

Aerial views conferred a tactical advantage to US border guards. Records of the Immigration and Naturalization Service, Record Group 85.

it, "lay in up a nearby crossing and sack 'em up."[64] Suspicion, surveil-lance, and distrust had all been built into the police infrastructure of the border by the early 1950s.

FALCON DAM

By the 1950s, dam building in US-Mexico watersheds was not new. In 1916, the US Bureau of Reclamation completed construction on Elephant Butte Dam on the Rio Grande in central New Mexico, the construction that changed the flow of the river that triggered a subse-quent river-straightening project in the 1930s. At the same time, work was afoot on the Boquilla Dam on the Conchos River in Chihuahua, a tributary of the Rio Grande. Boquilla was built with Canadian in-vestment and at the time was considered one of the largest dams in the world. Its construction continued despite the fighting of the Mexican Revolution, though in 1913 its one thousand workers and twenty engineers had to suspend work due to difficulties receiving shipments of materials via the railroad.[65] Then, in the depths of the Great Depression, the Bureau of Reclamation completed Hoover Dam on the Colorado River in 1936. It was a marvel of modern hydraulic engineering and a source of controversy between the United States and Mexico, since, after passing through five states, what's left of the Colorado eventually crosses the border into Mexico and drains into the Gulf of California.[66]

Unlike Hoover Dam, Falcon Dam, situated in the southern Rio Grande valley near the mouth of the river, was not a source of dip-lomatic controversy as the earlier water rights disputes were, nor did it rank among the most ambitious feats of hydraulic engineering. Grand Coulee Dam, for instance, on the massive Columbia River in Washington State, operated at 125,000 kilowatts throughout World War II to supply power to the insatiable aluminum industry used to manufacture war planes.[67] Both generators combined at Falcon—one in the United States, the other in Mexico—could produce only about half that. What did set it apart, however, was that it was the first major damming project on the international border itself. This meant that it was a joint construction project between the US and Mexican govern-ments, authorized by the terms of the 1944 treaty Utilization of Waters

of the Colorado and Tijuana Rivers and of the Rio Grande. The largely earthen dam took nearly four years to build, and when it was done, it was almost five miles long. It is a type of water barrier called "rolled earth-fill embankment," which means it was mainly constructed by creating a retaining wall of compacted earth, stabilized by compacted sand and gravel fill and protected by rock riprap.

Falcon Dam was designed for multiple purposes, including flood control and irrigation. One of its core functions, however, was to generate electricity. Though the spillway is located entirely on the US side of the border, water is diverted to a powerhouse located on the Mexican side of the border (see figure 3.10).[68] With the exception of

FIGURE 3.10.
Falcon Dam, 1971

Another aerial photograph taken by the IBWC. Views from above were critical not only to border policing and surveillance but also for designing and maintaining river engineering projects. Records of the International Boundary and Water Commission, Record Group 76.

the intake structure and the penstocks system, the Mexican power-house was identical to its American counterpart, and they were electrically interconnected. When completed, the dam stood 150 feet above the riverbed.[69] It retained a reservoir that, at its maximum capacity, held 3.98 million acre-feet of water, inundating the banks of the Rio Grande for miles upriver.[70]

By then, the ambitious Joseph Friedkin had risen in the ranks of the IBWC and had become commissioner of the entire agency. He oversaw the dam construction project. In 1953, President Dwight Eisenhower returned to Texas to meet his Mexican counterpart, Adolfo Ruiz Cortines, at the newly constructed Falcon Dam in the southern Rio Grande valley. Friedkin liked to quote what Eisenhower said at the occasion. As Friedkin remembered it, the president announced: "More than a mute monument to the ingenuity of engineers, the Falcon Dam is living testimony to the understanding and the cooperation binding our two peoples." Because it had been jointly built by both American and Mexican engineers and laborers, this was the kind of infrastructure project that lent itself to proclamations of solidarity and community. Friedkin relished these lines and sentiments, and he was proud of how the dam project had conquered the river. And as for complaints that the dam had negatively affected wildlife and vegetation, he easily dismissed them, saying, "I think, environmentally it has greatly enhanced the area." He noted the ballooning fish population and recreational facilities on the reservoir to make his case.[71] For him, environmental improvement was synonymous with engineers' ability to harness natural resources for human use, echoing the historian Mark Fiege's point that irrigators in the arid West saw habitat destruction as inevitable but were often very interested in the new environments that emerged from remodeled relationships between the built and natural worlds.[72]

The year after the dam was built, a torrential rain fell in the border region. The Rio Grande and two of its tributaries, the Pecos and Devils Rivers, filled to capacity, and above Falcon Dam, boundary commission workers measured the greatest water flow on record. The newly constructed dam held back the waters and prevented what would have been devastation in the towns of Harlingen, McAllen, Brownsville, and Hidalgo, as well as the agricultural lands around them. The areas above the dam, however, were not so lucky. The border towns of Del

Rio, Ciudad Acuña, Eagle Pass, Piedras Negras, Laredo, and Nuevo Laredo flooded, and all communications in and out of the towns were lost. Friedkin and other IBWC workers flew a small plane over the border to survey the damage, and saw that all the bridges joining the United States to Mexico had been destroyed by the floodwaters. Below the reservoir, however, he marveled at the dam's capacity to overcome the might of nature. He was happy to report that the river below the reservoir was nothing more than a "small, quiet stream," despite the carnage upriver.[73] From the point of view of the IBWC, part of the watershed at least had been conquered, taken back from the unpredictability of flooding.

Aside from flood control, the dam was also designed to expand irrigated agriculture in the southern Rio Grande valley. It succeeded in this, too. Stabilizing the water supply allowed growers in South Texas to double the acreage under production; by the 1980s, cultivated agricultural land had reached 800,000 acres. In the Mexican state of Tamaulipas, the expansion was even more dramatic compared to pre-dam levels, eventually reaching close to 600,000 acres under irrigation with river water.[74]

But the grandeur and fanfare of the first major dam on the US-Mexico border, the presidential ceremony, the pride in engineers' ability to dominate a river system, and the expansion of capitalist agriculture all obscured the experience of the people from the small towns of Zapata, Texas, and Ciudad Guerrero, Tamaulipas. There were probably only about one thousand people in Zapata, and they all shared the bad luck of living in an area that would be inundated after the reservoir was built. As in most towns along the international divide, the population was predominately of Mexican descent. Some had spent their whole lives living in the village, as had their parents and their parents before them. Some even had Spanish land grants that predated the American attack on Mexico in 1846 and Mexican independence. And yet despite this multigenerational claim to the area, they were forced to give up their land and move away from their homes.

Zapata's twin, a village named Ciudad Guerrero, was situated next to it, just across the river in the Mexican state of Tamaulipas. That town was also moved, but by the Mexican government. According to the Secretaría de Recursos Hidráulicos (Ministry of Water Resources), there were 440 homes in Guerrero, 291 of which were owned with clear legal title, while another 63 were either of indeterminate ownership, renters, or informal settlements—all referred to as *casos irregulares*. A substantial share of the town, or 85 houses, was used by federal employees, mainly the Comisión Federal de Electricidad (39 houses) and, of course, the Secretaría de Recursos Hidráulicos (40 houses). The remaining structures were occupied by officials from the CILA, the Secretaría de Marina Nacional (the marine branch of the Mexican Navy), and the Secretaría de Salubridad y Asistencia Pública (Ministry of Health and Public Welfare).[75] By the end of 1955, Recursos Hidráulicos had paid just over 3 million pesos in indemnities for both the destruction of the houses as well as agricultural land that surrounded the town.[76]

This was at times a contested process. Eustolio González Treviño, for instance, filed a complaint with Recursos Hidráulicos claiming damage to his property when it was "invaded by reservoir water." Unlike the ejidatarios who protested the destruction of their cotton fields during the Rio Grande Rectification Project twenty years earlier, González was a private landholder of fields and pastures totaling over 117 hectares. He wrote in formal Spanish, claiming he was not given any notice, and as a result lost land, some outbuildings on his property, and farm machinery and equipment. His property line was not extended to compensate for the underwater portions, and as a result, he was unable to plant a cotton crop in the first mild season after a five-year drought.[77] His request for $162,607 pesos in compensation was rejected; officials maintained that he should have taken the proper precautions, and any loss of property was due to his own imprudence, not the malpractice of the dam project.[78]

In global terms, however, compared to the most draconian forced displacements surrounding large-scale hydraulic engineering projects, the evacuation of Zapata and Guerrero went fairly smoothly. From Friedkin's perspective on the US side, echoing a well-worn colonial and technocratic mantra, the people were better off afterward. The IBWC built an entirely new town, also named Zapata. They built a new city hall, new schools, and a new water system, both for fresh water and wastewater. The people from Zapata drew lots for which plot they would receive in the new Zapata, and for those who lived in stick frame houses, the IBWC moved the houses themselves to the new site. Some people lived in adobe houses, however, and those dwellings could not be moved. They had to be abandoned, left to dissolve in the rising waters.

Like most traditional towns, space was shared in Zapata by both the living and the dead. The cemetery was as much a part of the town as the civic buildings, schools, and houses. The dead, too, had to be moved. For this work the IBWC brought in a Louisiana man, a specialist in negotiating disinterment, water tables, and public relations. According to Friedkin, he visited every family, brought them candy and flowers, and explained the care that would be used in handling the remains of their ancestors.

Having never seen a building project of this magnitude on the river before, some people doubted that the water could possibly rise as high as the engineers said it would. Despite the promises of a new and improved town, some residents refused to leave, standing fast in their doorways, remembering the courses their lives had taken in that very place. They stood there until the rising waters reached their feet, and, then, in tears, retreated.[79]

One thing Friedkin did not mention in his recollections of the Falcon Dam project and the relocation of Zapata was the Border Patrol. Perhaps he omitted this in an effort to underline what he saw as the more positive outcomes of a rebuilt city hall, schools, and houses. Or maybe, as someone who had worked closely with the Immigration and Naturalization Service and the Border Patrol on other construction sites, he simply took their presence for granted. In any event, Zapata was rebuilt to incorporate the presence of federal police in its midst. Included here is a reproduction of a plat map of New Zapata in 1953 from the point of view of the boundary commission, recovered in the archives (figure 3.11). A notation on the map indicates the town limit, laid out on a grid, which was the "area to be served by streets, water and sewer lines developed by I.B.&W.C." At its center was a park, and public spaces were woven throughout the town site. In addition, in the lower-right corner of the plat—the southernmost tip of the village—is a plot outlined in red on the original document. This was where officers of the Border Patrol lived after the relocation.

The southern part of town was the closest to the reservoir, the inundated site of the original settlement. Officials from the Federal Property and Resource Management took a photograph from the vantage point of the Border Patrol's houses (figure 3.12). State Highway

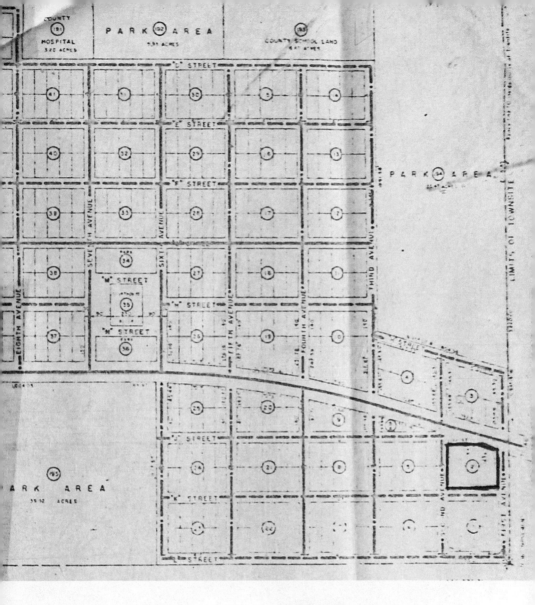

FIGURE 3.11.

Plat Map of Zapata, Texas (detail), 1953

The IBWC incorporated Border Patrol
residences (the outlined lot in the
lower right of the frame) into the plan
of the relocated town of Zapata after
the original site was inundated by the
reservoir created by Falcon Dam. Records of the International Boundary and
Water Commission, Record Group 76.

FIGURE 3.12.
View of Falcon Dam Reservoir from Zapata, Texas, 1965

View of the human-built lake from the Border Patrol residences.
Would they have considered this view picturesque? Records of the
International Boundary and Water Commission, Record Group 76.

83 runs off into the distance, transforming briefly into a bridge that joins Zapata to the other side of the artificial lake. Two flat-roofed structures occupy the middle ground, and in the background are the broad waters of the reservoir, beneath which generations of people from Zapata had lived in the old town site. This image was taken in 1965, thirteen years after the relocation, by bureaucrats tasked with managing transactions pertaining to federal real estate and property. It's possible they thought the view was a picturesque representation of the landscape, a good perspective for an auction.[80]

The experiences of the people in Zapata and Ciudad Guerrero stood in stark contrast to Eisenhower's proclamation that the dam was a testament to a smoothly functioning joint venture between the United States and Mexico and the "two peoples" of both countries. Such a statement refers primarily to intangible things: the diplomatic, technocratic, and economic connections between two nation-states. In this binary, there was no room for the actual people who inhabited the border region. People whose families had been rooted in that one spot for generations, for so long in fact that their most distant ancestors antedated the nation-state itself as a form of political organization. The construction of Falcon Dam, the transformation of the riverine ecosystem, and the inundation of Zapata and Guerrero attest to a fundamental characteristic of border history: the tension between individual lives in specific places on one hand, and massive federal works projects and high-level interstate relations on the other.

OPERATION CLOUDBURST/OPERATION WETBACK

Also standing in contrast to Eisenhower's words were the hardline crackdowns on Mexican migrant laborers by Eisenhower's old West Point classmate, former army general turned INS commissioner Joseph Swing. Swing had just retired from a forty-three-year career in the army when the president appointed him to head the INS. As a young lieutenant in 1916, freshly minted from the US Military Academy, Swing had gone with John Pershing into Mexico in pursuit of Pancho Villa on the ill-fated Punitive Expedition. Having cut his teeth in the mountains and deserts of Chihuahua and Durango during the Mexican Revolution, he then deployed to fight in the Great War.

He commanded the Eleventh Airborne Division in the Philippines during World War II, and had been retired for only three months when he received Eisenhower's nomination in 1954. Having been incubated in conflict zones for decades, he brought a militaristic outlook to the context of border labor control.[81]

Swing's signal achievement would be Operation Wetback in 1954, though Operation Cloudburst, the plan concocted the year before by Herbert Brownell Jr., the attorney general of the United States, is perhaps more instructive insofar as it reveals a new set of assumptions about the relationship between border policing and the built environment. In July of 1953, Brownell, the highest-ranking law enforcement officer in the country, made two trips to San Francisco. Both visits were kept secret. He spent all of his time at the Presidio. There on that base, first built in the eighteenth century by Spaniards on the fringe of the viceroyalty of New Spain, taken at gunpoint from Mexico by the United States in the war between the two countries, and once commanded by General John Pershing before he led his expedition into Mexico, Brownell met with representatives from both the Sixth US Army and the INS.[82] Eighteen men, including three generals, six colonels, two lieutenant colonels, the chief of the Border Patrol California branch, the INS district director from San Francisco, the district director from Los Angeles and his deputy, the chief of the Los Angeles Border Patrol section, and chief patrol inspectors from Chula Vista and El Centro, gathered there to discuss California's southern border. Together, under the direction of Brownell and his military counterpart, three-star general Joseph Swing, they drafted a detailed, classified plan to move the US military to the US-Mexico border.[83]

Operation Cloudburst was to be a deployment that had features of both military maneuvers and quasi–law enforcement operations, but it was to be directed exclusively at unarmed economic migrants— workers laboring outside the parameters of the Bracero Program. The plan that emerged from their meetings was not a mere sketch; these military and INS men produced a meticulously detailed and fully formed tactical document that could be instantly operationalized through a presidential proclamation from Eisenhower, though he never issued it. It imagined a level of aerial surveillance far more advanced than the watchtowers that still stood on the line, patrols in remote areas of the border region, and the commandeering of public roads for inspections.

The rollout was to consist of three components, the army working hand in glove with the INS: the "anti-infiltration operation" along the border itself, the "containment operation" that set up highway roadblocks and checkpoints, and the "mopping up" of the interior of California. General Swing assured the rest of the men at the meeting that once President Eisenhower authorized the deployment through presidential proclamation, five Globemasters would rumble to life, and within twelve hours hundreds of soldiers and their equipment would be on the line. In twelve days, the deployment would be complete. The regimental headquarters was to be at the Naval Air Station in El Centro, very near where the INS had recently complained about dilapidated border fencing, and from there 3,191 men would fan out along the border in two-man foot and jeep patrols working eight hours a day, seven days a week. Fifteen helicopters and as many light airplanes were to provide "aerial cover," and if more were needed, the army would keep them coming.[84]

In 1953, there were 1,079 Border Patrol officers nationwide, 208 of whom worked the Southern California border, a 232-mile stretch of land from the Pacific to Yuma, Arizona.[85] Operation Cloudburst, through its injection of military personnel into the California–Baja California border region, would have effectively tripled the size of the entire agency and swelled the ranks in Southern California by 1,500 percent. Most of the soldiers would have dedicated themselves to the "anti-infiltration operation" along the international divide itself, designed to prevent more unauthorized workers from entering. The containment operation required at least eleven roadblocks and inspection stations throughout Southern California, including Oceanside, Temecula, Brawley, Niland, and the desert roads in between. A mix of INS and military personnel would have run these checkpoints, with the INS officials dedicated more to inspection and the soldiers on hand for "transporting and guarding aliens." Their aim was to capture and command public use transportation infrastructure. Finally, the "mopping up" was to take place deep in the interior of California. The INS was to sweep the entire San Francisco district, focusing on farms, and there, too, the soldiers would serve as guards and use their equipment, possibly even the Globemasters, to remove unauthorized workers.[86]

The language of a draft press release, prepared but never released by Attorney General Brownell, was inflected with anticommunist,

Cold War rhetoric. It not only characterizes the border as a zone that needed to be brought "under control," by then a familiar refrain, but also described Mexican workers without contracts as possibly made up of the "most dangerous subversive classes." Due to this "invasion," he believed that the national security of the United States was threatened.[87] It was also meant to emotionally destabilize unauthorized workers: ". . . we will provide continuous strength all along the line; . . . we should be highly mobile; and . . . the psychology of the aliens involved will operate to this advantage."[88] In the final analysis, its militarism and unilateralism disqualified this plan from being operationalized. Nevertheless, the premises on which it was based prefigured not only future one-sided and semimilitarized initiatives by the United States but also the centrality of highway checkpoints, remote patrols, and fear in border policing tactics.

When Swing took over as INS commissioner, his first order of business in his civilian post was to launch Operation Wetback, the largest-scale deportation drive since the Great Depression, a modified version of Cloudburst. The INS claimed that, at the outset, it was expelling three thousand people per day, and by the end of the campaign, it had removed over 1 million unauthorized workers from US territory. Scholars have questioned the accuracy of these claims, but regardless of the exact numbers, what is important here is what Operation Wetback tells us about the way Swing and the INS conceptualized the space of the border region. As the historians Kelly Lytle Hernández, S. Deborah Kang, and others have explained, the policing initiative is comprehensible only within the complex legal, diplomatic, and cultural context of the US-Mexico guest worker arrangement known as the Bracero Program.[89] There was much at stake for the INS in the early 1950s, including negotiating expanded enforcement authority, cultivating the support of the Mexican American middle class, assuaging the concerns of the Mexican government that too many unauthorized workers were being admitted to the United States, and battling constant criticism from commercial growers who relied on undocumented workers.

Regardless of how many people the INS and Border Patrol actually expelled during these years, one thing is clear: much of the tactical success they achieved was accomplished by plugging into the existing built spaces of the border region and beyond. Roadblocks, or the commandeering of public use transportation infrastructure, were a key component. Other public spaces frequented by Mexicans and Mexican Americans, such as parks and places of leisure, were also targeted for raids. Perhaps most important, however, were work-sites. Federal police arrived unannounced at restaurants and hotels to inspect the staff. Sweeps of farms and ranches, including migrant camps, were also a core feature of Operation Wetback policing.[90] The expulsions of people from US territory by the INS followed a logic similar to that of the patrolmen who had advocated for more fencing around specific ports of entry only a few years earlier. Their idea of control was predicated upon both the construction of and interaction with the built world.

IN THE SPAN OF A SINGLE GENERATION, THE THIRTY YEARS between 1924 and 1954, the built environment of the border changed radically. The Border Patrol transformed from a threadbare organization—its first officers providing their own uniforms and sleeping in the county jail—to an agency run by a veteran of every war in the first half of the twentieth century who commanded a set of resources and personnel able to achieve the forced expulsion of workers at unprecedented levels. The natural landscape of the border region and beyond had also become an unrecognizable version of itself. Massive irrigation and damming projects throughout Northern Mexico and the American West had reshaped the terms of capitalist agriculture, and by extension, the meaning of labor and Mexican migration. These signal shifts in midcentury political, social, and environmental history are etched into the built environment of the US-Mexico border. The evidence of a coercive state became more and more clearly exhibited in the built world of the border region during these years. River rectification, as well as fence, tower, and dam building—all shared a similar ideological paradigm: that physical construction is a central means of affecting control over other people as well as the nonhuman world.

4

POLICE AND
WATERWORKS ON
THE BORDER

SYSTEMIC FLAWS

Much about border building in the 1960s held great promise for US-Mexico reconciliation and peaceful coexistence. Four of the Border Patrol watchtowers in El Paso were dismantled—a small gesture but symbolically rich. A nearly century-old disputed territory known as the Chamizal, also in El Paso–Ciudad Juárez, was finally resolved, and land was returned to Mexico. And a massive dam project, Amistad Dam, east of the big bend of the Rio Grande, seemed to provide permanent protection from flooding danger to residents on both sides of the border as well as a recreation area.

By the end of the decade, however, salinization problems in both the Colorado River and the lower Rio Grande pointed to how hydraulic engineering projects on border waterways were already proving to be unsustainable, or sustainable only at great additional cost. Also, newly elected president Richard Nixon's ill-fated policing venture, Operation Intercept, was an early salvo in the border "drug wars" that would come to color the region in the decades that followed. Like the human interventions on the border waterways, supply-side drug policing was also an unsustainable policy resulting in ever-escalating damage to human lives in both countries, as well as exorbitant outlays of public funds for enforcement. And though Operation Intercept did not in and of itself entail a building project, it nevertheless relied, like Operation Wetback before it, on the built environment. Where Wetback commandeered the roads of the border region and beyond, Intercept commandeered the ports of entry on the international divide itself. By 1970, early signs indicated that simultaneous state-sanctioned efforts to control all aspects of border water, manage a lucrative cross-border trade network, and police black markets could not be maintained indefinitely without significant impacts on the environment as well as on American and Mexican societies. The evidence of this can be read in the built environment of the international divide.

In the summer of 1964, not long before the groundbreaking of the Chamizal project, the INS "declared excess to its needs" four observation towers on the outskirts of El Paso.[1] These were the watchtowers so heralded by the first and second generations of Border Patrol officers, so instrumental to the establishment of the INS as the preeminent federal law enforcement presence along the US-Mexico divide. But after the towers had stood for twenty-five years, the INS had come to consider them salvage steel rather than tactical infrastructure. Rumors circulated that this was partly due to pressure from the Mexican government, but in any event, some of the most recognizable symbols of police suspicion and distrust along the border were removed.[2] In March of 1965, the holding agency, which was the INS, transferred ownership of the towers to the IBWC. All four were either in east El Paso or just outside of town, looking down on the agricultural land that was the site of the river-straightening project in the 1930s. One was on Carolina Drive, very near the river; another at the Socorro headgates; another seven miles east of that; and the final one seven and a half miles west of Fabens, Texas, a small town outside El Paso. The first two were both sixty feet high; the third, sixty-six feet high; and the final tower, the most rural, rose a startlingly tall ninety-six feet above the irrigated desert floor.[3]

The IBWC was interested in the structural steel the towers were made of. One was to be saved, moved, and repurposed for the future of radio communications in El Paso. The other three were meant to be taken apart and reused for IBWC operation and maintenance activities along the line.[4] Yet again, the INS and the IBWC were connected materially. Though a small episode in the larger history and landscape of border construction, the removal of these towers in the oldest and most important US border town, alongside the resolution of the Chamizal dispute and the successful construction of another dam that spanned the international divide, seemed to signal a turning point in US-Mexico border policy, a de-emphasis on policing and a turn toward a collaborative spirit. This was undergirded even more concretely by the inauguration of the Border Industrialization Program (BIP) in Mexico in 1965. If the Bracero Program had transformed the history of US-Mexico labor migration, controversial as it was, its quasi-replacement, the BIP, transformed the Mexican border region. It began with a handful of factories, or maquiladoras, all geared toward making products for export, and has since proliferated into a massive industrial belt that triggered rapid population growth and urban expansion in Mexican border towns. It was heralded—without data, as Jorge Bustamante points out—by the Secretaría de Industria y Comercio (Ministry of Industry and Commerce) as a panacea for social and economic challenges ranging from underemployment to the elimination of widespread prejudice about the low quality of Mexican goods.[5] The Programa Nacional Fronterizo (PRONAF), also a federal initiative, prepared the way by paving roads, building railroad spurs, extending electrical and water grids, and constructing industrial parks. The program upended policy in Mexico that privileged domestic manufacturing for national markets by carving out both the legal and physical spaces in which predominately US firms could operate in Mexican territory without the standard duties and regulations that usually restricted foreign capital.[6]

In the last chapter, we saw a range of border construction projects that confronted previously unbuilt areas on both border land and border water. They responded to "untamed" nature and new, experimental immigration policy. Some of the same dynamics remained in place in the next phase of border policing and waterworks: tensions between local populations and federal policy, binational collaboration in dam building, and links between policing and transportation infrastructure. Increasingly, however, as this chapter shows, the built environment of the border evolved as a response to other border construction projects, and, especially in light of the near-simultaneous rise of the BIP and Nixon's "war on drugs," the ports of entry began to embody the ever-deepening contradictions embedded in policies designed to accelerate sanctioned economic exchange on the one hand while seeking to decelerate black market commerce on the other.

THE CHAMIZAL

The Chamizal dispute was at once a testament to American bad-faith negotiations, Mexican nationalism, and the unpredictability of a desert river. The land in question was the most significant territorial dispute between the United States and Mexico since the war between the two countries ended in 1848, and though the Chamizal involved only about 630 acres, the controversy over that territory lingered for nearly one hundred years. Between 1966 and 1969, it also became a major border construction site that profoundly reshaped the built environment in El Paso–Ciudad Juárez. Or, in the words of Bob Ybarra, former secretary of the IBWC, "These were the years when the earth was actually moved."[7] Historians have shown the effects the dispute had on people who were forced to relocate and have ruminated on the meaning of the project in terms of Cold War politics, international law, and diplomacy.[8] It also fits, as I show here, into the larger history of border building. Like so many other border construction projects, it produced benefits for some as well as excruciating losses for others.

Bob Ybarra was born in El Paso, went to Texas Western College (now the University of Texas at El Paso), and graduated with degrees in history and journalism in 1968. That was the year the Mexican government massacred hundreds of student protesters in Mexico City, and when Mexico's Border Industrialization Program had begun to gather momentum. Ybarra worked as a journalist right out of college. The changing shape of Mexican politics and the border economy made a big impression on him, and he wrote about it. Thanks in large part to his weekly column called "Border Briefs," he was recruited by the IBWC as a "kind of trouble shooter." His parents were Mexican Americans from Tucson who had an abiding interest in teaching their children Spanish and maintaining a sense of Mexican history. He recalled conversations from his childhood in which the story of the Chamizal came up—a piece of Mexican territory accidentally ceded to the United States by an out-of-control river. But when he asked his teachers in grade school about it, they quickly dismissed it, saying, "'No. You're crazy. There's no such thing as that.'"[9]

Nestor Valencia, the former head of the El Paso City Planning Department, had a different childhood perspective on the Chamizal. He was also born in the El Paso area, in Ysleta, and also went to Texas Western College, where he studied art and government. He was inspired by artists and drawn to visual production, everything from cartoons to cartography, interests that would eventually inform his work for the city during the Chamizal project. Unlike Ybarra, however, his parents had immigrated from Mexico and had instilled in young Valencia a sense not only of Mexican history but also of Mexican

ORDOVA ISLAND

RELOCATED RIVER CHANNEL

CD. JUAREZ
CHIHUAHUA

EL PASO, TEXAS

UNITED STATES
MEXICO

JUNE 4. 1966

nationalism. Amid childhood discussions at home about *patriotismo*, *la patria*, and *los héroes*, the question of the Chamizal was a common topic. His parents' exaggerated perspective was a counterweight to Valencia's teachers' complete dismissal. For Ybarra's immigrant parents, always harboring dreams of one day returning to Mexico, "everything was Chamizal to them." They thought it encompassed most of El Paso and half of the valley east of the city.[10] As adults, both Ybarra and Valencia, through their work in the IBWC

FIGURE 4.1.
The Chamizal, 1966

This construction project required the complete relocation of the Rio Grande. The dotted line is where they carved its new channel, lined in concrete. Records of the International Boundary and Water Commission, Record Group 76.

and city planning in El Paso, came to understand the border differently from their teachers and parents. They came to see it in terms of concrete, demolition, excavation, and construction.

As was its custom, the IBWC documented and conceived of the

project from the air. One such aerial photograph was taken looking east in the summer of 1966, just before groundbreaking on the project took place (figure 4.1).[11] It depicts the exact geography of construction. The (yellow) dotted line glued to the photograph makes it clear that the Chamizal agreement entailed not only the transfer of land from the United States to Mexico but also a fundamental restructuring of both cities, including the relocation of the river itself. The bulk of the land transfer was around the bulge of Cordova Island, but as can be seen from the gap between the proposed river channel and the existing bed of the Rio Grande in 1966, a longer section of river was to be moved north as well, ceding a strip of land stretching out along the international divide toward west El Paso–Ciudad Juárez. This photograph also makes it clear that despite the abstractions of territorial sovereignty and nationalism, there were numerous physical structures and people living and working in the contested territory, and for them the Chamizal project had tangible implications.

The Chamizal encompassed 596 houses and sixty-five tenements and was home to hundreds of people.[12] To make way for the construction, the residents were forced to move, whether they liked it or not. This was not the first time a border building project had displaced local residents. Just over a decade earlier, the people of Zapata, Texas, and Ciudad Guerrero, Tamaulipas, were evicted from their homes by the federal governments of the United States and Mexico to accommodate the expanse of the Falcon Dam reservoir, completed in 1954. But unlike the residents of Zapata, some of whom still held the title to their properties through the authority of Spanish land grants, those living in the Chamizal had a much more nebulous claim to their land and houses. In the end, however, the difference between a deed and title conferred by the antique authority of the Spanish Crown and a semi-ephemeral settlement on contested territory mattered little; the residents of both Zapata and the Chamizal were forced to leave just the same.

The uncertainty of the Chamizal's territorial status contributed to an atmosphere of disregard toward the area by those living outside of it. In the words of J. Samuel Moore, an El Paso lawyer who worked at a firm involved in the initial failed arbitration in 1911, the dispute "acted as a chiller insofar as active sales and purchases of land in the Chamizal. And what that resulted in was a very low level of improvement, both residential and commercial."[13] From the outside, many people saw the area as not worth investing in or developing. Bob Ybarra echoed that sentiment, saying, "If you wanted to buy property in the Chamizal[,] there was a cloud on that title."[14] It was a precarious place to live, an area that drew people with a certain kind of self-sufficiency about them.

Nonresidential buildings were also located in the Chamizal. Many of them were businesses, such as Rosebud Lumber, customs brokers, an iron works establishment, and a broom factory. Perhaps the largest among them was Peyton Packing Company. Among the equipment that had to be moved during the relocations was a bone grinder, a head rack and jaw puller, a pneumatic head splitter, a beef eviscera hoist, a hog shackling hoist, a hog scalding tub, a dehairing machine, an eviscerating table, and a head conveyor.[15] The plant reeked. The odor of dead and processed animal flesh would have been a familiar smell to all who lived in the area or frequented it.[16] The Chamizal also contained a city dump, collecting the trash of El Paso along the border.[17] The area was a liminal space in every sense, a repository of things offensive to smell and sight.

But this was not necessarily how it was experienced by the people who made their lives there. William Bass, for instance, when asked about Cordova Island, replied, "Oh, yes! That was a beautiful little island. . . . That was a nice place because there was corn [and] chile."[18] This laudatory description stands in stark contrast to the way the Border Patrol often talked about the same place, as a tactical nightmare and smuggling zone. Bass bought a house there in 1947, the year after he came home from the navy. Aside from that, he worked for the Southern Pacific Railroad for forty years and liked living in the Chamizal because it was close to the rail yards on Piedras Street. He painted the house every year, inside and out, and thought the neighborhood was the friendliest in town; when one person had a party, everybody went. His house, like most of the others in the neighborhood, was made of adobe bricks brought over from Mexico. He loved it so much that, years later, after it had been demolished in the excavation, it still sometimes appeared in his dreams, just as it was when he lived there.[19]

Bass lived in one of the more expensive houses. Feliciano Hinojosa, the former president of the Chamizal Civic Organization, commented on the range of dwellings found in the area, many of which were more humble constructions: "Some of them were like shacks, some of them were half nice. Some of them, they didn't have any electricity, no running water [and had] outhouses for the bathroom." Some, he explained, had been built in pieces, each room added separately as the family acquired enough money to build it.[20] William E. Wood, one of the appraisers sent into the area to assess the value of the properties, also pointed out that there were often multiple houses built on the same lot, each one built sequentially as families expanded.[21] The built environment reflected the complexity of social relations in that area, not just within Mexican-descent families with long-standing ties to the area but also across racial and ethnic lines. It also reflected a resilient autonomy and the extent to which interpersonal ties, a sense of community, and a shared sense of space mitigated the absence of basic utilities like water and power.

In addition to the houses, people, and businesses that had to be moved as part of the settlement, government and commercial infrastructure was also reconfigured. The maps produced by the IBWC identify the structures the commission thought were most relevant (see figure 4.2).[22] The Peyton Packing Company is near the center, and various schools are also included, several of them in the Second Ward of El Paso (or el Segundo Barrio, pictured in the lower left of the frame), as well as the Escuela de Agricultura (School of Agriculture) in Ciudad Juárez. Just to the right of the center of the frame, a US Border Patrol station is also noted, just south of a trucking company. This building was crucial to the system of policing and surveillance that had been a permanent part of the city's landscape since the Mexican Revolution. And as part of the Chamizal resolution, it was incorporated into Mexican national territory. When the river was finally relocated and the territorial cession was complete, the Mexican government tore down nearly every structure on that land. Gone were the traces of the packing plant, the dump, and the houses. In their place, a park was built, a memorial to the recovery of Mexican land. But they did not raze the Border Patrol station. Instead, in keeping with a long-standing series of connections between border policing and water management, they converted it into the new headquarters of the Mexican section of the boundary commission, the Comisión Internacional de Límites y Agua.[23]

The Chamizal project also had important implications for the physical infrastructural connections between the United States

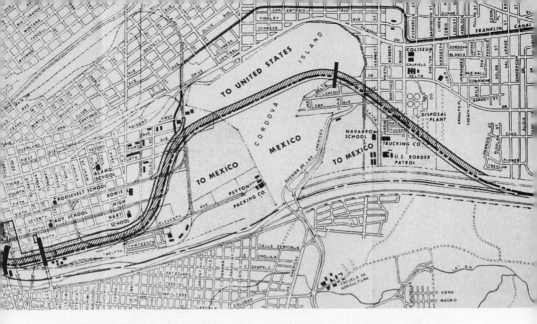

and Mexico. If you look closely at figure 4.1, you can make out four bridges in the lower-right foreground of the frame. The outer two bridges, visibly wider than the two between them, were for pedestrians and vehicles. They flanked the two main railroad bridges, one dedicated to the Santa Fe Railroad–Ferrocarril Nacional de México, the other to the Southern Pacific–Chihuahua al Pacífico. All four were constructed at the exact level of the streets, smooth and flat transitions from one territory to the other. Since the Chamizal agreement called for the relocation of the river in this area, completely new, longer bridges had to be built to accommodate the new location of the river border. Another construction document depicts the scope of the bridge renovation (figure 4.3).[24] The port-of-entry inspection facility was enlarged on El Paso Street, which would soon be one of the key sites of Operation Intercept, along with the export control building on Stanton Street. The bridges were also elevated, which required even more elongation to allow for the grade of the ramp to ascend and descend the bridge.

Nestor Valencia explained that the bridges were elevated to facilitate the increasingly complex interaction of transportation infrastructure along the line. Raised bridges meant that cross-border trains

FIGURE 4.2.
Chamizal Properties (detail), 1966

A US Border Patrol station in the contested territory was transferred to Mexican ownership after the Chamizal dispute was settled. It was then converted into the headquarters of the Comisión Internacional de Límites y Agua. Records of the International Boundary and Water Commission, Record Group 76.

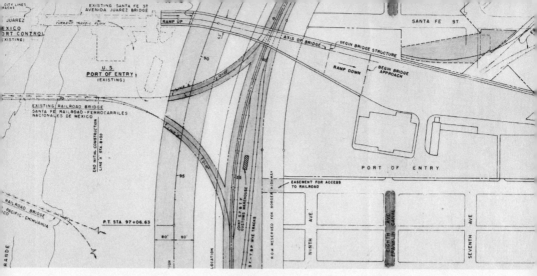

could now pass underneath them instead of blocking traffic as they crossed the roads. It also facilitated the construction of a new border highway that ran parallel to the international divide. In part, it helped make way for the increasingly more complex economic connections between the United States and Mexico in the years to come. The implementation of Mexico's Border Industrialization Program in 1964 coincided with the Chamizal project. Valencia pointed out in an oral history years later that the eleven small maquiladoras that had been built in Ciudad Juárez by 1969 would eventually balloon to include hundreds more.[25]

Many people did not like the new bridges. The expansion and, above all, the elevation were major disruptions in the topography of the built environment in El Paso. Some criticized the project, calling it a "'monument to concrete.'"[26] Others joked that they were so high, battleships could pass underneath them.[27] Perhaps the most irate of all was the former mayor of Ciudad Juárez, René Mascareñas Miranda. The son of refugees from the Mexican Revolution, he was born in 1913 in Los Angeles, though he eventually returned to be both the president of the Juárez chamber of commerce in 1954 and the

FIGURE 4.3.
Chamizal Relocation Ports (detail), 1966

The port of entry inspection facility was expanded as part of the Chamizal construction project, and the old Franklin Canal was "obliterated" and moved to run alongside the railroad tracks and the river border. The ghost image of the former riverbed, irregular in its banks, contrasts with the uniform geometry of the channelized riverbed running down the center of the image. Records of the International Boundary and Water Commission, Record Group 76.

mayor from 1956 to 1959. He called the new bridges "unos monstruos," or monsters, that had "separated, divided, and created distance" between two border communities.[28]

Finally, in addition to the housing, commercial, and infrastructural relocations, the Chamizal agreement was also centrally concerned with managing water. Ray Daguerre, also the descendant of refugees from the Mexican Revolution and the former administrative assistant to Joseph Friedkin, the IBWC commissioner, offered a succinct history of the river border: "After the War of 1848[,] the Mexican Survey Commission had no interest in irrigation at all, no interest in division of water between countries; the only interest was, let's say, that the river *was* the boundary. They didn't even care what the river did. They were just lucky to map the river and say, 'This is it.' The question began to arise in the late [18]80s—what to do when the river moves?"[29] This is a good summary. The first boundary survey team in the 1850s, like other contemporaneous border surveyors, could not accurately determine longitude, and in some places incorrectly mapped the western land border. And as the centrality of irrigated agriculture, the density of human settlement along the river, and the complexity of US-Mexico economic connections all increased over time, so, too, did the degree of human intervention in border waterways. In other words, the Chamizal dispute was, at its heart, about the failure to control water and the dissonance between the law and unmanaged hydrological processes.

The territorial dispute was rooted in the evolution of the law and the evolution of the river itself. To understand this, we have to backtrack momentarily to the nineteenth and early twentieth centuries. The Treaty of Guadalupe Hidalgo that ended the war between the two countries and first established the boundary line did so only vaguely. Article V states that where the Rio Grande forms the border, from El Paso–Ciudad Juárez down to the Gulf of Mexico, the international boundary would lie with the deepest channel of the river. In the El Paso–Ciudad Juárez region, however, the Rio Grande is a desert river, running through loose terrain prone to erosion. This meant that the river often shifted course, all too evidently to those who survived a massive flood in 1864, among others. In 1884, a new treaty was adopted by both countries to try to address the hydrological idiosyncrasies of the river that the Treaty of Guadalupe Hidalgo had ignored. By the time this document was drafted, the land that would eventually become the Chamizal had already been accidentally ceded to the United States because the river had jumped its riverbed. The 1884 treaty laid out the conceptual framework that would fuel the controversy well into the twentieth century. It states that the border should follow the "original channel," even if it became "wholly dry," so long as the river changed path through "slow and gradual erosion and deposit of alluvium."[30]

But no one knew the path the river had taken before the floods of the 1860s. No survey had ever been conducted. So when the US and Mexican governments agreed in 1911 to an arbitration hearing to adjudicate the territorial integrity of both nations, the Americans claimed that the river had changed course through slow and gradual erosion and accretion, meaning the United States kept the territory, whereas the Mexicans claimed its path shifted through violent avulsion, making it Mexican land. Eugene Lafleur, a Canadian jurist, was brought to El Paso to help determine the matter as a neutral third party. The deliberations took place at what was then the Sheldon Hotel, several hundred feet from the border. During the hearing, they heard gunshots from Ciudad Juárez; the revolution in Mexico had just begun.

The arbitration continued nonetheless, and swayed by testimony about nineteenth-century floods in which trees, entire houses, and riverbanks were swallowed by an out-of-control Rio Grande, Lafleur ruled that two-thirds of the territory should be returned to Mexico. The change in the river's course, he concluded, had been violent, not slow and gradual. Many in the United States were outraged; some Texans thought the Canadian legal scholar had been bribed. The United States rejected the decision and did nothing.[31] The law alone was not enough to solve the border problem. Ultimately, the definitive solution would emerge in the context of physical construction, a building project.

But it was not just the Rio Grande and its channel that mattered. There was also the Franklin Canal to contend with on the American side, the diversion project Mexican officials had protested at its inception decades earlier. With every new project, the vision of the IBWC was edging closer and closer to efficiency, symmetry, and visual simplicity along the border line. A document of that vision shows how the Franklin Canal was redesigned to fit within the newly streamlined infrastructure of the border—highway, river, canal, and railroad all neatly lined up in parallel, all running unencumbered underneath the newly raised cross-border bridges (figure 4.4).[32] The canal's purpose was to divert river water to irrigation outside El Paso, part of the 1930s canalization project in the region. Though it was very close to the border, it wasn't actually a part of it, so the Bureau of Reclamation built it to connect to the American Canal that carried water from the American Dam, a diversion dam built by the IBWC. A Mexican counterpart, known as the Acequia Madre, also diverted water for irrigation outside Ciudad Juárez. The elevation of the river downstream was actually lower than the agricultural land, and since pumping was expensive, the best option for a gravity diversion was up near the smelter. In both cases, this meant that large irrigation ditches ran directly through the most heavily populated areas of both cities.[33]

The irrigation ditch that originated in a bilateral controversy had evolved to represent a division of class and ethnicity within El Paso. The Franklin Canal was an open waterway, nearly the width of a city street, that ran through one of the poorest areas in town, the Segundo Barrio. Joseph Friedkin recalled that "it used to go right down Sixth Street . . . right through those tenements. And it was a sewer almost. And the kids swam in it and we had drownings right through those tenements."[34] Nestor Valencia echoed this, saying, "We were losing a lot of children through the highest density neighborhood, which is in South El Paso. Every summer people would drown there. Many lives were lost." The relocation of the canal out of this neighborhood, inserted neatly to fit with the rest of the border infrastructure along the international divide, was in part an effort to solve this problem. As an extra precautionary measure, they decided to "protect it with necessary fencing."[35] But people kept drowning.[36] This time, they likely included unauthorized border crossers.

A common feature of both the canal and the river relocations was that they were encased in concrete. In one sense, this was the completion, at long last, of the river rectification begun in the 1930s. The straightening of the Rio Grande three decades earlier was hindered in part by the fact that the land upriver from Cordova Island lingered in dispute. To the water managers, concrete was central to a definitive solution to the complete mastery of the wayward river. "First we concrete-lined the channel so there'd be no future problems," Friedkin said, adding, "you don't want a channel shifting around between two

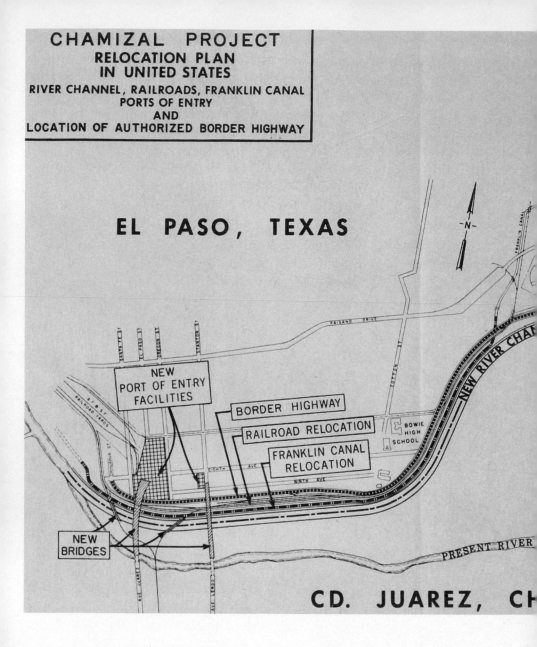

CHAMIZAL PROJECT
RELOCATION PLAN
IN UNITED STATES
RIVER CHANNEL, RAILROADS, FRANKLIN CANAL
PORTS OF ENTRY
AND
LOCATION OF AUTHORIZED BORDER HIGHWAY

EL PASO, TEXAS

NEW
PORT OF ENTRY
FACILITIES

BORDER HIGHWAY

RAILROAD RELOCATION

FRANKLIN CANAL
RELOCATION

NEW
BRIDGES

NEW RIVER CHAN

PRESENT RIVER

CD. JUAREZ, CH

BOWIE
HIGH
SCHOOL

PAISANO DRIVE

FRANKLIN CANAL

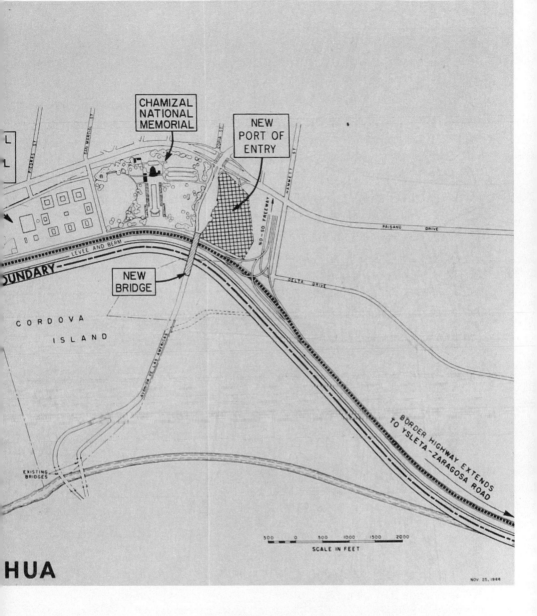

FIGURE 4.4.

Chamizal Relocation Plan (detail), 1966

The vision for the remodeled border between El Paso
and Ciudad Juárez was one of order. The railroad,
border highway, new riverbed, and the Franklin Canal
were all aligned neatly parallel to one another. Records
of the International Boundary and Water Commission,
Record Group 76.

cities. Also, less right of way was required, less width of channel, when you have it concrete-lined."[37] This updated concrete section of the river was 4.35 miles long upon completion. It was a trapezoidal channel; the bottom width was 116.2 feet, the top 167 feet, with a maximum depth of 19.7 feet. The bottom was also fitted with a 60-foot-wide trapezoidal low-flow channel that is 4 feet deep. Since the river often runs very low due to agricultural diversions in New Mexico, the sloping walls of the embankments have become popular canvases for graffiti. The newly fixed, durable trench for the river could accommodate 24,000 cubic feet of water per second, a number that was calculated by adding the historic runoff from a 1935 storm in Las Cruces; arroyo flows between Caballo Dam at Leasburg Dam, both in New Mexico below Elephant Butte; releases from Caballo Dam; and the base flow of the Rio Grande.[38] After nearly a century of concern about the river's location, and after over thirty years of river building projects in that region, the Rio Grande was finally shortened, straightened, canalized, channelized, and immobilized to the specifications of border builders.

After the excavators, concrete mixers, bulldozers, and other heavy building and demolition equipment had ceased their work, the border between El Paso–Ciudad Juárez had been remade. In the end, 193.16 acres had been transferred from Mexico to the United States, while 437.18 acres were transferred from the United States back to Mexico. After nearly a century of debate, Mexico had regained a bit of its territory. That this territory fell in the most densely built and populated area along the border mattered, resulting in a more complex construction project than would have been necessary almost anywhere else along the international divide. The two countries divided the cost equally, and after relocating and building a new river channel, lining it with concrete, and remaking five bridges, the US and Mexican governments had spent $86.7 million.[39]

The complexity and expense of this project also lent themselves to a particular kind of border pageantry, a tradition of political performance on the border in which presidents meet on the line to speak in platitudes about the US-Mexico border and US-Mexico relations. This, too, was linked to construction. On December 13, 1968, Lyndon B. Johnson and Gustavo Díaz Ordaz met at the border. In his remarks, Johnson heralded the achievements of the builders: "An unpredictable river has been converted into a controlled source of water—water for irrigation, water for electric power, water for recreation—for Mexicans and Americans alike." They convened on that day not to dedicate the new border line; that had been done about a year earlier. Rather, they were there to dedicate the new concrete channel itself. Continuing his speech, Johnson said that the "finest thing I know to say about our two countries . . . is that . . . we have no armies patrolling our borders." For him, border peace was tied to environmental manipulation, construction, and commerce. "Peace is the active development of physical resources," he said, and the IBWC "has shown us in concrete terms how peace and understanding can bring about economic, social, and educational development."[40]

In his remarks, Díaz Ordaz echoed many of these sentiments, but also referenced another massive border building project that had just been completed—Amistad Dam. "The construction of the imposing Amistad Dam to make these waters, that previously were only a source of problems for the two nations and the people living along the banks of the river, produce electric power and render the land they irrigate fertile," was to the Mexican president another victory in the construction of the border, tied as so many were to increasingly higher energy-dependent societies and commercial agriculture.[41]

AMISTAD DAM

The huge flood in 1954, downriver from the big bend of the Rio Grande, made a lasting impression on border builders. For as long as people had settled near the river they had grappled with its overflows. Since both human settlement and agriculture often depended on very close proximity to its waters, simply moving somewhere else was not an option for many. Instead, people chose to build their way to flood safety. Structures began accumulating on and around the Rio Grande, and by the twentieth century, federal agencies constructed the largest of these waterworks. Flooding in the Mesilla Valley of New Mexico had been brought under control by the construction of Elephant Butte Dam in 1916. Flooding of El Paso–Ciudad Juárez had been managed by the straightening of the river in the 1930s, and the completion of Falcon Dam in the southern Rio Grande valley in 1954, just months before a huge flood, narrowly averted disaster at the mouth of the river. Hundreds more smaller-scale structures managed the waters of the Rio Grande, including diversion dams, levees, and canal systems. But despite the extent of river projects between 1916 and 1954, and despite the success of Falcon Dam in reining in the floodwaters, the damage created above the dam propelled people like Joseph Friedkin, who had by then become the commissioner of the US section of the International Boundary and Water Commission, to begin planning yet another massive storage dam on the international divide.[42]

The greatest effects of the flood, however, were experienced most forcefully not by high-level policymakers, but rather by the people on the ground in the flood zone. Since much of the Rio Grande's water is siphoned off for irrigation in El Paso–Ciudad Juárez and farther north in New Mexico, the bulk of the floodwaters in 1954 came from the merging flows of the Rio Grande and two of its tributaries, the Pecos and the Devils Rivers. These two smaller rivers both converge on the border river just north of Del Rio–Ciudad Acuña, which generated a massively increased flow that swept down the basin through the border towns of Eagle Pass–Piedras Negras and Laredo–Nuevo Laredo. No one knew how many people died. The border towns were severed from one another when the bridges connecting them were washed out entirely. The streets were inundated, killing some and completely destroying property.[43]

Amid the devastation of the flood, Presidents Dwight Eisenhower and Adolfo Ruiz Cortines agreed that the border needed another dam, even though construction would not begin for several years, during the administrations of their successors. This new construction would be the most massive structure ever built on the border river, designed to hold 5.5 million acre-feet of water, about 2¾ times larger than the Elephant Butte reservoir, nearly 1½ times larger than Falcon Dam reservoir, and unlike Falcon Dam, which was primarily an earthwork construction, this new barrier was to be made largely of concrete.[44] Engineers from the United States and Mexico began drawing up plans. They broke ground in 1964 and worked for five years until the dam was dedicated in 1969, this time with two new presidents standing atop it, Richard Nixon and Gustavo Díaz Ordaz. In his dedication speech, Nixon quoted a line from Eisenhower's dedication of Falcon Dam fifteen years earlier, when he had called it "'a living testimony to the understanding and the cooperation binding our two peoples.'" Nixon went on to point out that the original proposed name of the structure was to be Diablo Dam, or "Devil Dam," though "President Eisenhower thought that was a rather ominous name for a dam and President Adolfo López Mateos suggested that the name be changed to Amistad, meaning "friendship" in Spanish.[45] Much more significant than his dedication of the dam, however, was Nixon's declaration of the "war on drugs" in 1971. On the border, this ongoing conflict would begin soon after the Amistad Dam dedication, with Operation Intercept. This initiative set into motion a series of policies that would help transform the international divide into one of the most antagonistic, combat-oriented, and heavily built police landscapes in American history, upending the notion of *amistad*.

In stark contrast to the impending unilateralism of Intercept, however, the dam's construction required extensive bilateral coordination. Due to its gigantic reservoir and the quantity of concrete used to build it, the dam was the most significant geological manipulation in US-Mexico border history. It required a sounding of the earth like no other border building project. When completed, the 2,182-foot-long concrete portion of the dam towered 254 feet above the riverbed. Flanked on both sides by a total of 30,018 feet of earth embankment, 21,347 feet of which were in Mexico, the concrete dam was constructed using forty monoliths and was fitted with sixteen spillway bays, each with 50-foot-wide and 54-foot-high tainter gates. It was a gravity structure, designed to use the weight of its own mass between its heel and toe to resist the pressure of the water. Of the just over 5.5 million acre-feet of storage capacity, 0.55 million acre-feet were reserved for silt and dead storage, 3 million for conservation storage, and 2.11 million for flood control capacity and superstorage.[46]

Falcon Dam was constructed in a rural but not entirely unpopulated area. As part of creating its reservoir, two small villages, Zapata on the US side and Ciudad Guerrero on the Mexican side, had to be destroyed. The Chamizal construction, on the other hand, took place in an urban area and required the complex reconfiguration of bridges, railroads, and the river itself, as well as the displacement of people. Amistad Dam, however, was not only the largest construction of its kind on the border but also the most remote. Even though it was only a few miles north of Del Rio–Ciudad Acuña, the expanse of the reservoir to the north and northwest extended into some of the most unpopulated areas in Texas and Coahuila. Nevertheless, both the American and Mexican governments had to acquire rights-of-way from local ranchers, for which the ranchers were paid between fifty and seventy dollars an acre. Though the IBWC owned the dam, the National Park Service managed the reservoir as a National Recreation Area. Some of the first people to buy boats to take out on the water were local ranchers who, like the people from Zapata in 1954, never thought the water could get so high. Unfamiliar as they were with watercraft, they first boarded their boats wearing Stetson hats that blew off and high-heeled boots that slipped out from under them on deck.[47]

On the Mexican side, the small town of Ciudad Acuña, a few miles downriver of the dam site, was suddenly overtaken by major federal projects. The mayor of the town, Jesús María Ramón Cantú, wrote to the Secretaría de Recursos Hidráulicos to get a clearer idea of what parts of town had been designated part of the "federal zone" of the dam project.[48] The regional director, Oscar González Lugo, wasn't sure, and wrote with some urgency to his superior in Mexico City requesting precise maps of the city that designated which private houses would have to be expropriated not only as part of the broader operational zone of Amistad Dam but also for the urban revamping projects of PRONAF.[49] In this context, the major disruption to border people and their property was not the inundation of the reservoir, but rather the secondary effects of how the border region had to be reorganized to accommodate border building of various kinds. For instance, in 1962, in anticipation of dam construction, the Secretaría de Recursos Hidráulicos slated four houses in Las Cuevas, an ejido on the outskirts of Ciudad Acuña, for expropriation and indemnification. The humble concrete-and-cinderblock homes of María Salas, José Alvarado López, Calixto Navarro Martínez, and Domingo Franco Robles were nowhere near the proposed basin of the reservoir, the site of the dam itself, or even an area designated for PRONAF development. Instead, their properties were seized because they were in the way of the proposed access road for dam construction.[50] This, too, is a core feature of border construction: the logistics and materiality of moving heavy equipment to building sites along the international divide is a key component of the process but one that is often overlooked.

Even though the Amistad Dam construction did not significantly disrupt contemporary human settlement in the area on a scale commensurate with the Rio Grande Rectification Project, Falcon Dam, or

the Chamizal, it nevertheless entailed a massive reconfiguration of the natural landscape that set it apart from other projects. One aerial photograph captures a view from Mexican airspace, looking southeast at the first stage of construction on the US side (figure 4.5).[51] In this photograph, the river has been diverted to allow for the concrete placement of the stilling basin, a feature of the dam designed to slow down the flow of water. In the middle distance, the machinery and buildings necessary for the aggregate processing, cooling, and concrete batching sit atop a zone completely denuded of vegetation. In the background, the flat, semiarid

FIGURE 4.5.
Amistad Dam Site
(detail), 1965

During the 1950s and 1960s especially, the US and Mexican governments constructed hundreds of dams, many of which held back river waters in the American West and the Mexican North. Dams of this size on border water, however, were rare. Amistad Dam was only the second to be built. Records of the International Boundary and Water Commission, Record Group 76.

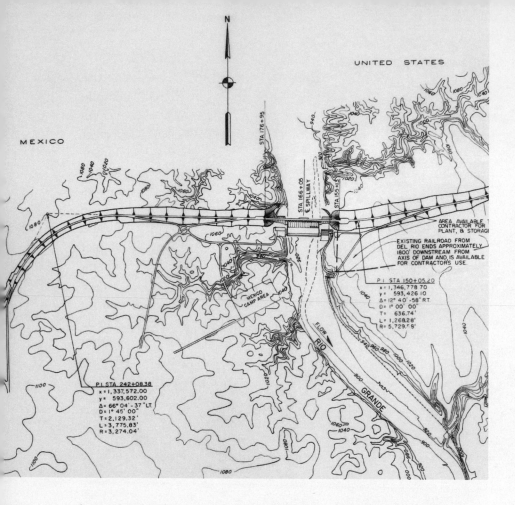

N

UNITED STATES

MEXICO

STA 176+95

€ SPILLWAY
STA 166+05

STA 155+15

AREA AVAILABLE T
CONTRACTOR FOR
PLANT, & STORAG

EXISTING RAILROAD FROM
DEL RIO ENDS APPROXIMATELY
1800' DOWNSTREAM FROM
AXIS OF DAM AND IS AVAILABLE
FOR CONTRACTORS USE.

P.I. STA 150+05.20
x = 1,346,778.70
y = 593,426.10
Δ = 12° 40'·58" RT.
D = 1° 00' 00"
T = 636.74'
L = 1,268.28'
R = 5,729.58'

MEXICO
CAMP AREA

RIO

FLOW

GRANDE

P.I. STA 242+08.38
x = 1,337,572.00
y = 593,602.00
Δ = 66° 04'·37" LT.
D = 1° 45' 00"
T = 2,129.32'
L = 3,775.83'
R = 3,274.04'

karst landscape recedes into the distance. The wing and strut of the IBWC
plane intrude into the frame, recalling
the tradition of aerial surveys carried
out by the boundary commission, most
notably in 1947 and 1948 to prepare for
the construction of the western boundary fence.

A detail from one of many documents
produced by engineers in the Army
Corps of Engineers and the IBWC in
preparation for construction envisions
the dam site in terms of the regional
topography (figure 4.6).[52] The flood of
1954 was a powerful impetus to begin

FIGURE 4.6.
Amistad Dam Topography
(detail), 1965

In part, this top-down, topographic view of the border
recalls the "planos" produced
by the boundary survey in the
1890s. This map, in contrast, was
produced not to help legislators
understand the political division
between the two countries,
but rather to help engineers
understand how to sync the built
environment of the dam with its
surroundings. Records of the
Army Corps of Engineers, Fort
Worth Division, Record Group 77.

designing the dam, though the first IBWC study to determine the most feasible location was in 1948. They settled on a site one-half mile below the confluence of the Rio Grande and the Devils River.[53] As can be seen by the densely bunched contour lines around the river valley, which runs nearly north to south at this point on the border, this is a region in which the river has cut a canyon through the surrounding landscape. The massive concrete section of the dam was fitted into the canyon, but this rendering also shows the extent of the earthwork embankment snaking through the surrounding landscape, its segments resembling vertebrae from above. The dotted line depicting the "natural ground line" was excavated to construct the embankment. Before the excavation, the "natural ground" consisted of terrace alluvium, or silty sand, clay, and gravel, but this was unsuitable for the embankment foundation. On the map, it is simply referred to as "overburden." Workers dug down until they hit the rock line, either Georgetown Limestone or Del Rio Limestone.

A crucial complement to the topographic map was the geological map of the site that depicts the construction site in terms of sedimentary rocks of the Quaternary and Cretaceous periods (figure 4.7).[54] In the center right of the map, the Rio Grande and Devils River converge and the dam axis is plotted across the riverbed. Over the course of centuries, the rivers carved channels down through the layers of alluvium, gravel, clay, and Buda Limestone until the water hit dense Georgetown Limestone. The engineers were interested in the exact geologic composition of the entire construction site. To ascertain this, they systematically took samples by boring at one-thousand-foot intervals into the earth. Each boring hole was drilled between seventy-five and eighty-three feet deep, and core samples were extracted that included information about the hardness, grain, chert particles present, styolites, manganese oxide composition, and fossils.[55] Could the limestone bed viably support a massive concrete structure that in turn had to resist the pressure of millions of acre-feet of water? The karst structure of the geology complicated this, as it was riddled with sinkholes and fault lines. Sinkholes are denoted with an "S" on the map, faults indicated by broken lines. They are everywhere around the dam site, and the dam axis weaves through them, not only undulating over the surface of the earth but also dodging the weak points within it.

The international border bisects the dam. Construction proceeded

FIGURE 4.7.
Amlstad Dam Geology (detail), 1965

A view of the border very few people saw or had the
formal training to understand how to interpret—a
bilateral, geological map, emphasizing types of rock,
upthrown or downthrown fault lines, and sinkholes—all
critical information for border builders on both sides of
the international divide. Records of the Army Corps of
Engineers, Fort Worth Division, Record Group 77.

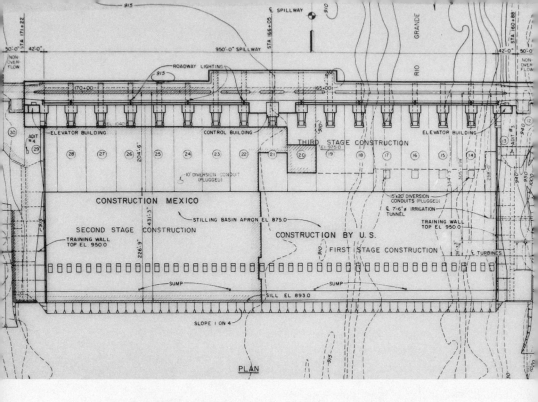

PLAN

in multiple stages, beginning with excavating diversions, constructing cofferdams, placing the embankment and riprap, and concluding with the removal of cofferdams and installing the gates and machinery into the concrete section.[56] One blueprint labels the stages as "Construction Mexico" and "Construction by U.S.," as both American and Mexican engineers and laborers worked simultaneously from the same blueprints and geologic and topographic surveys (figure 4.8).[57] In the section shown

FIGURE 4.8.
Amistad Dam Scope of Work (detail), 1965

A detail from one among dozens of Amistad Dam blueprints. These documents guided both the on-site engineers and the laborers during the construction process. Records of the Army Corps of Engineers, Fort Worth Division, Record Group 77.

in this detail, the plan for the dam is superimposed upon the topography of the river valley; the curvilinear contour lines contrast with the rectilinear lines of the dam construction. The border passes through the center, following the riverbed. Though Mexican construction took place on the American side on Monoliths 20 and 21, and though US construction took place on the Mexican side on the installation of the spillway gates, the international border perfectly bisects the control building mounted atop the dam, designed for bilateral boundary commission meetings.

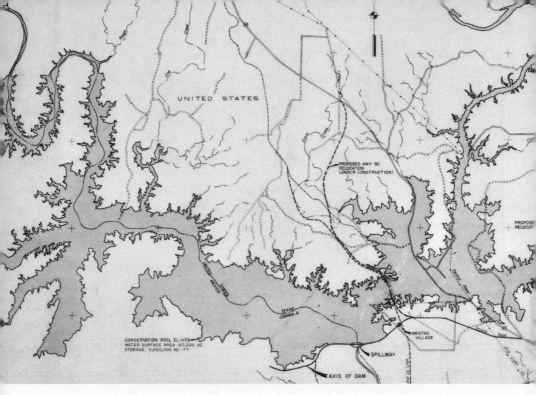

UNITED STATES

PROPOSED HWY 90
RELOCATION
(UNDER CONSTRUCTION)

PROPOSE
RELOCAT

TEXAS
COAHUILA

RIO GRANDE RIVER

CONSERVATION POOL EL 1170
WATER SURFACE AREA 67,000 AC
STORAGE 3,550,000 AC-FT

AMISTAD
VILLAGE

SPILLWAY

AXIS OF DAM

In the end, not only had the dam site itself transformed the topography of the riverbed; the reservoir it created remade that region of the border. The jagged edges of the human-made body of water show how the dam raised the water level high enough to fill the ancient canyon the rivers had cut through the sediment, and also how the lake crept into the myriad arroyos and washes that fed the Rio Grande basin during heavy rains (figure 4.9).[58] The international border, which, according to the 1884 treaty, was still located at the deepest channel, was also inundated. The widest part of the reservoir is around four miles wide, and yet across this expansive surface of water, the border is not a straight line. Rather, the international divide winds its way through the lake, marked by a string of buoys that follow the path of the riverbed deep underwater.

Amistad Dam was a triumph of logistics, the most complex structure ever created on the US-Mexico border. It required the coordination of

FIGURE 4.9.
Amistad Dam Reservoir Area (detail), 1965

When the dam became operational, the border river expanded on both sides, filling side canyons and arroyos, and it widened the riverbeds of both the Rio Grande and the Devils River. The actual location of the international divide, however, remained fixed in the deepest original channel. Records of the Army Corps of Engineers, Fort Worth Division, Record Group 77.

multiple federal bureaucracies in both the United States and Mexico and constant collaboration between engineers, geologists, and laborers on both sides of the line as well. It was also a triumph over the unpredictability of nature. Upon completion, it brought the discharge of four different rivers—the Rio Grande, the Conchos, the Pecos, and the Devils—under human control. Its construction solved the flooding problem in the border region between the big bend and Falcon Dam, and it solved a silt accumulation problem in Falcon Dam's reservoir by accumulating silt itself.[59] Other sections of the border, however, in particular on the Colorado River and in the southern Rio Grande valley, were already starting to show signs of environmental degradation due to related waterworks on and around border rivers.

RIVER CLEARING AND SALINITY CONTROL

The closing lines of LBJ's speech at the dedication of the concrete-lined channel for the Rio Grande in El Paso in 1968 embodied a central assumption of border building. He explained that "long after our words of today are gone and forgotten, something more important is going to endure—channels between men, bridges between cultures . . . these, my friends, will never pass away if we are true to our heritage."[60] His use of physical structures as symbols for larger cultural and political ideals is not unusual. What is of particular importance here, however, is the presumption that physical structures are everlasting, that they are durable enough to exist into an indeterminate future, carrying with them the high ideals of the societies that built them in the first place. And indeed, as the journalist and writer Marc Reisner points out, dams might be among the longest-lasting structures humans have ever built.[61] But already by the 1960s, the built environment of the border had begun to contribute to degraded water quality and create havoc within the irrigation systems it had been designed to facilitate. So while the structures may indeed survive for many generations into the future, the structures' interaction with and relation to the natural environment transformed relatively quickly and sometimes dramatically. Confidence remained that technological expertise and engineering prowess could fix these problems, though border building began to take a different focus. Instead of responding to challenges posed by nature itself—flooding, shifting riverbeds, harnessing and exploiting water in arid landscapes—border construction began to be more and more compensatory, responding to challenges created by the built environment itself.

The two main forms of compensatory border building in the 1960s had to do with water management: vegetation clearing and desalinization. Agricultural lands around the "limitrophe section" of the Colorado River, the area around Yuma, Arizona, where, for about twenty-four miles, the river forms the US-Mexico border, had been subject to flooding since at least the turn of the century. Between 1905 and 1912, the Bureau of Reclamation built levees there as part of its Yuma Project, though an overflow between 1905 and 1907 created massive flooding in California's Imperial Valley, creating the Salton Sea, now infamous for its toxicity. After the completion of the Hoover Dam in 1935, as well as subsequent damming projects on the Colorado, the threat of flooding at its mouth was greatly diminished. Nevertheless, the threat of overflow still persisted, largely because, in the absence of a steady flow of water, thick vegetation that clogged the waterway had grown in the river's channel.[62]

In Minute No. 217 in 1964, both the US and Mexican sections of the boundary commission agreed to begin vegetation removal to ensure flood waters could pass through unencumbered and thereby keep the river border in place.[63] They documented their work, as usual, with aerial photography. One example from this series was a photo taken in 1965 looking north, upstream, from an altitude of about eight hundred feet (figure 4.10).[64] In the right third of the frame, the West Main Canal of the Yuma Project glides along the edges of fields, and to its left, the Yuma Levee runs alongside the floodway of the Colorado. The river bulges to the west, surrounded by agriculture on all sides. A companion photograph documents the same space just after the first strip disking, the method used to excavate the vegetation that had grown up in the channel (figure 4.11).[65]

Another photograph in the series shows a different area of the river from only two hundred feet above the ground, looking north toward Morelos Dam (figure 4.12).[66] Morelos Dam was built in 1950 by the IBWC, the last of fifteen dams on the main stem of the Colorado, not counting the hundreds more on its tributaries. The "after" photograph documents the same area after it had been denuded of most of its

riparian plants (figure 4.13).[67] The excavation of flora in 1965 was successful according to both sections of the boundary

FIGURE 4.10.
Colorado No 8, 1965

commission, though it was not a permanent solution. To compensate
for the massive development on the Colorado River and the ways those
building projects fundamentally reshaped the nature of the waterway,
vegetation clearing had to be carried on consistently, year after year,
as the plants grew back in the area where the river had been reduced
to a trickle. Between 1965 and 1981, with the exception of 1967 and
1970, every autumn was spent clearing and reclearing the riverbed.[68]

Damming projects on rivers altered the riparian ecosystems surrounding the waterways, and they also transformed the composition
of the water itself. By the 1960s, it had become abundantly clear, not
just in the border region but also across the globe, that high-intensity
irrigation, especially in marginal zones, carried with it the scourge
of salinity. Salinization was an ancient problem, as old as irrigation

itself. "Salt," which is a generic term that refers to a range of compounds including calcium carbonate, zinc sulfate, barium chloride, sodium bicarbonate, phosphates, nitrates, and hydrates, clusters around the roots of plants, interrupting their lifecycles, sometimes catastrophically. The threat is particularly acute in arid lands where irregular and sparse rainfall has led to high concentrations of salt. Part of what makes desert plants hardy is their high tolerance for salinized

FIGURE 4.11.
Colorado No 8A, 1965

These two photographs taken from an IBWC plane flying low above the ground show a section of the Colorado River before and after riverbed clearing. To the boundary commission, the denuded riverbed was preferable. Records of the International Boundary and Water Commission, Record Group 76.

earth. Irrigation, however, brings with it both nonnative plants and a hydrology out of sync with soil composition. By the 1970s, commercial agriculture in places otherwise as dissimilar as Pakistan, Peru, Afghanistan, Syria, Iraq, and India had begun losing massive tracts

of land to salinization. This was also true in the American West and Mexican North, giving rise not only to widespread doubt in

FIGURE 4.12.
Colorado No 11, 1965

the ongoing feasibility of maintaining such practices but also to new government research institutions, principally the Salinity Control Laboratory, housed in the Department of Agriculture and located in the San Joaquin Valley of California, infamous for its poor drainage. The solution, if there was one, many hydraulic engineers thought, had to include more building.[69]

Both Lyndon B. Johnson and Gustavo Díaz Ordaz were aware of this accumulation problem. In the winter of 1966, before construction on Amistad Dam was fully completed, the two presidents met at the dam site. Relieved that the Chamizal dispute farther upriver had finally been settled, Johnson looked forward to better relations with Mexico. During the meeting at the construction zone, chosen to emphasize recreation, conservation, and generally good relations between the

o #11-A: Aerial oblique
n 5/5/65, altitude 200 ft.
diately below Morelos Dam,
ing upstream after clear-
work.

two countries, Díaz Ordaz expressed his concern about the salinity of the Colorado River.[70] In contrast to the comparatively smooth operations at Amistad Dam, the tetra-borders of California, Arizona, Baja California, and Sonora, all clustered around the mouth of the Colorado, had become a quintessential example of US-Mexico environmental strife, as well as extreme hydrological intervention.

A major water treaty between the United States and Mexico, signed in 1944, authorized dam construction on the main channel of the Rio Grande and changed the name of the bilateral commission from the International Boundary Commission/Comisión Internacional de Límites to the International Boundary and Water Commission/Comisión Internacional de Límites

FIGURE 4.13.
Colorado No 11A, 1965

More before and after aerial photographs taken by the IBWC. From their point of view, a riverbed stripped of its vegetation made it easier to manage. Records of the International Boundary and Water Commission, Record Group 76.

y Aguas, a pivotal shift in both the legal history of border construction as well as the more explicit acknowledgment of the connections between the "boundary" and "water." Under this treaty, Mexico was allotted 1.5 million acre-feet of water a year from the Colorado River. This was a small fraction of the massive river's discharge, and since the treaty was signed, the amount of water delivered had diminished rapidly due to high-intensity agricultural cultivation on the US side. During the 1950s, an average of 4.24 million acre-feet of water per year crossed into Mexico. By the 1960s, it had already been nearly quartered, reduced to 1.52 million acre-feet.[71] This not only produced the vegetation clogging problem discussed above but also was accompanied by increased salinization.

In part, salinization was due to decreased flows that resulted from the staggering construction on and diversion of the Colorado. This factor alone, however, did not fully account for the salinity problem. The Gila River, which for five years between 1848 and the Gadsden Purchase in 1853 formed part of the US-Mexico divide, joins the Colorado in this section of the border region. And like the Colorado, the Gila basin had come under heavy management and exploitation by the 1960s in the service of commercial agriculture. Its waters were managed by the Wellton-Mohawk Irrigation and Drainage District, created by the Arizona state legislature in 1951, and to maintain ground water levels below the crop root zone, they began pumping from aquifers.[72] Had the flow of the Colorado not been so diminished, it would have diluted the saline waters and delivered usable irrigation water to Mexico. By the early 1960s, the salinity had increased from the former annual average of around 800 parts per million total dissolved solids (TDS) to almost 1,500 parts per million. According to Mexican standards, anything above 1,300 parts per million TDS was unusable. The Mexican government protested in 1961, claiming that the treaty had been violated.[73]

After continued pressure, the United States began to alter its river operations in 1963 to respond to Mexican complaints. In 1965, the two governments reached a five-year agreement, codified in Minute No. 218, which, unsurprisingly, involved more construction. The United States built a twelve-mile-long concrete line channel designed to accommodate 353 feet per second of water. It extended from the junction of the Gila and Colorado Rivers to Morelos Dam, where it could either be diverted into the main Colorado River flow or not, depending on the quality of the water. They called it the Main Outlet Drain Extension, and along with seasonally staggered pumping of higher- and lower-quality wells in the Wellton-Mohawk water district to correspond with Colorado River water releases upstream, the drain did manage to slightly reduce salinity.[74] The idea was to increase the amount of water flow, which would in turn decrease seepage and clear out some of the salt buildup. It was not enough, though, and in the early 1970s, the two countries revisited the issue.

By then, both Johnson and Díaz Ordaz were out of office, replaced by Richard Nixon, who was largely uninterested in Latin America, and Luis Echeverría, whose campaign was supported by northwestern Mexicans angry about their water problems. In 1972, Nixon sent Herbert Brownell Jr. to the border as his special representative. Brownell, the former attorney general and draftsman of Operation Cloudburst—the unrealized, draconian plan to use the US Army to forcibly expel unauthorized Mexican guest workers in 1953—worked for over a year with a team composed of representatives from the Department of State, the Department of the Interior, the Army Corps of Engineers, the Environmental Protection Agency, the Council on Environmental Quality, the Office of Science and Technology, the Office of Management and Budget, the Domestic Advisory Council, and, of course, the IBWC. Their objective was to come up with a plan to desalinate the water allotted to Mexico. Their findings were incorporated into Minute No. 242, titled "Permanent and Definitive Solution to the International Problem of the Salinity of the Colorado River."

The overweening faith in technical expertise was still in place. The title of Minute 242 suggests that an eternal remedy to a problem that had plagued agricultural civilizations since ancient times did indeed exist, and that it could be used to resolve the water dispute on the US-Mexico border. The "permanent and definitive" solution was more construction. One part of the renovations focused on the All-American Canal, the huge irrigation ditch INS officers in the early 1950s had hoped to use as a deterrent to unauthorized migrants. A forty-nine-mile section of this channel was lined with concrete to salvage 130,000 acre-feet per year that had been seeping into the earth. A desalination plant was built on the Colorado to remove saline compounds from return flows coming out of the Wellton-Mohawk basin. They extended the canal from Morelos Dam to the Santa Clara Slough, near the Gulf of California, in order to divert the salt-loaded water produced by the plant, the "reject stream," as well as salinized return flows from the Wellton-Mohawk. In addition to this, both nations were limited to pumping no more than 160,000 acre-feet per year out of the ground within five miles of the international border. It took until 1977 to fully implement all the provisions of Minute No. 242.[75]

The salinity problem was not limited to the Colorado-Gila zone. In the Texas-Tamaulipas border region, a similar problem had cropped up in the 1960s, although this time the source of the salt loading came from the Mexican side. Again, the issue arose in a meeting between the American and Mexican presidents. In fact, Díaz Ordaz brought it up in his official remarks at the dedication of the channelized Rio Grande connected to the Chamizal project. "The first months of 1969 will see the completion of the work we are doing also on the course of the Rio Grande at a place called El Morrillo [sic], to solve a problem of salinity that Mexican waters were causing in United States lands," he said as he stood atop the newly built concrete channel bisecting El Paso–Ciudad Juárez.[76]

The San Juan River, the southernmost Mexican tributary of the Rio Grande, had been extensively canalized by the 1960s to support agriculture in the region. After water was diverted to the fields, the runoff was contained in a large ditch known as the Morillo Drain. Measurements taken between 1960 and 1964 revealed an average salt load of 10,000 parts per million, almost six and a half times higher than the salt levels at the mouth of the Colorado. This resulted in the average annual delivery of 400,000 tons of salt to the Rio Grande. Downriver, this water was then used for irrigation on the American side, and in the most extreme cases, entire fields of small plants were killed, choked by the compounds in the water. The water commissioners from both countries responded with construction. They built a pumping plant and divergence structure close to the mouth of the drain, and then excavated a new twenty-three-mile-long channel that connected to fifty-two preexisting miles of channel. This new system of canals, alongside the electrical pumps that had a capacity of 106 cubic feet per second and a pumping lift to 16.5 feet, was able to segregate the salinized water from the Rio Grande, diverting the former directly into the Gulf of Mexico. The project cost $1,380,000, evenly split between the United States and Mexico, even though all construction took place in Tamaulipas. In fact, agricultural interests in the United States were so concerned with salinization that one-half of the US funding came not from the federal government but rather from local interests, including thirty-four water districts, twenty cities, and 235 individuals.[77]

The demands of high-intensity agriculture in the marginal landscape of the tetra-borders around the mouth of the Colorado, as well as in the humid zone of the Rio Grande delta, had led to multilayered built environments that were first designed to feed water into crops, then modified and remodified to compensate for the side effects of those initial diversions. And despite pretensions to permanence and engineering mastery, this compensatory building was rather a testament to processes that were bound to collapse eventually. One tangible example of this unsustainability came as part of the agreement of Minute No. 242 in 1973: high-water-use agricultural land was bought and "retired" by the IBWC to mitigate water overuse in the Wellton-Mohawk basin.[78] But it was not only water management along the border that began to show signs that it could not be sustained. Border policing, too, especially under the Nixon administration, quickly revealed the fantasy of sustained control over the border to be just that, a fantasy, one also tied to the built environment of the international divide.

OPERATION INTERCEPT

O peration Intercept was a disastrous episode that unfolded along the US-Mexico border in 1969. The chaos it produced revealed yet another unstable feature of the border's built environment: the unsustainability of punitive antidrug policy in the context of cross-border transportation infrastructure designed to accelerate and facilitate commerce. Intercept was the first major border policing initiative directed specifically at illicit drugs, particularly marijuana.[79] It devolved almost instantly into a logistic and diplomatic catastrophe, collapsing in only twenty days. The plan was alluringly simple: eliminate shipments of illegal drugs from Mexico to the United States by physically inspecting every person and vehicle that crossed the border.

Breaking with the custom of much more lax inspection at ports of entry, Operation Intercept incurred a tremendous cost—the relentless searches reduced the constant and lucrative cross-border traffic to a near standstill.

The Nixon administration unilaterally built Operation Intercept on simplistic assumptions about the border that even then appeared bizarre to those who understood the interconnectedness of the United States and Mexico. A week after the Intercept rollout, conservative Arizona senator Barry Goldwater contemptuously declared, "'Operation Intercept is an example of how bureaucrats and legislators without vision can destroy so many years of effort on behalf of extremely cordial interamerican relations. . . . The man who ordered it must be a mental retard.'"[80] The US embassy in Mexico City agreed, and though Ambassador Robert McBride expressed his dissent in more graceful terms, he was just as concerned about the reckless unilateralism of the policing initiative. In addition, the Bureau of the Budget found the emphasis on marijuana instead of "hard" drugs like heroin and LSD indefensible.[81] Declassified documents reveal that a central motivation for Operation Intercept was to force Mexico into a drug crop defoliation program, and the border debacle did indeed help produce closer dialogue and collaboration in antidrug policing in Mexico.[82]

Yet in the context of the built environment of the border region, the operation was important not so much for its policy objectives but for how it interacted with the built spaces of the international divide and for the transition in border policing it heralded. Intercept took place on the cusp of a major rural highway construction boom in Mexico that would ultimately help increase legal traffic across the border. So, though it was a policing initiative designed to gain operational control of the international divide and therefore protect US territory from the purported scourge of illegal psychoactive substances, what it actually revealed was the resilience of the physical connective tissue joining the United States to Mexico.[83] And crucially, building on the intensity of the Intercept deployment, subsequent border policing initiatives began to incorporate more and more militaristic tactics and hardware.[84]

On September 21, 1969, on the heels of nearly a decade of successful bilateral construction projects on the line, the Nixon administration rolled out Operation Intercept along the US-Mexico border in the context of both the PRONAF and the BIP. They proudly called it the "largest peacetime search and seizure operation by civil authorities" in US history.[85] The basic idea, like so many others in the history of law enforcement, seemed intuitive to the architects of the operation.[86] Simply search every person and motor vehicle entering the United States from Mexico in hopes of severing the northbound flow of illegal drugs. In other words, commandeer the ports of entry.

A total of seven federal agencies collaborated on Operation Intercept.[87] The most predictable of the lot, the Bureau of Customs and the Immigration and Naturalization Service, conducted the vast majority of inspections at the land ports of entry. They were accompanied by the Bureau of Narcotics and Dangerous Drugs, one of the antidrug agencies that Nixon would ultimately consolidate into the Drug Enforcement Administration (DEA) in 1973. Though the bulk of the initiative centered on the ports, the coast guard and the navy handled sea patrols in the Pacific and the Gulf of Mexico, the Federal Aviation Administration sent its flight logs to the Operation Intercept command, and the General Services Administration provided logistical support.

This panoply of organizations brought to bear an array of cutting-edge technology, infusing many new layers of hardware into the landscape of border surveillance. The coast guard used cutters to halt and search suspicious craft in US waters, and the navy piloted the same torpedo boats it used to hunt Viet Cong in Southeast Asia.[88] The Customs Bureau and Immigration Service established a command center on Terminal Island, Long Beach, California, which coordinated twenty-three radar installations that stretched all the way to Brownsville, Texas.[89] Customs officers flew both pursuit planes and observation planes over the open country in between the ports. This dramatic outlay of military hardware was undergirded by legal provisions expanding the purview of the federal agents policing the border. The Federal Aviation Administration began requiring preflight plans from all flights originating in Mexico, and Customs and Border Patrol agents were granted new authority to force down private planes that seemed suspicious.[90]

Despite this impressive geographic coverage, however, the bulk of the police work was carried out at the ports of entry. By the late 1960s, a growing body of jurisprudence had continually reinforced what legal scholars call "the border search exemption."[91] This meant that law enforcement activity at the border could be more invasive and expansive than in the interior of the United States, where the definition of a "reasonable" search was more rigid. Vested with this authority, federal officers during Operation Intercept inspected every single person and vehicle that crossed the US-Mexico border, with or without probable cause. Under normal circumstances, border inspectors stopped only one crosser in twenty that they thought looked suspicious enough to warrant a more thorough search. During Operation Intercept, they stopped everyone. Customs and immigration officials conducted a primary inspection of every single vehicle, which meant peering under the hood, the trunk, leaning into the car to inspect the seats and what might be behind or between them, as well as pounding on door panels to echolocate hidden contraband. This could be done in a few minutes, but under the new border interdiction program, one vehicle in twenty went to secondary inspection, which could take at least a half hour and often involved hoisting the vehicle in the air to dismantle some or all of its constituent parts. Those on foot were also subject to increased searches. During the first week of Operation Intercept, border law enforcement inspected nearly two thousand pedestrians in a tertiary search that often involved stripping naked.[92]

High-intensity border inspection of this sort is extremely difficult to sustain. Though officials claimed Operation Intercept would go on indefinitely, the initiative quickly developed stress fractures and collapsed in a matter of weeks.[93] Customs and Border Patrol agents had been slogging through twelve- to fourteen-hour shifts and ultimately inspected over 4.5 million border crossers, regardless of citizenship status. In the end, the police had seized a few milliliters of morphine and Demerol, a handful of codeine and Percodan tablets, 1.5 kilos of heroin, sixty pounds of peyote, seventy-eight pounds of hashish, scarcely a quarter ounce of cocaine, and about a ton and a half of marijuana.[94] Even by 1960s standards, this was a paltry haul, though officials claimed that the objective of Operation Intercept was not to confiscate drugs but to deter smuggling altogether and thereby drive up street prices to make them unaffordable to youth.[95] This notion was also undermined when it became clear that the radar system they had developed to police the skies above the border was incapable of detecting an untold number of low-flying aircraft running drugs from airstrip to airstrip.[96] The entire notion of physically policing and controlling the flow of drugs looked more and more like an unattainable fantasy, an unsustainable policy that could not be resolved, regardless of how elaborate the technology involved.

The logistical implications of inspecting everyone and everything that crossed one of the busiest borders in the world were also devastating. Within hours after Operation Intercept went into motion, lines at the ports of entry backed up for many miles. For instance, at the San Ysidro port between San Diego and Tijuana (by then one of the epicenters of the US-Mexico border), it could take as long as four hours just to get to primary inspection, though some claimed that six hours was more accurate during rush periods. At the inspection stations, the end of the line stretched too far into Mexico to see, though the incessant cacophony of car horns protesting the egregious wait times was a constant reminder that the thousands upon thousands of people waiting to cross the border hadn't gone anywhere. During an interview with a *New York Times* reporter, one inspector leaned out of his booth to hear the din of horns and declared, "'They're playing our song.'"[97]

These clogged ports of entry were waypoints in a continental system of exchange. By 1970, highly developed countries like the United States and France had started to experience problems of congestion in their highway networks. Mexico, on the other hand, had far greater problems with communication and integration of its road systems. In fact, the United States and Mexico were nearly mirror opposites of one another at that time in terms of road infrastructure. Much of the interstate highway system in the United States had been constructed by then, though these trunk roads represented only 20 percent of roads in the United States. The other 80 percent were feeder roads, local and regional routes that connected rural hinterlands to major markets. In Mexico, however, the highway landscape was reversed. Just over 80 percent of roads were trunk highways, and much of the countryside lacked easy access to major arteries of transportation.[98] This imbalance harkened, in part, all the way back to the Porfiriato of 1876–1911, during which president Porfirio Díaz helped convert Mexico into a de facto extension of the western US resource frontier. This meant privileging north-south railroad trunk lines that connected to US territory and markets.

To remedy this roadway imbalance, in the 1970s, Presidents Luis

Echeverría and José López Portillo each launched substantial rural roadbuilding campaigns between 1970 and 1982, but at the time of Operation Intercept, the shape of Mexico's transportation infrastructure system spoke to Mexico's history of uneven geographic development that privileged certain industries and left large sections of society outside mainstream markets.[99] It also spoke to the fact that a central purpose of the trunk roads was to physically join Mexico to the United States and vice versa.

It was not just the routes that mattered, though; it was also the character of the roads themselves. They became more durable over time, able to withstand heavier vehicles. Before 1950, highways in Mexico were designed to accommodate 13.6-ton trucks; in the 1950s and 1960s new roads were built for 24.5-ton trucks; and after 1970, new highways were built to support the weight of 32.7-ton vehicles. The increases correspond to greater volume in commodity markets as well as in long-distance trade.[100]

Especially after the Second World War, the United States and Mexico constructed an elaborate legal and physical infrastructure to facilitate the movement of over 4.5 million migrant laborers (the Bracero Program) as well as a crushing tonnage of animals, machinery, and oil. By the late 1960s, the two nations had literally been built into and upon one another, and all of this translated into an impossible policing challenge. A well-established history of smuggling and black markets already existed in the border region, and indeed in American history more generally.[101] Contraband trade is a predictable constant of free market capitalism as well as physical interconnectedness.[102] In Mexico especially, much of the transportation infrastructure network had been specifically designed to accommodate and facilitate cross-border truck and vehicle traffic. Operation Intercept was an attempt to interrupt an infrastructural inertia that had been building for over one hundred years; had rapidly expanded since the 1940s; and with PRONAF and the BIP, promised to gain even more momentum.

Nixon was largely focused on the Soviet Union and Asia and was particularly dismissive of the Spanish-speaking countries in the Western Hemisphere, confiding once to Henry Kissinger, "'Latin America doesn't matter.'"[103] Yet Mexico, along with Canada and Great Britain, shared one of the longest and most complex relationships with the United States.[104] This was evidenced by the volume of traffic across the border, as well as demographic shifts in Northern Mexico. In 1969, there were thirty-one official land ports of entry between the United States and Mexico, and Operation Intercept affected each of them. Measured in terms of human movement, the US-Mexico border had by then become the most important land boundary of the United States, despite the fact that the US-Canada border is twice as long and was also a nexus of trade. During the war years of the 1940s, the balance shifted: more people began to legally cross the Mexican border than the Canadian border. By the year Operation Intercept went into effect, around 67 percent of all sanctioned land entries into the United States were in the US-Mexico border region, totaling around 216 million entries per year, or around 590,000 every day—a daily migration both epic and ordinary.[105] This relentless movement across the US-Mexico border in the 1960s reveals the extent to which markets in both countries had become integrated. A significant part of this flux across the international divide had been facilitated by the Border Industrialization Program, initiated just four years before Intercept began.[106] In 1969, there were 108 maquiladoras along the entire border. Three years earlier there were only 57.[107] They multiplied fast. The border trucking industry boomed, too. In northern states like Chihuahua and Tamaulipas, the number of truck companies nearly doubled between 1965 and 1970; hundreds of trucks were added to existing fleets, and freight increased in states like Baja California Norte and Coahuila by millions upon millions of tons.[108] Notwithstanding the awkward twenty days of Operation Intercept, 1969 was the first year US imports from Mexico cracked the $1 billion mark.[109]

Business was booming, and with it came a demographic shift as the factories pulled workers to the Mexican North and swelled the populations of the border towns. In 1960, just over 1.4 million people lived in all the Mexican border towns combined, but by 1970 that number had soared to 2.1 million.[110] The 1960s, after the 1940s, saw the biggest population surge in US-Mexico border history, and both surges were fueled by the momentum of the US-Mexico economic relationship. The complex economic system that existed between Mexico and the United States in 1969 did not come about by accident, nor were the majority of its working parts informal. The social, physical, and legal infrastructure that held the two countries together was painstakingly developed over the course of decades, as the federal governments of both nations moved ever closer to economic interdependence. The logic of Operation Intercept did not take any of this into account, so in its efforts to stem the flow of drugs, it also crippled the flow of everything else, sending devastating shockwaves through the border economy on both sides of the line.[111]

Intercept reverberated from Washington to Mexico City but was felt most acutely at the local and regional level. Robert T. Hudgins was a customs inspector who worked in El Paso during the operation. Born in Boise, Idaho, raised in California, and disabled in World War II, he described the difficulties some Mexican laborers faced in terms of hydraulic development, or the lack thereof. In Coahuila, he said, "You can't scratch a living out of the land. There's no irrigation, it's just desert. What're you gonna live on?" Faced with this challenge, many answered the call of growers in the United States, though in his estimation, this was often a pyrrhic victory. He rattled off a list of counties—Hudspeth, Culberson, Presidio, Jeff Davis, Ector—places in the Chihuahuan Desert scrub of West Texas that Hudgins believed were home to virtual slave owners. "People that for years have been running slavery," as he described them. "We're talking about slavery, like in the South before the Civil War. The wets come over from Mexico, they work for 25 cents an hour, 20 cents an hour. That's slavery they go into."[112]

Within this larger context of hardship and exploitation, however, he recounted how his job as an inspector at the ports of entry in El Paso before Intercept was relatively low-key: "You never opened a trunk; and if you did, and you didn't catch a load of dope or somethin', you got your rear end eat up. It was a greeting service. We didn't enforce the law, nobody really cared." To underline this porousness even more starkly, he explained how he adopted his son from Mexico, and when he brought him across the line with the proper paperwork, "nobody *looked* at 'em."[113] The negative experiences endured by hundreds of thousands of other people of Mexican descent as they confronted police in the border region stood in stark contrast to Hudgins's placid view of the line, but his point nevertheless speaks to the extent to which Operation Intercept acted as a watershed on the international divide that signaled the beginning of a new era of tension along the line.

Bob Ybarra remembered how the bridges in El Paso–Ciudad Juárez were expanded in the 1960s to anticipate increased trade.

"You're talking about eight lanes [on the] Bridge of the Americas [and a] big inspection facility with room to grow, and grow, and grow," he recounted, also pointing out that "there was criticism that it was over-built." During the 1970s, the opposite proved to be true. The Border Industrialization Program had gathered momentum, and soon even more bridge remodeling had to be carried out, not just to expand the number of lanes, but also to retrofit the structures to accommodate the increased weight of nonstop truck traffic. To Ybarra, Intercept marked the turning point. Since then, he stated flatly, "The world is changed."[114] The next epoch in border history would bring with it more and more compensatory building to respond to the impossible task of both policing and facilitating large-scale trade.

Even in 1969, during the fledgling years of the border industrialization boom, any interruption to border traffic was a major undertaking. In the words of Arthur Adams, a Border Patrol officer working in El Paso at the time, "you had to take drastic measures."[115] These drastic measures—the thorough inspections on the bridges—devastated local businesses that were dependent on the regular comings and goings of ordinary people in both border cities. Héctor Chánez Aragón was one of those shopkeepers. He was born in Madera, Chihuahua, but as a young boy had to flee his hometown due to death threats his father, a political dissident, received. After escaping through small towns like Matachí, Temósachic, Tejolocachic, and Cocomorachic, they ended up in Ciudad Juárez. In high school, Héctor ended up in El Paso, gravitated toward "electrical trades," and took a field trip to Lubbock as part of the Vocational Industrial Club of Texas. There, for the first time, he encountered a sign outside a restaurant, ubiquitous in many parts of Texas: "NO DOGS, NO MEX." Back in El Paso, a town populated overwhelmingly by Mexican-origin people and ostensibly somewhat friendlier, he eventually opened an electronics and furniture store on Stanton Street. But when the Chamizal settlement was resolved, he and his business partner were afraid their store would be included in the territory returned to Mexico. It wasn't; the cutoff missed them by a block. Nevertheless, the bridge construction rerouted cars, and their business suffered. Operation Intercept, however, was a financial catastrophe for their store. He and the other shopkeepers from Stanton and El Paso Streets got together and all sent a letter directly to Nixon explaining their situation, to no avail.[116]

For many people on the Mexican side, however, according to the former mayor of Ciudad Juárez, René Mascareñas Miranda, the damage was more than economic. Along the entire border line, from Tijuana to Matamoros, he had heard people explain how the operation was an affront to their dignity. *"Pagaron el pato."* Ordinary people bore the brunt of a police program that cast aspersions on an entire nation, and they suffered the shame of shakedowns on cross-border routes they had taken for years, largely unencumbered. In Mascareñas's view, the episode had set cordial relations between the two cities back fifty years, creating a tension that hadn't been experienced since Pancho Villa attacked Columbus, New Mexico, in 1916 and set off Pershing's Punitive Expedition into Mexico. One word he used in Spanish to describe what had been damaged was "amistad," an ironic echo of the recently constructed dam by the same name. For Mascareñas, only *"fronterizos,"* or border people, could truly understand how Operation Intercept had disrupted border history.[117]

In these stories, we can see more examples of that now-familiar disconnect and tension between the immediate physical spaces of the international divide and their integration into larger continental and federal systems. For those who lived near the line, cross-border bridges and ports of entry were often part of a concrete, personal geography. For the federal officers who conducted the inspections and the politicians who concocted the plan, border infrastructure was simply something that could be commandeered and transformed into a chokepoint amid the hemispheric geography of black markets.

Meanwhile, an absurd quality settled on the diplomatic fallout in Mexico. Scarcely two months before Operation Intercept, the United States had sent the first human beings in history to the moon. Though the ephemeral radar cordon strung out along the US-Mexico border had proven incapable of detecting many low-flying aircraft transporting drugs, the US space program had successfully engineered the moon landing. Upon their return to earth, the lunar astronauts set out on a victory lap through twenty-six countries.[118] Mexico was their first stop, and they arrived to great fanfare just days after Operation Intercept had crippled border traffic of all kinds. The astronauts rode triumphantly through the streets of Mexico City adorned with gigantic Mexican *charro* hats. Onlookers threw rose petals. Waxing philosophical, Neil Armstrong declared that from a height of 128,000 miles he had looked down upon Mexico and the United States and "'could see no border between our countries.'"[119] Mexican president Gustavo Díaz Ordaz, however, could.

Díaz Ordaz, who had been present with Johnson at the major border construction sites of the 1960s, took advantage of the mammoth crowds and the international press coverage of the astronauts' visit to articulate the shock and confusion that had set in among many of his fellow citizens and members of his government. In a speech to the Apollo 11 crew, their wives, and an array of journalists, he went off script to describe what he saw as a "'bureaucratic mistake'" that had "'raised a wall of suspicion'" between Mexico and the United States.[120] Functionaries back in Washington balked, many in their ignorance still confused as to why Mexicans did not appreciate a unilaterally deployed police operation along their northern and most important border. Reverting to an old stereotype about Latin Americans, they simply explained away the increasing hostility emanating from Mexico by saying, "For whatever reasons, Mexican national honor seems to have become involved." This thread of Mexican "honor" and "pride," and Mexicans' great sensitivity about both, runs throughout the US diplomatic correspondence on Operation Intercept. In the press, US government spokespeople backpedaled and apologized for the diplomatic rupture with Mexico, though a now-declassified memorandum reveals that the plan all along was to keep the Mexicans in the dark. The memo states that government officials in Mexico were "not in any sense . . . consulted on the Operation during the planning stage, because the agencies responsible for the Operation insisted that advance consultation with the Mexicans would lead to damaging leaks."[121]

THROUGHOUT THE DECADE OF THE 1960S, THE UNITED STATES and Mexico spent well over $100 million on building projects on the international divide. The two largest construction sites, the Chamizal and Amistad Dam, were celebrated as shining examples of US-Mexico cooperation and partnership. They also embodied an ideology about the natural world and the proper relationship between water and human civilization. In bringing border rivers under control, however, hydraulic engineers also produced side effects. Thanks to irregular discharge due to so many upstream diversions, vegetation grew wild in the bed of the Colorado River, which in turn created a new flooding threat. In addition, the water allotted to Mexico from Colorado had become salinized due to high-intensity irrigation on the US side. A similar problem cropped up in the Texas-Tamaulipas border region around the Morillo Drain. These symptoms had been produced by the built environment itself, and the response was more layers of construction to mitigate the systemic flaws in the earlier layers of building. Water policy in the border region and beyond had begun to show serious signs of deterioration, and as hydraulic engineering projects expanded, the system became ever more precarious. Border policing, too, had reached a turning point. The widespread use and construction of transportation infrastructure in the border region, meant to connect markets in the United States and Mexico, had also accelerated black markets deemed anathema to American society. The highway systems of the two countries, like the railroads before them, had brought with them phenomena that could not be controlled. The Nixon administration tried, briefly, to get a grip on smuggling, but control proved elusive. In the decades that followed, new forms of both building and policing would take hold in the border region. And more and more, border construction would turn to compensatory building: physical, concrete attempts to use the built environment to respond to unsustainable laws and environmental practices.

BUILDING THE BORDER OF TODAY

From the straightening of the Rio Grande in the 1930s to the construction of Falcon Dam in the 1950s and Amistad Dam in the 1960s, the largest building projects on the US-Mexico border for much of the twentieth century centered on hydraulic engineering. The International Boundary and Water Commission, the lead agency of these river projects, had also been instrumental in early border fence construction, especially between 1948 and 1951. These barricades, as well as other kinds of police building, were executed on a much smaller scale than waterworks, and the vast majority of the early border fence was intended to keep animals at bay, not people. Toward the end of the century, however, the balance flipped. Police building, in particular barriers and surveillance infrastructure, became the dominant form of construction on the line, even as the long-standing tradition of expanding transportation infrastructure between the two countries accelerated.

Building projects on and around border waterways from the 1970s on were predominantly geared toward managing the limited utility and negative effects of previous waterworks. Flooding and silt accumulation that resulted from damming and canalization was met with even more excavation, vegetation clearing, channeling, and damming. In this sense, I argue that riverine construction had much in common with newly installed police infrastructure. Nearly all police construction was designed to manage the negative effects of incoherent, self-contradictory, and failed policies regarding immigration and banned psychoactive substances. Both are examples of compensatory building.

Especially since 1990, the idea of border fencing as a potential solution to a range of social problems was reinvigorated and underwent several new iterations, each one more aspirational than the last. And after the attacks of September 11, 2001, a political shift took place as well. For the first time, politicians, much more so than the police themselves, as had been the custom for much of the twentieth century, began to advocate for border barriers. Also, the old preoccupation with surveillance on the border was supplemented and expanded with new technological innovations designed to enhance visibility and lend law enforcement an even greater tactical advantage.[1]

Meanwhile, powerful multinational businesses lobbied for market deregulation and trade liberalization.[2] They succeeded, and the North American Free Trade Agreement (NAFTA) of 1994 was the most concrete result of their efforts. This, too, involved colossal construction projects to open new ports of entry, renovate old ones, and expand road systems to accommodate increased truck traffic across the border. In short, though much of border building since the 1970s was meant to help manage the side effects of unsustainable previous practices in the built environments of both water management and policing, the solutions were themselves expansions of the same built environments throughout the border region.

Scholarly writing about recent border history has been dominated by social scientists and political theorists rather than historians. Social scientists have relied heavily on interviews with migrants, politicians, and border policymakers, as well as statistical analysis, to understand the recent history of the international divide. Much of their work is focused on militarism within law enforcement, activist organizing in opposition to both increased border policing and free-trade ideology, and the punitive dimensions of the so-called war on drugs.[3] Political theorists have framed their analyses of borders more abstractly in terms of neoliberalism, globalization, and sovereignty. Many have concluded that the nation-state itself is unsustainable as a form of political organization due to sustained competition with supranational organizations and multinational corporations, the widespread privatization of social goods and services, international migration, the militarization of policing, subnational extremist groups, and massive ecological degradation accompanied by permanent climate refugees.[4]

From this point of view, the fortification of nation-states with physical barricades, in light of the massive opening of borders to facilitate the transnational circulation of capital, appears desperately anachronistic. Scholars who have focused on border barriers in particular have often made arguments that highlight hypocrisy in government policy, practical inefficacy, and historical amnesia.[5] Historians of the "drug wars" and of territorial sovereignty itself have come to similar conclusions about the internal inconsistencies of criminal justice paradigms and the decomposition of the nation-state.[6] Borders, either implicitly or explicitly, figure centrally in their claims.

Drawing on the insights of this diverse scholarship, I examine in this chapter the history of the border since the 1970s, focusing on the various physical construction projects that have been built on the line. Recent border building has much in common with the past and has in many ways simply extended the scope of preexisting construction. Flood control projects on the border rivers; border fencing; long-distance, cross-border trade; and the modification of the natural landscape to achieve these ends all have decades-old trajectories. Even the enlistment of the harsh environments and topography as weapons in border policing's arsenal has historical precedents. Especially in the context of police and commercial building, however, the scale, durability of materials, and political will that drove border construction in this period broke with past precedents and likely signals that a new epoch of even more extreme compensatory building projects lies ahead.

WATERWORKS

By the 1970s, the stretch of the Rio Grande between Fort Quitman and Presidio-Ojinaga was one of the last zones of the river that had not yet been completely dammed, channelized, canalized, or straightened. Nevertheless, those 198 miles of waterway felt the effects of all the previous modifications upstream. Often, due to increased water use upriver, reservoir regulations, and decreased runoff, this section of the Rio Grande was a mere trickle. Sometimes long periods of time went by when no water at all ran through the river channel there. During periods of heavy rain, flash floods rushed into the river valley from large tributary arroyos in the surrounding desert and brought with them huge deposits of sediment, which, coupled with the irregular flow of the river, resulted in a constantly shifting channel. This meant that, once again, the exact location of the international boundary itself came into question as small tracts of land separated and shifted from one side of the bank to the other, just as they had around urban sections of the river in the nineteenth century. To make matters worse, much of the riverbed had "insidiously become choked" with salt cedars, a nonnative species also known as tamarisk, which further disrupted the flow. These plants are nearly impossible to kill by fire, drought, freezing temperatures, hypersalinity, complete submersion, or repeated cutting at ground level.[7] Nearly 130 years after the Treaty of Guadalupe Hidalgo had delineated the border on paper, and after hundreds of adjudications and land transfers, both large and small, to fix the US-Mexico border in place, there were still some remote regions where the exact location of the international divide was uncertain in the late twentieth century.[8]

The boundary commissioners of both the United States and Mexico met the day after Christmas, 1979, in Ciudad Juárez and collectively worried about the remote places where the Rio Grande had completely dried up. They agreed that "its character as the boundary [would] be completely lost in large sections of the reach" if its channel wasn't stabilized through more human intervention.[9] In other words, well into the decade during which, as the sociologist Timothy Dunn has shown us, the US government began to incorporate high-tech and exorbitantly expensive military equipment such as night-vision goggles and helicopters into border policing, there were sections of the divide where the border was still vague, and where border water was at risk of accidentally becoming border land due to overexploitation of the river. In response to the indeterminate location of the river by the 1970s, the IBWC launched the "Rio Grande Boundary Preservation Project." The idea was to restore the Rio Grande. This did not mean a return to the unpredictable, wild, and meandering path of the desert river. Rather, the project was meant to ensure its cartographic precision through more excavation and straightening.

The last major boundary treaty between the United States and Mexico was signed in 1970 and dealt specifically with the issue of the as yet unfixed border.[10] Despite the fact that the US and Mexican governments had been repeatedly surveying both the land borders and rivers since the 1850s, much of this mapping had been in response to specific boundary problems and was not tied into the national geodetic network, designed to provide a consistent coordinate system for latitude, longitude, and other geospatial measurements. And though the boundary surveys of the nineteenth century have garnered the lion's share of attention by historians interested in border making, there was yet another international boundary survey conducted during the 1970s that has been all but forgotten. It is important to remember, however, because of what it tells us about the persistent tension between border environments and border builders.

In 1972 and 1974, the IBWC flew its planes over the Rio Grande, and in 1973 and 1975, over the Colorado to conduct yet another aerial survey of the border. Using the Transverse Mercator Projection, they produced controlled photographic mosaics at scales of 1:20,000 and 1:10,000. The exact location of the border was determined by engineers from both countries, and in places where the Rio Grande ran dry, they used the channel where water was supposed to flow.[11] This final mapping, which completed a process that had begun over 120 years earlier, was accompanied by another resurrected nineteenth-century practice: the erection of boundary markers on the western border.

Between 1975 and 1980, the US and Mexican sections of the IBWC installed supplemental boundary markers to complement those footed in the 1850s and 1890s. Though much of the fencing built between 1948 and 1951 still existed on the western land border, hundreds of miles remained unmarked by any human built structure. The new monuments were not evenly distributed, but rather were concentrated in certain places based on the logic of urban and commercial expansion, or the areas that had seen "the most rapid development growth along the boundary." This was most evident along the California–Baja California border, between the Colorado River and the Pacific Ocean. The IBWC thought both in terms of the physical features of the landscape and the built environment of the border, so they described this region as the space "between Monument No. 206 and Monument No. 258." The US section of the IBWC placed 126 markers in that stretch of land, and the Mexican section placed 127. More supplementary markers were also placed between Monuments 108 and 204A on the Arizona-Sonora border for similar reasons.[12]

They did this because they were concerned that "the precise location of the boundary [could not] be readily determined by people along the border because most of the monuments [were] so far apart."[13] They built two types of border markers, both made of concrete and buried in concrete bases. One was 7 inches square, with two feet pro-truding above ground and three feet below, reinforced with a ⅝-inch deformed iron bar. The other design type tapered from 9.8 inches at the base to 6.7 inches at the top, in keeping with the obelisk form of the nineteenth century, though only 15 inches were visible above ground, with 9 inches underground. It was reinforced with a ⅜-inch steel bar.[14] These small structures, in conjunction with the new river mapping surveys, represented the IBWC's conviction that the border should be as legible as possible, both in a cartographic sense and in a concrete, physical sense. They also represented the extent to which border marking corresponded to expanding population zones. Many sections of the border were ignored, that is, no new markers were placed there. This was especially the case in the New Mexico–Chihuahua border region, which had experienced either slow or non-existent changes in urban development and industry.

Other parts of the international divide, however, posed different challenges for engineering and border construction. The Rio Grande delta, near the mouth of the Rio Grande and the Gulf of Mexico, had the opposite problem from the desert section of the river between El Paso–Ciudad Juárez and Presidio-Ojinaga. Instead of a dry riverbed clogged with silt and tamarisk, the Rio Grande in its southernmost valley was prone to disastrous flooding. Apart from the major con-struction projects of Amistad and Falcon Dams and the subsequent heavy fencing after 1990 on the western boundary, this is perhaps the most intensely built part of the international divide. In essence, the Rio Grande is almost a different river in this area. Aside from the storage dams that regulate discharge, its flow is largely determined by dozens of small tributaries in both northeastern Mexico and south-western Texas, and the climate is not arid like the western border but rather humid, prone to heavy rains of long duration.

There was a long history in the lower valley, not of big water proj-ects, but of constant small engineering interventions on waterways. The threat of flooding came not only from the unpredictability of nature and climate but also from the changing relationship of human settlement and land use along the Rio Grande. According to official documentation by the IBWC, flooding danger increased with the ar-rival of the first railroad between 1904 and 1906.[15] Not coincidentally, this dovetails with historians' accounts of the widespread disposses-sion of Mexican Americans in the region. The railroad increased land values, which led to higher property taxes that many people of Mexican descent were unable to pay. Subsequently, much of the ranchland in the region that had been geared to local and regional economies was consolidated and repurposed for high-intensity commercial agriculture.[16] The IBWC also noted the risk to the "rapid development of urban areas and irrigated agriculture," which meant that more property of higher value was subject to inundation when the river overflowed.

Some of the early twentieth-century farmers built their own private levees to hold back the floodwaters, and when that failed, they banded together to form flood control organizations to pool their resources. The private waterworks they constructed weren't strong enough, however. In 1925, after two disastrous floods in 1919 and another in 1922, Cameron and Hidalgo Counties began construction of more robust waterworks based on plans developed by the Bureau of Reclamation. These included digging channels in the floodplain that could divert excess waters, as well as smaller diversion dams. The counties had invested more than $5 million by the end of the 1920s to stem the threat of flooding, but it wasn't enough. It became clear that the resources of the federal governments of the United States and Mexico would be necessary to manage the landscape of expanding commercial agriculture and the uncertainties of the Rio Grande's discharge in a wet, subtropical climate.

The IBWC became the primary border water builder in the delta after 1932, strengthening, lengthening, and excavating new levees and channels. A massive flood in 1958 demonstrated that they had not solved the problem, as did Hurricane Beulah in 1967. Falcon Dam proved useless to control it; they closed the gates to hold back the water in superstorage, but upward of thirty-five inches of rain fell below its reservoir, leading to a peak discharge at the mouth of the Rio Grande of 220,000 cubic feet per second, 50 percent larger than the maximum expectation on which flood control waterworks were constructed at the time. By the 1970s, over six hundred structures and 14,600 acres of interior floodways were spread across 180 river miles in the lower Rio Grande valley, collectively known as the Lower Rio Grande Flood Control Project.[17]

Between 1979 and 1983, the US Geological Survey and the US Customs Service—another collaboration between land managers and law enforcement—worked together to produce a "simulated natural

color" image series of the US-Mexico border. The Mexican Dirección General de Geografía del Territorio Nacional (General Office of Geography and the National Territory) took high-altitude infrared photography at a scale of 1:80,000, then the images were rescaled to 1:25,000 to produce 203 maps of the border region. A detail from one of these maps (figure 5.1) helps illustrate the complexity of the built environment in the Rio Grande delta.[18] The American city of Brownsville occupies the upper half of the frame, and the Mexican city of Matamoros, the lower. Each city is surrounded on all sides by an almost phantasmagoric array of semigridded fields. The photograph is bisected by the river border, twisting and bending its way through both urban space and agricultural land. It is a precarious landscape characterized by thorough development along one of the most intractable sections of the Rio Grande.

FIGURE 5.1.
Brownsville Port of Entry (detail), 1983

The Rio Grande delta region contains the curviest part of the border. It is still heavily engineered, however, not only by a dense combination of urban and agricultural development but also by a complex system of flood control dams and channels. United States–Mexico Border, Color Image Map Series, U.S. Geological Survey and U.S. Customs Service, 1979-1983, Perry-Castañeda Map Collection, University of Texas Libraries.

The last major border water construction project in this area was the Retamal Dam, completed in 1975, which was the culmination of a multigenerational battle against the power of water in the valley. Two types of dams were built on the US-Mexico border: storage dams and diversion dams. Falcon Dam and Amistad Dam are the only two storage dams, massive reservoirs capable not only of flood control but also of producing electricity. More numerous are diversion dams. These are much smaller structures designed to reroute water or otherwise control its flow for the purposes of irrigation or managing floods. American Dam and International Dam, built in 1938 and 1940, respectively, managed water diversion around El Paso and diverted water into the Acequia Madre in Ciudad Juárez. Morelos Dam on the Colorado River, built in 1944, served a similar purpose. Anzalduas Dam was the first major diversion dam built south of the Falcon Reservoir. Construction was completed in 1960 when it became clear that Falcon Dam and smaller flood control measures could not protect the south valley. Retamal was the last in a long series of waterworks on the US-Mexico river border designed to protect the increasingly dense human settlement and agricultural production on its banks.

Both design and construction costs were split evenly between the two countries. The structure was developed by a private contractor called Leeds, Hill and Jewett, Inc., Consulting Engineers, alongside Mexico's Secretaría de Recursos Hidráulicos. Mexican workers excavated the bypass channel, built cofferdams and steel pile cutoff walls, and laid concrete for the base and abutments. They also installed commemorative monuments. American workers built the four interior piers and the control building, and provided the gates and two emergency generators. The dam they built was thirty-three feet high, designed to permit the passage of up to 20,000 cubic feet per second through eighty-two-foot-wide and twenty-four-foot-high gates. In an effort to finally solve the flooding problems that had plagued the area since the beginning of the twentieth century, they also installed two manually controlled side gates, each forty feet wide and twenty-nine feet high, that could accommodate 10,000 cubic feet per second in the event the water rose higher than anticipated, which it always had.[19]

Meanwhile, around the same time, the Tijuana River was being channelized at the opposite end of the border. By the close of the 1970s, there was scarcely an inch left of any of the border rivers that had not been subject to a building project of some sort. The 1970s saw the final push to control and manage every cubic foot of water on the US-Mexico border. Another photographic map from the 1979–1983 aerial survey reveals a starkly different border landscape from the southernmost Rio Grande valley (see figure 5.2).[20] Instead of an undulating, serpentine river border, the boundary between California and Baja

California is a straight line bisecting the center of the frame. And unlike the Colorado River and the Rio Grande, which have their headwaters in the United States, the Tijuana River originates in Mexico and drains into California. It crosses the border near the center of the photographic map, which itself was created in 1979, the same year the Tijuana River channelization was dedicated.

The concrete work is visible from many thousands of feet in the air in this detail from the USGS and Customs map series. As the river passes through the city of Tijuana, its bed forms an almost completely straight diagonal line. The river flows 5.3 miles through Southern California before it empties into the Pacific. In 1964, hoping to develop the area around the river for urban, commercial, and recreational use, the city of San Diego preemptively began asking the

FIGURE 5.2.

San Ysidro Port of Entry (detail), 1979

The trapezoidal concrete lining of the Tijuana River—on the Mexican side—is one of the most clearly identifiable features of this border zone. United States–Mexico Border, Color Image Map Series, U.S. Geological Survey and U.S. Customs Service, 1979-1983, Perry-Castañeda Map Collection, University of Texas Libraries.

IBWC to design and construct a flood control project. Environmental concerns and disagreements about land use delayed the project for several years; Mexico began construction in 1972, the United States not until 1978. The original plan for the US side, prepared in consultation with the Army Corps of Engineers, was meant to be a concrete-lined trapezoidal channel to guide the river water all the way to the ocean. Ultimately, however, advocates for leaving the final section of the Tijuana Valley as open space won out, and the segments of the river that were channeled in concrete were built primarily on the Mexican side. There, on the south side of the border, a 2.7-mile-long and 230-foot-wide concrete-lined ditch manages the flow of the river, and the concrete channel extends only 1,223 feet into US territory.[21]

Nevertheless, major though less visible construction also took place on the US side. A private contractor called Kasler Corporation won the $6,666,666 contract to reshape the mouth of the Tijuana River.[22] The work they did was not lined in concrete, and was therefore less conspicuous, though it nonetheless transformed the river channel. At the end of the concrete-lined zone, just north of the border, Kasler, in conjunction with the Army Corps of Engineers, built a 3,700-foot-long flared energy dissipater. This constituted a widening of the river channel as well as filling it with massive amounts of grouted stone and dumped stone that was meant to create turbulence in the water and slow down its flow. Beyond that, earthwork levees flanked the river basin, ranging from twelve to twenty-three feet high.[23]

By the 1980s, the Tijuana River, the Colorado River, and the Rio Grande had all been fundamentally reshaped, work that had unfolded in various stages over the course of the twentieth century. The speed at which the water flowed, its quantity, its direction, its path, and its destination had all been modified through building projects along nearly every river mile. Had human beings not settled so densely along the border, and had they not dedicated themselves to higher- and higher-intensity irrigated agriculture, many of these building projects would have been unnecessary. The built environment of urban and agricultural expansion required the rivers to be rebuilt, however, and the ecological and hydrological consequences of that rebuilding then had to be managed, often through more construction. Yet despite the exhaustive scope of water management on the border for so many decades, the biggest projects had been completed by the 1980s. The western land border, however, was a different story. There, a renewed momentum was gathering for barrier construction, and the most intense phase of building on border land had yet to begin.

POLICE BUILDING

By the late 1970s, the Western Land Boundary Fence Project of 1939–1951 was a distant memory to many interested in government border policy, if they remembered it at all. With the bulk of construction taking place between 1948 and 1951, the IBWC in conjunction with the INS, the National Park Service, and the Bureau of Animal Industry built 237 miles of border fencing between the Pacific Ocean and El Paso. At the time, it had been the biggest border fencing project in American history, spurred in large part by the outbreak of foot-and-mouth disease in Mexico in 1947. Nevertheless, immigration border police took full advantage of the situation to advocate for more extensive and durable fencing around the ports of entry where they worked. The IBWC spent $765,789 building the final stage of that border fence, though in 1951 Congress cut off appropriations for border fence construction and maintenance, claiming it had achieved its objectives because foot-and-mouth had been contained.[24]

For twenty-six years the subject of border fencing languished as a major issue in the federal government of the United States, though in 1977 it was reinvigorated by new funding for proposed border fences in El Paso and San Ysidro.[25] Beginning in the 1970s, more than ever before, the border became a national-level preoccupation in the United States and an increasingly valuable political tool in elections. More and more US politicians and policymakers began to zero in on the border to cast it as a region that posed a threat to American society, and those two border towns were the places where the majority of unauthorized crossings took place.[26] The historian Oscar Martínez explains how the proposition turned into a controversy on the border. The INS announced plans for the new fencing in October of 1978. At the same time, one of the builders who had been contracted to construct the fence bragged that it would cut off the toes of anyone trying to climb it. Apparently, he claimed, part of his fence design included razors. The media dubbed the proposed fence the "Tortilla Curtain." The

Mexican government protested alongside local activist organizations such as the Coalition Against the Fence in El Paso. Bill Clements, an oilman Republican who was soon thereafter elected governor of Texas, denounced it, joining Robert Krueger, a Democratic senatorial candidate, also from Texas. Mexican American organizations, such as the League of United Latin American Citizens and the Mexican American Legal Defense and Education Fund, also criticized it. Presidents Jimmy Carter and José López Portillo discussed these concerns about the fence in 1979, and ultimately the project was scaled down.[27]

This kind of resistance and bipartisan opposition would soon be overwhelmed by the border fence builders of the 1990s and beyond. That is not to say that there would not be widespread opposition to subsequent border fences, but rather that border builders—often led by politicians, not police—pushed forward with greater impunity toward bigger and bigger projects. The moment of opposition surrounding the "Tortilla Curtain" is also interesting because the proposed fence design did not differ significantly from the border fences put in place in the late 1940s, though the level of controversy surrounding it suggests the dawn of a more contentious kind of border politics.

By August 1978, three months before the official announcement that new fences would be built, the INS had already produced a detailed guide to materials and exact specifications of three different types of border fence. This information was then furnished to contractors to perform the construction. The Houston contractor's comments about severed toes and razors on the fence helped galvanize opposition to the border barrier, though no actual razors were used in the INS's design. Some important modifications do, however, mark the "Tortilla Curtain" as a stepping-stone construction between the fences on the western boundary from the 1940s and 1950s and the much larger and more durable barricades built after 1990.

INS specifications for the late-1970s border fence, called the "Border Control Fence" in official documents, are only slightly updated from the fencing built between 1948 and 1951.[28] Like previous fencing around the ports of entry, its stated purpose was to be a "barrier capable of inhibiting and deterring the passage of unauthorized persons," and at around ten feet tall, the three designs were of similar height to the old fences. Like previous fences, posts were sunk in a concrete footing or apron meant to prevent tunneling, and much of the actual

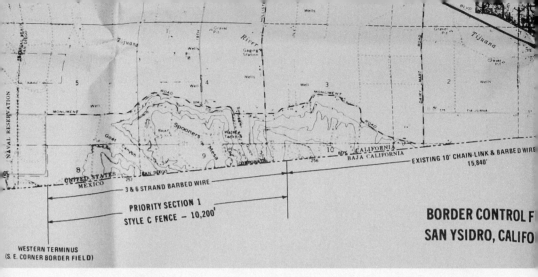

fencing material was chain-link, though of a stronger variety. The chain-link fabric was either zinc, aluminum, or vinyl-coated steel, helically woven into a one-inch diamond mesh with a minimum breaking load of 1,290 pounds. This was a tighter weave than the 2" × 2" pattern from earlier fencing.[29]

There were at least two more significant updates, however, that distinguished the design of the Border Control Fence from preexisting fences. In all three Border Control Fence styles, at least one-third of the fencing fabric was expanded metal rather than chain-link. This was more difficult to cut through, but perhaps more importantly, official INS specifications dictated that sections of expanded metal grating shall be "randomly sheared to result in open and sharp edges." Similarly, the "selvage," or leftover chain-link material at the top of the fence, was supposed to be modified into sharp edges. Again, INS specifications were clear: "The fabric shall be twisted and barbed by twisting the wire in a closed helix of 1½ machine turns equivalent to 3 full twists, and cut at an angle to provide sharp barbs."[30]

The 1948–1951 border fencing, at least the sections that surrounded the ports of entry, did include multiple strands of barbed wire mounted on top of the chain-link on separate arms as well, and in this way it was also a fence hostile to human passage. Interestingly, however, only "Style B" of the Border Control Fence included any overhanging components, and though this 1970s fencing was not outfitted with barbed wire, the selvage was still meant to be twisted into points.[31]

INS maps detailing the proposed location of the Border Control Fence also reveal several key aspects of border fencing at the time

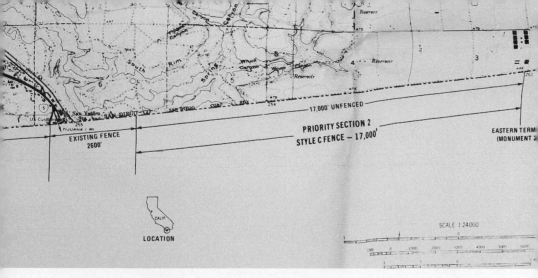

(see figures 5.3 and 5.4).[32] According
to official documents, the siting of the
fence in both places referred to one
of the oldest types of border construction: the nineteenth-century survey
monuments. In El Paso, the western
terminus of the fence was meant to
coincide with Monument 1, while the
eastern terminus of the San Ysidro
fence was slated to coincide with
Monument 253. In El Paso, Monument
1 marks the beginning of the western

FIGURE 5.3.

Border Control Fence, San Ysidro,
California (detail), ca. 1978

Unlike in the nineteenth-century
"planos" and the Amistad Dam topographic maps, Mexican territory is
completely ignored in these maps,
cartographically gesturing to the
unilateralism of recent border
fencing projects. Records of the
International Boundary and Water
Commission, Record Group 76.

land border on one hand, and the spot where the Rio Grande becomes
the international divide on the other.[33] That part of the border is also
significantly obstructed by Cristo Rey, a craggy mountain that makes
crossing there extremely difficult. In Southern California, however,
there is no significant topographic feature that might have informed
the INS's decision to end the fence building at Monument 253. I suspect this instance is a good example of how various kinds of border
construction inform one another. Faced with the uncertainty of how far
to extend the fence line east of the port of entry, a preexisting survey
marker might have served to help dictate an arbitrary stopping point.

The El Paso fence proposal from 1978 had much in common with
the hand-drawn fence proposal from 1947 (see chapter 3, figure 3.3).
Both focus on the downtown area where the primary international
bridges were located and where cross-border traffic was highest. The

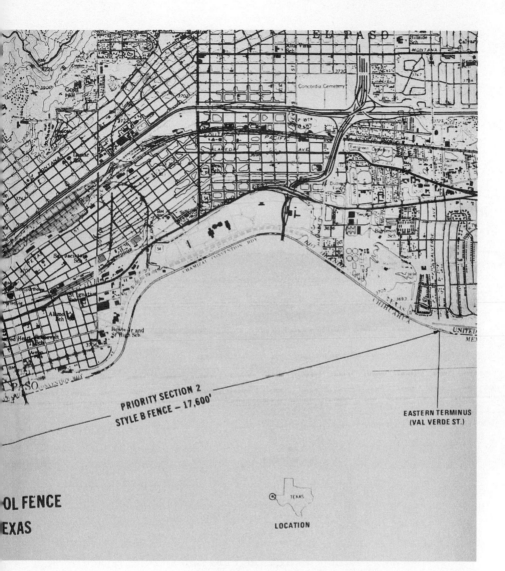

FIGURE 5.4.

Border Control Fence, El Paso, Texas (detail), ca. 1978

The Rio Grande Rectification and Chamizal projects had firmly fixed the location of the river border
between El Paso and Ciudad Juárez. US government
officials wanted to build more durable fencing along
the river's northern bank in the late 1970s. Records of
the International Boundary and Water Commission,
Record Group 76.

1978 map also includes much more detailed information about the urban plan, which was of particular interest to border police worried that unauthorized crossers could blend in quickly and easily to their surroundings. In Southern California, on the other hand, the 1978 map included much more detailed information about transportation routes than the 1953 border fence map (see chapter 3, figure 3.6), another cartographic predecessor of the 1970s fence proposals. In the earlier map, only major highways and railroads were included to signal a distinction between chain-link fencing around the ports of entry and ranch-style fencing in remote regions. In the 1978 map, however, even local dirt roads are included, which seems to suggest that border police were paying greater attention to tactical mobility in semirural areas. We can also see in the San Ysidro map the extent of existing fencing. Before the Border Control Fence was built, 28,640 feet of fencing were already in place, all of it constructed with sections of barbed wire.[34]

It is also important to note that, unlike the border fence map produced in 1953, these are topographic maps. They include contour lines that signal not only changes in elevation but also the relative steepness and form of the physical landscape. Border police were also attentive to the interplay between the built environment of policing and the natural world in fencing proposals from 1947 and 1948. Even then, they paid attention to how waterways, such as the All-American Canal in Southern California, could assist as deterrents to unauthorized crossers. They were particularly interested in artificial lighting because the night posed a great tactical disadvantage; border patrolmen couldn't see and felt overwhelmed in the dark. The IBWC, the fence-building agency, also conducted detailed studies of the landscape to assess the relative difficulty of construction. In addition to these similarities to earlier fence design, we can read the contour lines on the 1978 maps as a further step in enlisting the natural environment in border policing measures. The "prevention through deterrence" model the Border Patrol developed in 1993 not only incorporated increased manpower and shifted the tactical organization of border police but also included "hostile" terrain, a combination of topography and climate, into its strategy.[35] The contour lines here can be understood as evidence of an ever more detailed police reading of the natural landscape, and the arid climate and extreme heat that once plagued government officials in the nineteenth-century boundary surveys were being deployed against unauthorized crossers.

Finally, it is significant that these border fencing plans were designed only for two ports of entry along nearly two thousand miles of the international divide, completely ignoring remote regions and smaller ports. Much of the impetus of earlier fence building came from the 1947 foot-and-mouth disease outbreak in Mexico, which meant that the border fences built between 1948 and 1951 were a joint production of the IBWC, the INS, and the Bureau of Animal Industry. In the 1970s, however, the focus on animals and remote areas had nearly completely fallen away as political attention shifted toward the two largest human migration routes in and around the two largest border town complexes. In this way, too, we can understand the Border Control Fence as a stepping stone between earlier fencing and subsequent barrier construction. When remote regions came back into focus among policymakers in the years before the passage of the Secure Fence Act of 2006, they were framed in terms of human movement, not animal diseases, marking both a continuity of form and a break in concept from earlier fencing.

In the 1990s, a greater consensus between policymakers, lawmakers, and border police began to gain momentum. Historians and social scientists have documented the internal inconsistencies, inefficacies, and lethal byproducts of increased border policing during these years and to the present day. The literature focuses largely on the politicization of the border in US national discourse; how the various "wars" on drugs" have contributed to punitive, sometimes lethal, state responses; the criminalization of migrants; and the symbolic qualities of border policing.[36] Starting in the 1990s, the Border Patrol, armed with an ever-expanding budget, hired new agents at a breakneck pace. The agency grew from just over 4,000 agents in 1992 to over 21,000 in 2011.[37] This expansion was largely in response to a new political will, shared by many Republicans as well as Democrats, oriented around perceived dangers that were typically framed in terms of changing demography, smuggling, terrorism, or some combination of all three. The root causes of these phenomena were typically unrelated, but they nevertheless spawned more homogeneous political thought about border policing. Unauthorized cross-border traffic in these years was frequently cast as a permanent emergency for which more policing was always part of the solution.[38]

The built environment does not figure prominently in much of this scholarship, however, and when it does appear, it is often analyzed for its rhetorical dimensions. Nevertheless, perhaps the clearest indicator of the expansion of police authority and coercive power in the border region is the built environment and infrastructure that accompanied the ballooning of border law enforcement. Arrest at the border, holding for deportation, forced removal from the United States, as well as permanent or semipermanent imprisonment within the United States all required massive building projects to accompany them. Most of the deportation infrastructure is intentionally out of sight. The fence is not; it is deliberately monumental, meant to be seen, an emblem of idealized stability amid a continental system of constant movement.[39]

As the political theorist Wendy Brown explains, the recent building boom on the US-Mexico divide is not an isolated phenomenon. She points to various kinds of border barricading on the South Africa–Zimbabwe border; the line between Saudi Arabia and Yemen; the borders between India, Pakistan, and Bangladesh, as well as other kinds of border fortifications in Uzbekistan, Turkmenistan, Botswana, Egypt, Brunei, and others. To her, these construction projects are embedded in a landscape that "signifies the ungovernability by law and politics of many powers unleashed by globalization and late modern colonialization, and a resort to policing and blockading in the face of this ungovernability."[40] Put a different way, this is compensatory building: physical construction designed to respond to wide-reaching policies that apparently cannot be sustained without simultaneously creating greater and greater inequalities both within and across societies.

The year 1990 was a watershed that marked a new era of heavier, more durable, more expensive, and more politically motivated barriers on the US-Mexico divide driven by both increased global connectivity and an increased social and governmental aversion to risk. Responding to mounting public perception that the border was "out of control," the San Diego Sector of the Border Patrol took it upon itself—using the broad powers granted to the attorney general to guard international borders—to build the first rigid fencing along the US-Mexico divide.[41] It was a cheap construction project. The labor came from within the Border Patrol itself, as well as the Army Corps of Engineers and the National Guard. No outside contractors, always more expensive than government labor, were used. The fence was made of sheets of carbon steel. The metal was military surplus, used

during the Vietnam War for improvised landing strips, which effectively reduced the budget for materials to zero.[42]

It was imagined in part by the San Diego Sector Chief Gustavo de la
Viña, the architect of Operation Gatekeeper in 1994. Like generations
of Border Patrol officers before him, he thought of the fence as a local
solution to serve local operational needs. The San Diego Sector did not
seek to expand their fencing concept across the entire boundary line,
though similar fences were copied around Campo, Yuma, Nogales,
Naco, and Douglas.[43] Because they were solid sheets of metal, these
fences were opaque, which posed a tactical problem: agents could not
see what was happening on the other side. They made do with what
they had, built relatively few miles of fencing, and did so rather slowly.
The San Diego fence was fourteen miles long upon its completion,
more or less along the same stretch of land previously fenced multiple times with chain-link and barbed wire. They stopped building
after fourteen miles because early 1990s fence construction was not
intended to stop people from crossing the border entirely, but to divert
traffic outward into remote areas.[44] Though this was a local project,
the far-flung provenance of its materials mattered. Designed for a military conflict on the other side of the globe, the appearance of these
landing mats on the US-Mexico divide signaled the extent to which
the physicality of border building fit into global contexts in ways that
it had not before.

It quickly became clear to both elected and appointed officials
that shows of force on the border and barrier infrastructure could
be leveraged toward political victories and increased funding for
certain government agencies dedicated to the use of physical coercion. Other federal institutions began thinking more seriously about
border fencing, including the newly inaugurated Office of National
Drug Control Policy and Sandia National Laboratories. The ONDCP,
established in 1989 as an outgrowth of the Reagan-era "drug wars,"
blurred the lines between economic migrants and smugglers by fram-
ing the border in terms of a single problem—a lack of control, which
was a familiar refrain. Sandia National Laboratories was older than
the ONDCP, founded in 1948 as one of the scientific engines of the
burgeoning nuclear weapon industry, and it regarded the border as
a design challenge. In 1993, working closely with the ONDCP and
the Immigration and Naturalization Service, Sandia's engineers and

scientists produced the first theoretical plan for fencing on a much larger scale along the border.[45] Here, too, border building was inserted into a larger nexus of engineering expertise that linked it to Cold War–era armament manufacture, breaking with smaller-scale fencing projects of the past.

By the mid-1990s, local Border Patrol–driven initiatives in San Diego and El Paso had ricocheted back to Washington. In 1996, President Bill Clinton signed the Illegal Immigration Reform and Responsibility Act into law. A Republican-sponsored bill that passed easily through both houses, it funded more fencing on the border and increased the purview of immigrant imprisonment. Using Sandia's design of a multiple-layered and permanently lit fence line, construction began on a new secondary fence reinforcing the original San Diego landing mat barrier.

The attacks on September 11, 2001, added terrorism to a growing list of potential border threats, increasing the momentum toward the accumulation of police infrastructure that had already been building for at least a decade.[46] The effects of September 11 on the border manifested bureaucratically through the shuffling of the Border Patrol out of the Department of Justice and into the newly created Department of Homeland Security. Also, it translated into an added determination by Congress to fund and legally support the widest possible array of police activity on the international divide.[47]

The Real ID Act of 2005 exemplified this. With overwhelming Republican cosponsorship and support (written by Rep. James Sensenbrenner of Wisconsin), some Democratic dissent, and dissent from both the libertarian Cato Institute and the civil rights–oriented American Civil Liberties Union (ACLU), the statute was designed to increase the federal government's ability to regulate the entry and exit of noncitizens. Much of this revolved around bureaucratic mechanisms such as state licensure and information databases. But there was a physical dimension as well. It made large-scale border barricade building legally unstoppable. The law authorized the Secretary of Homeland Security to waive all legal requirements that might impede the construction of barriers along the international divide. This was an exceptionally wide-ranging authority, with few precedents in US history. The Congressional Research Service found only one analogous law that legally inoculated a building project to that extent—the 1973 Trans-Alaska Pipeline Authorization Act.[48] This makes sense, since fencing and pipeline building projects are quite similar. Both are long, linear construction sites that, because of their length, cut across dozens of ecosystems and cross an uneven landscape of public and private land. And they were both driven by powerful interests within and outside the government.

This expansiveness also translated into a wider range of justifications for policing. By 2006, border security had become, in the words of Kevin Stevens, the senior associate chief of Customs and Border Protection (CBP), "an all-threats issue," encompassing every imaginable uncertainty and doomsday scenario, ranging from terrorism; to animal, plant, and human pathogens; to banned psychoactive substances.[49] Momentum was gathering for a major fencing project. The Republican-dominated House of Representatives had just passed a bill in 2005, H.R. 4437, that called for 854 miles of double-layer tall fencing—no vehicle barriers—wired with lights and cameras. In 2006, the Senate passed a more bipartisan fencing bill, S. 2611, that called for only 370 miles of triple-layer fencing, plus 500 miles of vehicle barriers. Neither became law, but both signaled a widespread political readiness for major police construction on the border.

The former Border Patrol chief of the El Paso Sector, Silvestre Reyes, then a Democratic US Congress member, opposed a fencing project of this scale, despite the fact that he had been instrumental in reinventing a more militaristic kind of border policing just over ten years earlier. He said it was a waste of money and advocated instead for hiring more Border Patrol agents. T. J. Bonner, the president of the National Border Patrol Council, agreed, and said Sandia's assessment in 1993 had proved to be wrong on all counts.[50] Like their Border Patrol forebears from the 1940s, they didn't see the purpose of a long-distance barrier. They advocated for increased hiring instead, to focus more manpower on operations around the ports of entry. But when it became clear that all aspects of border policing, from hiring to tactical infrastructure, could expand with new appropriations, a hard consensus emerged about fence construction across party lines and between agencies. Thus, the will to build came less from practical necessity than it did from the perception of unlimited threats and seemingly guaranteed appropriations. This impetus also set recent barrier construction apart from previous iterations that had been tied to concrete policies or specific events, such as the treaty obligations of the Bracero Program or the outbreak of foot-and-mouth in Mexico. Instead, this was border building and policing as a way of life.

Since the days of the Mexican Revolution and Prohibition, the Mexican border had been seen as suspect, tawdry, and dangerous in the eyes of many US policymakers, but the new political atmosphere that emerged toward the end of the twentieth century converted these threadbare suspicions into robust physical construction. The Secure Fence Act of 2006 was the culmination of this momentum, the law that laid the groundwork for the barrier system of today. It was sponsored by the hard-line immigration restrictionist Peter King, a Republican Congress member, and was cosponsored by forty-one other Republicans and one Democrat; it passed easily through both houses with significant Democratic support, including then senators Barack Obama and Hillary Clinton. Since 1990, when the first landing mats went up as fencing in San Diego, the Border Patrol had built 75 miles of fencing by 2006, all around urban areas.[51] The Secure Fence Act mandated 850 miles of barriers, though this number was reduced, to the great chagrin of some of the original proponents of maximum fencing, to 700 miles by the 2008 Consolidated Appropriations Act (P.L. 110–161). Barriers were in fact built, and in record speed. Within three years, 306 miles of tall pedestrian fencing and 301 miles of vehicle barriers were in place, standing as the most fixed and permanent features amid a massive outlay of new agents, more vehicles, more aircraft, and more technology.

In the first big fencing projects of the early 1990s, design played a minor role in the construction process. The Border Patrol had a limited labor supply and access to only a narrow range of materials. Building the post-2006 barriers was a much more complex process, however. The Engineering and Construction Support Office of the US Army Corps of Engineers planned and oversaw the project. These engineers and planners were part of an institution with a history that stretches back to the founding of the country; the corps has been a constant feature of all manner of building projects and public works, both civilian and military, and had previously participated in many of the hydraulic engineering projects on the border. To physically build the border fence, they siphoned laborers from the US National Guard and military units from the Department of Defense's Joint Task Force North, founded in 1989 as a counter-drug element of the US Army. The Department of Defense understood their employees' work on the border as an important practice exercise, preparing them for the routines of tactical infrastructure construction elsewhere in the world.[52] Echoing military thinking during the Mexican Revolution, the border was once again converted into a sort of training ground for the US armed forces preparing for combat operations somewhere else on the globe.

By 2008, despite a history of bad contract management by the Border Patrol, including weak oversight, frequent managerial turnover, and incomplete implementation of programs, CBP turned to private contractors to take over major aspects of border fence construction.[53] A quintessential example was "Border Fence K" in El Paso, which demonstrated the close relationship between police infrastructure in the local context of the border region and a much larger history of infrastructure construction in the United States.

In 2009, over one thousand workers and six hundred pieces of equipment convened along a thirty-eight-mile stretch of land in El Paso and its outskirts. They were there to take part in a $170 million building project. Some of the equipment had been custom made specifically for this project. The pride and joy was the "Iron Pony," a twenty-five-foot-tall, nine-foot-wide movable scaffolding system that helped the workers build at an astonishing rate—about half a mile a day. It took them just four months to build a structure along the US-Mexico border unlike any that had existed before.[54] Made of steel mesh and footed in a concrete base, the new fence dividing the two oldest border towns stood nineteen feet tall. One of its segments wound along the river only feet from Monument 1, the obelisk the first boundary survey footed to mark the border during the first boundary expedition. But unlike that obelisk, whose position was arranged by the binational group of the boundary commission, Border Fence K was a unilateral project, erected not on the international divide itself, but rather on US soil, set back from the line. And unlike most previous border fencing made of barbed wire, chain-link, and other light materials, Border Fence K was exceptionally rigid and durable, designed to exist long into an indeterminate future.

The general contractor for the Border Fence K project was Kiewit Corporation, a building company that had been winning government contracts since World War II. Kiewit got its first big project in 1939 when the firm was hired to build Fort Lewis, an army base in Washington State. After President Dwight Eisenhower's directive to construct the interstate highway system in 1956, Kiewit built more highway miles than any other contractor. Its coal-mining interests were even used to provide energy for the production of the first atomic bomb. The "Iron Pony" they built in El Paso was only one small innovation in decades of government megaprojects. And, in keeping with the long history of interconnectedness between police building and water management along the border, Kiewit also helped build the Kay Bailey Hutchison Desalinization Plant in El Paso. It opened in 2007, at the same time as border fence construction was under way. It's the largest inland brackish water desalinization plant in North America, designed to help stave off a water crisis in El Paso due to a desiccated Rio Grande and contaminated aquifers.

The Department of Homeland Security, the bureaucracy responsible for overseeing the construction of the border barriers, referred to them as "tactical infrastructure." This points to their ability to divert and slow down unauthorized cross-border traffic and therefore act as a "force multiplier" for the Border Patrol. Like other force multipliers, such as radar, infrared night-vision goggles, seismic sensors, helicopters, and other devices used to extend the capacity of the human senses, the barricades on the international divide are not understood by law enforcement as a complete solution to buttress the national territory but rather as one among several means toward achieving tactical advantage within a given policing sector.

The wider public calls these barriers the "border fence," but in actuality they are an amalgamation of well over a dozen different designs, ranging from huge, heavy bollards to expanded metal mesh. They stretch across 653 miles of the nearly 2,000-mile-long international divide, and only 353 of these miles constitute what could legitimately be called a fence, that is, a very high structure intended to deter or brake human crossing. The other 300 miles are vehicle impediments, some sunk into concrete, some prefabricated off-site and simply placed on the ground by small cranes.[55] Some of the prefabricated variants are the nostalgically named "Normandy-style" barriers in reference to the tank traps deployed on the Normandy beaches on D-Day (see figure 5.5).[56]

From a builder's point of view, the Normandy-style barriers are the easiest to set in place. They are fabricated off-site, then trucked out to remote locations such as the border between Chihuahua and New

Mexico (figure 5.5). There, they are fitted together with steel sleeves. The main component for this kind of construction is not the technical know-how of the workers themselves, since there is no need either to mix concrete or to negotiate major topographic impediments. Rather, the most crucial tool is the access road, purpose built for border barrier construction in remote regions like this. Another photograph I took in the same area as figure 5.5, highlights this (see figure 5.6).[57] New Mexico is on the left, Chihuahua is on the right, and a long string of Normandy-style barriers recedes into the vanishing point in the lower left of the frame. More notable than the barriers, however, is the smoothly graded, gravel-lined road that accompanies it. Though rough dirt paths were there already to service the ranch fencing in that area, this wide road did not exist before border barrier construction.

Despite the totalizing aspirations of the most ardent fencing proponents in the US government, the construction process in remote areas ran up against some of the same logistical problems as did the boundary surveys of the nineteenth century and the fence construction projects of 1948–1951. Along the western boundary in particular, materials and equipment were hard to move out into the desert, far from access roads of any kind, and for the same reason it was hard and expensive to move laborers out there as well. Barriers made of inflexible, heavy materials, especially those footed into concrete, meant that the construction site preparation had to be more extensive. This meant that before the workers built the fence, they had to build new roads.[58] It is also important to understand that roads like this first served for construction access, but then took on a second life as they were incorporated into the policing tactics of the Border Patrol. They were repurposed to become "drag roads," dirt roads intentionally smoothed and resmoothed by border police in an effort to identify human footprints and track down people who crossed without authorization.

Among the fence's most vehement supporters in Congress, all vehicle barriers were seen as a disgraceful evisceration of the original concept, which called for nothing less than the true fortification of the United States with high pedestrian fencing. It is a curious fact that this unprecedented barricading of the border, never before attempted with any seriousness in remote areas, could be upon its completion both an extraordinary monument to policing and judged as a failure to "do enough." I took another photograph just east of Columbus,

New Mexico, to illustrate one of the spots where the steel mesh pedestrian fence and vehicle barriers meet (figure 5.7).[59] The graded access road runs through the foreground. To my eye, there is a kind of absurd quality

FIGURE 5.5.
Normandy-Style Fencing, 2013

Prefabricated vehicle barriers separate New Mexico and Chihuahua. Photograph by the author.

to a monumental fence that ends, seemingly arbitrarily, in the middle of the desert. But, as has been well documented, the geography of fencing also has a tactical function for border police: it is designed to push people out into the open country, where the hostility of climate and topography can be enlisted in the service of law enforcement.[60] In other words, the fence was meant to end, not continue along the entire border line. This was in part a means of reshaping the geography of unauthorized crossing by diverting migrants into remote areas.

Yet despite the preference for criminal justice–based policy solutions that had taken root in Congress, in the racist right, in the executive branch, and in law enforcement agencies themselves, people were still resisting police infrastructure building in the 2000s. Fence construction in Texas posed special problems. The cultural geographer

J. B. Jackson once wrote that Americans "inherited a veneration of private land, of private territories," and nowhere was this more obvious than in Texas.[61] When Texas was converted from an independent, irredentist nation to a US state in 1845, it retained its public lands, unlike the western states of the Mexican Cession after the Mexican-American War. By maintaining control of its own lands and then selling them off rapidly, Texas had already established the most complete private property regime west of the Mississippi by the close of the nineteenth century.[62] Thus fence construction in Texas, a twenty-first-century building project, encountered a nineteenth-century problem. In California, Arizona, and New Mexico, close to half of all land was still owned by federal and state governments in the 2000s, making real estate acquisition for fence construction run relatively smoothly. And, of course, the IBWC had already built hundreds of miles of fencing on the western border. But in Texas,

FIGURE 5.6.
Border Fence Road, 2013

The international divide is visible here largely because of the graded access road. It was built to move equipment and laborers into the remote country between New Mexico and Chihuahua to set up vehicle barriers. Photograph by the author.

FIGURE 5.7
Pedestrian Border Fence End, 2013

As in earlier border fencing projects, most barriers
were not tall "pedestrian" fencing. Here, just east of
Columbus, New Mexico, the pedestrian fence stops
and vehicle barriers begin. Photograph by the author.

the federal government manages just over 1 percent of the nation's second-largest state. Thus, a significant cost to building in Texas, even along the border, was land acquisition. Individuals, cities, and even the Brownsville branch of the University of Texas filed hundreds of lawsuits to halt fence construction. In every case, the Department of Homeland Security exercised its eminent domain powers to forcibly build through private property, leaving a landscape of ranchland, cities, and farmland split, sometimes bizarrely, by fencing.[63]

Barrier construction also entailed direct environmental manipulation, not just the deployment of climate and topography as a weapon. In addition to the legal complexities of building fences, the vegetation of Texas also posed special problems. The new barricade building was driven not only by a nationalist vision and an obsession with control but also by a particular vision of the natural landscape. In South Texas, the climate is humid and subtropical, very different from the arid desert ecosystems of much of the western border region. That wet climate came with much more dense plant growth, including the massive proliferation of Carrizo cane, a nonnative species brought to the region centuries ago by Spaniards. Like other cane species, the Carrizo variety grows wild, fast, and tall, which produces a tactical nightmare for border police. As J. B. Jackson pointed out, the problem of visibility is a classic military preoccupation, where any given landscape is simply "a kind of setting or empty stage," interesting only insofar as it helped or impeded military maneuvering.[64] Border police and builders imagined the border region in similar terms, and found too much plant growth problematic. This meant that the fence construction process also included efforts to transform the botanical landscape through massive cane eradication programs that used a combination of herbicides, shredders, and excavators to kill and remove the plants.[65] They were attempting to reshape the riparian growth of South Texas into the complicit, unobstructed landscapes of the western deserts, the idealized military landscape, where Border Patrol agents could see unencumbered for miles across the dry plains, scrublands, and dunes.

Surveillance and sensing technology was another sort of tactical infrastructure central to the more recent phases of border building. The sociologist Timothy Dunn has tracked infusions of military hardware into border policing since the late 1970s. He found that night-vision scopes in the Border Patrol's possession jumped from 66 between 1978 and 1980 to 335 between 1981 and 1988, and that during the same time frame, five airborne infrared radar systems were deployed in helicopters for the first time, and the helicopter fleet itself had expanded from two to twenty-two.[66] During and after the 1990s, these were supplanted by machines that were categorized under the heading of "change detection capability." They included periodic overflights by unmanned aerial systems, subterranean unattended ground sensors, remote video surveillance systems, and imaging sensors, all complemented by agents' portable surveillance systems and mobile video surveillance systems. This equipment was linked to integrated fixed towers as well as to relay towers that consolidated the video, seismic, thermal, and photographic information at the nearest Border Patrol station.[67]

But despite vast improvements in technological sophistication and rapid communication, as well as increases in research and design budgets, the accretion of new high-tech surveillance systems in the border region actually represented a continuation of a very old tradition—the preoccupation with visibility. The Border Patrol's "leverage technology," which includes the mobile and fixed video surveillance systems as well as night-vision devices, heat sensors, personal radiation detectors, radiation isotope identification devices, and Z backscatter X-ray vehicles, all function as visual prosthetics, designed to amplify and enhance the human eye.[68] This was, at its essence, a high-tech, updated version of the watchtowers used in the 1940s, aided by drastically increased public spending and political commitment. Critically, however, the promise of technological omniscience over the border often exceeded its capability. Developed in 1998, the Integrated Surveillance Intelligence System, or ISIS, was found by a congressional review to be "a camera and sensor system that was plagued by mismanagement, operational problems, and financial waste." A subsequent techno-surveillance project, the Secure Border Initiative, or SBInet, didn't fare much better. According to a 2010 study by the Government Accountability Office, it took longer than expected to set up, cost more than anticipated, and didn't work very well.[69]

Yet despite these shortcomings, the Border Patrol also created more technologically advanced choke points along roads and highways beyond the international divide itself. Again, the problem of visibility was paramount, and public transport infrastructure was incorporated into the project of border policing as it had been during Operation

Wetback of 1954 and Operation Intercept of 1969. As of 2005, thirty-three primary inspection stations, or permanent checkpoints, had been strategically placed in the interior of the United States along major and secondary highways between twenty-five and seventy-five miles from the line. These were all fixed facilities with hardwired communications that included outbuildings for short-term imprisonment, paved shoulders with enough space for vehicle lifts, and gamma ray machines large enough to inspect tractor trailers. These permanent checkpoints were supported by additional tactical checkpoints on smaller roads, which were much smaller in scale and impermanent; much of the equipment had to be hauled there by truck. But their shifting positions, designed to give the element of surprise to unauthorized traffic, were often quickly undermined by cell phone countersurveillance.[70]

This accretion of police infrastructure under the ground, in the air, along the international divide, as well as terraforming, access road building, and the commandeering of public highway systems, all constituted the physical manifestations of a virulent, but not uncontested, enforcement mentality in American political thought that looked to coercive state measures to respond to increasingly complex phenomena. The physicality of the new barriers, through their materials, design, and legal authorization, separated recent border building from previous police construction. Nevertheless, when the Congressional Research Service studied the border fence upon its completion in 2009, it came to the same conclusion as many scholars: it does not, and cannot, succeed in its purported mission to stop illegal entry and the illegal movement of contraband.[71] It was overbuilding designed to compensate for an unsustainable immigration system, unsustainable "drug wars," and an unsustainable politics of scapegoating noncitizens. Far more successful at achieving its stated goals, however, was the infrastructure of cross-border commerce.

TRANSPORTATION INFRASTRUCTURE AND BRIDGES

Though barricades have attracted the most attention, two major construction projects along the border have been ongoing since the early 1990s: one dedicated to police infrastructure, and the other dedicated to the infrastructure of commerce. The tremendous surges in police building in the 1990s and 2000s evolved in tandem with increases in market complexity and interconnectedness that in turn ushered in a greater sense of vulnerability for many. As the sociologist David Garland puts it, the "pursuit of freedom—moral freedom, market freedom, individual freedom—brings with it the risk of insecurity and the temptation to respond with repression."[72] In this sense, the border construction complex expressed the newest problem of American freedom: an ironic sense of liberty that is achieved through an increased police presence embedded in enlarged transportation corridors designed to accelerate and increase the movement of people and commodities, which is counterproductive to the police purpose.

The unilateralism of the border barricading was possible only because it did not interrupt the US-Mexico trade relationship. Authorized commercial traffic across the border dwarfs everything else and expanded during the years of furious barricade construction. The border region is a porous zone for both countries through which enormous wealth passes, facilitated by an ever-growing highway system. From this point of view, the political scientist George Gavrilis's assertion that "borders are institutional zones, not lines of separation between states . . . [They] regularize and structure contact and interaction between states" is particularly relevant.[73] In 1985, just before Mexico joined the General Agreement on Tariffs and Trade (GATT)—the first major step in liberalizing its trade policies—the United States and Mexico traded goods worth $33 billion dollars a year. By 2015, the two counties were trading $530 billion annually.[74] This circulation of capital is dependent on the built environment, that is, the infrastructure of overland transportation.

The centerpiece of the neoliberal restructuring of the US-Mexico economic relationship was the free trade agreement, or NAFTA, in 1994. It was designed to lower tariffs and trade barriers at the borders and join the markets of Canada, the United States, and Mexico into a North American trading bloc.[75] Partly in preparation for this increased economic activity, the Mexican Secretaría de Comunicaciones y Transportes (Ministry of Communication and Transport), under the administration of President Carlos Salinas de Gortari, initiated the Programa Nacional de Autopistas (National Highway Program) between 1989 and 1994. The agency described it as one of the most ambitious road infrastructure projects in the world at the time. It included lane expansion, surface improvement, and rural road construction—all oriented around six main axes, three of which led to the border.[76]

The year 1989 was also the first time Mexican-domiciled trucking companies were granted authority to travel within the United States. Most carriers had sister companies in the United States and operated according to the business model known as "drayage." Mexican truckers drove goods through Mexico, crossed the international border, and entered a "commercial zone," a strip of about twenty miles inside US territory that encompasses most of the border towns. There the truckers offloaded their goods to their American counterparts, who then drove to destinations throughout the United States.[77] When NAFTA went into effect, Mexican trucks were supposed to be granted wide access to US territory beyond just the "commercial zone" of the border region, but the United States repeatedly violated that provision. In retaliation, the Mexican government imposed $2.4 billion in annual tariffs on agricultural and manufacturing goods between 2009 and 2011. Ultimately, the United States capitulated after the NAFTA Arbitration Panel found the United States in breach of its obligations. The unilateralism of barricade construction was impossible to replicate in the context of trade, where Mexico had far more leverage.

Between 2011 and 2014, the US Department of Transportation and the Federal Motor Carrier Safety Administration conducted a large study of cross-border long-haul trucking that offers valuable insight into the nature of bilateral commercial infrastructure.[78] In the three years during which they collected data, trucks from fifteen different Mexican freight companies crossed the border 28,225 times.[79] Around three-quarters of these border crossings passed through a single port of entry, Otay Mesa, California. Nearly all the rest went through two ports around El Paso, Texas. This all corresponded to improved and expanded highway infrastructure on the Mexican side. And even though the majority of these trucking companies still had licenses to operate only in the border commercial zone, Mexican-domiciled trucks drove 1.2 million miles through the border states—overwhelmingly in Texas and California—and just over 255,000 miles through nonborder states.[80] From the vantage of cross-border trade, the international divide all but disappears; the transportation infrastructure that makes such lucrative US-Mexico commerce possible is continental in scope and, not coincidentally, follows a layout very similar to that of the nineteenth-century transcontinental railroads.

Especially since the 1960s, high-speed and high-capacity highways

have been, like the railroads before them, the most important connective tissue between the United States and Mexico. Human-built
pathways joining disparate locales have a multimillennial history, and
as J. B. Jackson points out, they have always brought with them a
sense of danger, harboring the potential "to introduce unwanted
outsiders into the self-sufficient community or house."[81] The proliferation of ports of entry in recent years has exacerbated this ancient
anxiety as more and more traffic can, and does, cross the international
border. As of 2017, there were fifty-two operational ports of entry on
the US-Mexico border. That includes twenty land ports and twenty-
eight bridges, one of which, the B&M Bridge between Brownsville
and Matamoros, doubles as a railroad bridge, as well as three more
dedicated railroad bridges. That does not include the ferry crossing at
Boquillas del Carmen in the Big Bend area, the western land border
railroad crossings, or the historic and now closed suspension bridge
(the only one of its kind) between Roma, Texas, and Ciudad Miguel
Alemán, Tamaulipas.[82]

What is more important than the number of ports, however, is their
rapid proliferation, renovation, and expansion in recent years. It is crucial to note that especially around San Diego–Tijuana, El Paso–Ciudad
Juárez, Laredo–Nuevo Laredo, and the southern Rio Grande valley,
ports tend to form clusters. This bunching is related to highway systems; many new road spurs and entirely new ports were constructed
to accommodate massive increases in truck traffic after the free trade
agreement was implemented. Texas-Mexico bridges are particularly
instructive in this regard, especially since US-Mexico trade is largely
geared toward Texas industries and traffic. Of the twenty-eight vehicu-
lar border bridges in Texas, excluding railroad-only bridges, every
single one except for the Juárez-Lincoln Bridge and the crossing over
Falcon Dam have been rebuilt, expanded, improved, or constructed
from scratch since 1990, the year heavy wall building began in San
Diego. In addition, as of this writing, thirteen more ports are proposed
along the border. There is no precedent for either this scale or speed
of port construction and renovation in border history. It promises
to exaggerate the side effects that border building has already been
scrambling and failing to attend to for nearly half a century. In this way,
these port expansions likely signal a new era of compensatory police
building ahead.

Though the IBWC monitors and manages some aspects of nearly all border construction, it owns only four crossings in Texas—the two atop Amistad and Falcon Dams, the Fort Hancock–El Porvenir bridge east of El Paso–Ciudad Juárez, and the Bridge of the Americas, first constructed in 1967 as part of the Chamizal border relocation. Only the Presidio Bridge is owned by the state of Texas; nineteen are owned by cities or counties; and four, the B&M Bridge, the Weslaco-Progreso International, Los Ebanos Ferry, and the Rio Grande City–Camargo crossings, are privately owned. Thirteen are dedicated exclusively to commercial traffic, and of those, eight are designated hazardous materials crossings.[83]

Each of these port expansions deepened the complex interdependence between the United States and Mexico. Each new port opening required a bureaucratic coordination between municipal and state governments, including the Mexican Servicio de Administración Tributaria (Tax Administration), the Secretaría de Comunicaciones y Transportes, as well as the Secretaría de la Defensa Nacional (Ministry of National Defense), tasked with the construction of inspection facilities on the Mexican side.[84] The cost of grading and laying of new spurs and new roads to connect the ports with highways, as well as bridge

construction across the river border, spiraled into hundreds of millions of dollars. For instance, two satellite images demonstrate the transformation of the desert landscape between 1985 and 2014, during which time the Port of Santa Teresa, New Mexico, was opened in 1992 (figures 5.8 and 5.9). Urban sprawl on both sides of the line, new center-pivot irrigation agriculture plots, and feeder roads accompanied the new port construction.[85]

The renovation and expansion of existing ports also posed significant design and construction challenges. For instance, private architecture and engineering firms undertook what a trade journal called a "maelstrom" of a building project freighted with "hellish" logistical challenges: the remake of the San Ysidro port of entry. It connects the San Diego and Tijuana metropolitan zones and is perhaps the busiest port in the world, funneling 50,000 vehicles daily. They used 300- and 550-ton hydraulic cranes to erect a cable-stayed canopy system that relied as heavily as possible on preassembled, panelized, prefabricated, and modularized building elements. That port expansion project alone cost $741 million, far exceeding the exorbitant per-mile costs of the border fence surrounding it.[86]

FIGURE 5.9.
Santa Teresa, New Mexico, 2014

Santa Teresa, New Mexico, was formerly a quiet area in the desert, but in 2014, officials recorded over 1 million crossings through this new port of entry. Google Earth Pro.

Different types of roads make up the cross-border mega system, and the new landscape of ports and barriers has produced a greater variety of pathways on and around the border than ever before. From the point of view of cultural landscape studies, J. B. Jackson distinguishes between "national" highway systems on the one hand, which have over centuries traditionally been built for soldiers and capital, and on the other, regional "vernacular" roads that serve the needs of local transit.[87] Jackson talks about vernacular roads as "flexible, without [an] overall plan . . . a system which is isolated, usually without maintenance," which makes them the "bane . . . of a government wanting to expedite military . . . traffic." This is certainly true for heavy, long-range deployment and mobilization.[88] The border barricades and the police that accompany them have produced new kinds of local roads, however. In an unusual reinvention of the vernacular road, the incessant, remote military-style patrolling by civil police on the border has generated a semiformal road system used nearly exclusively by law enforcement. The dirt roads created to build and place the barriers are examples of this. These police roads thus take on the core feature of major highway systems—they expand the capacity of the state—despite the fact that they are sometimes improvisational and remote. In other words, the access roads police use in far-flung areas can be understood as a new kind of "police vernacular."

Migrants seeking to avoid detection by the state have also built vernacular roads. Or, more accurately, they have abandoned roads entirely and reverted to the ancient footpath.[89] These low-impact, unauthorized routes are blazed precisely to avoid the teeming infrastructure of both commerce and police; they are used so that the travelers who take them might remain unseen within the larger border apparatus of heightened visibility. For Jackson, national highway systems are inherently political because they join "all the spaces which constitute the territory of a community or state."[90] This certainly holds true if we imagine roads as contained within political boundaries. They rarely are, though, which is only to say that Jackson was right, but in a broader sense. Transportation infrastructure is also political because it binds territory together across international boundaries and disrupts the presumptions of territorial sovereignty. Whether we adopt the point of view of unauthorized border crossers seeking to avoid sanction by the state, or the point of view of corporate lobbyists pressing the state toward certain economic policies, roads are political but not in a "national" system, only in a continental one.

MUCH HAS BEEN WRITTEN ABOUT THE INEFFICACY, IDEOLOGICAL incoherence, and racism of recent border policy, as well as how border policies have helped shape larger inequities across class and racial lines in both countries. This chapter demonstrates the extent to which these policies have a physical form and have manifested themselves in a seemingly endless string of construction projects, all of which have emerged, in one way or another, from the painstaking process of border fixing that came to be definitely resolved only in the 1970s, after well over a century of treaty making, aerial photography, surface mapping, surveying, and river monitoring. The border barriers adjacent to this fixed line evolved in a very short time from local, cheap, and purposeful building projects to long-distance, exorbitant infrastructure megaprojects that did not accomplish what their supporters wanted them to do on the border, although they did help consolidate a neonativist political base. By 2009, upon completion of the hundreds of miles of mandated barriers, the Congressional Research Service and Customs and Border Protection were fully aware that the fence could in fact create the appearance of "working" by diverting unauthorized traffic away from cities, or even away from entire Border Patrol sectors. But in the aggregate, illicit traffic more or less continued as it had before. After the fence, however, this traffic was accompanied by thousands of migrant deaths, many due to hyperthermia as they traversed lonely, clandestine footpaths.[91] Seeing this, the fiercest critics of the border policing apparatus have called it a "killing machine," a supreme manifestation of structural violence that absolves itself through the neoconservative belief in perfect, individualistic free will, in every migrant's "choice" to break the laws of authorized entry.[92]

The new fence was also accompanied by increases in unauthorized activity designed to subvert the physical barriers to further contraband enterprises.[93] Attacks on tactical infrastructure create significant ongoing costs, referred to by government officials as "maintenance." The barriers are constantly assaulted with saws, torches, and sometimes even heavy equipment. Stone age technology—the tunnel, the catapult—can still consistently defeat the techno-national fencing megaproject. This is a new antistatism of the twenty-first century, oriented toward the demolition or incapacitation of the infrastructure of power, further evidence that the constructions are meant to compensate for unsustainable policies that reveal their weaknesses in ever more extreme manifestations.

Yet despite these inefficiencies, both politicians and policing agencies themselves have demanded more border policing, regardless of expert opinion or political opposition from below in border communities and elsewhere. In this vein, the political scientist Peter Andreas has written about how scale-ups in border policing came to be self-reinforcing in recent years. The very existence of the border policing apparatus implied the severity of the threat level and therefore justified more police power on the border.[94] To my eye, this is a result of the self-perpetuating nature of institutions and of an argument embedded in the very physical existence of durable border barriers. Infrastructure begets more infrastructure. A short border fence implies that a longer border fence might be necessary, and an ephemeral border barrier implies that a more permanent one might need to take its place. In short, the built environment produces new ways of thinking, of imagining space, of believing.

Yet the border fence was not the only building project on the US-Mexico border since 1990. Only when we examine the recent history of tactical infrastructure on the line in the context of trade infrastructure—ports, more roads, more truck traffic, and more traffic in general—can we fully apprehend the source of tension surrounding an international divide that is built to be both open and closed at the same time.

When the one thousand laborers; the engineers; the concrete, steel, and rebar suppliers; the trucking companies; and the slope paving and erosion control workers finished construction on Border Fence K in El Paso, they left behind more than a pedestrian barrier between twin cities, and more than a monument to political theater and public relations opportunism. They left behind an emblem of our time, perhaps one of the purest examples. It's a time when the meaning of national territory has changed, though we do not yet have a name to refer to the new configuration.[95] A time when an enforcement mentality is easily shared by many in both major political parties in the United States and major political parties in Mexico, many of whom have forgotten about rehabilitative, welfarist, and universalist alternatives.[96]

A time when the logic of "free" markets and deregulation have seeped into the realms of government, common speech, and policymaking— with the glaring exception of policing.[97] The physicality of the fence is its most exceptional quality; the durability of steel and concrete guarantees that this border structure could be with us for much longer than its predecessors, perhaps as long as the dams on the border rivers. And like the dams that produced new ecological environments around them, the fence has transformed the social and political fabric around it. Like all permanent structures, it has come to influence the way we think about and understand the border. So long as the border fence stands, awkwardly positioned amid both local communities and a continental system of exchange, it will continue to lend its rigidity and its weight to policing as an organizing concept in American life.

EPILOGUE

I return now to the premise with which I began the book: few people from the United States or from Mexico have been to the international divide that separates our two countries. Fewer still are familiar with the environmental diversity of the vast border region or the complexities of its built world. Long stretches of road pass between gas stations, cell phone coverage can be intermittent or nonexistent, the heat can be extreme, and few mainstream touristic destinations are to be found in the area. But it is not just inconvenience and discomfort that keeps people away. Aversion also plays a role. The notions that the border is an intrinsically dangerous place and that deserts are nothing more than "wastelands" are now threadbare stereotypes, though they remain as resilient now as they ever were.

In the border region, limited resources and the strictures of US immigration law prevent many northern Mexicans from crossing to explore the American Southwest, and many Americans who live in the border zone have no interest in going to Mexico despite their legal and financial ability to do so. Also, many border dwellers take for granted certain aspects of life in harsh ecosystems at the edges of national territory: lush green fields in the desert made possible by large-scale irrigation technology, ditches winding through neighborhoods, "hard" water pumped from brackish aquifers, the feeling of cactus spines in the flesh, cemeteries without grass, adobe buildings, the dust storms in the spring and the "monsoons" in the summer, the unmistakable smell of creosote in the infrequent rain, endless semi truck traffic on the highways, highway checkpoints, and the constant presence of federal police and soldiers, along with their equipment of surveillance, fortification, and war.

Yet even people who live in the border region are often surprised and disoriented when they first visit a far-off place on the same long international divide. Radical differences in humidity; divergent linguistic practices in English, Spanish, or "Spanglish"; attitudes of Border Patrol agents and inspectors at the ports of entry; the sensation of crossing the border over land instead of on a bridge, or vice versa; the appearance, and even smell, of different crops in the fields; and the distinctive appearance of various types of border barricades can all provoke a sense of displacement alongside uncanny recognition for border people traveling along the vast expanse of the line.

The past, too, is often elusive, even for those who have made their lives near the border line. In this regard, the built environment that has undergirded the most significant social, political, and economic transformations in the border region has had the simultaneous effect of obscuring these histories. In part, this is because the most durable construction projects—transportation infrastructure, the current border fence, and the dams—have succeeded in projecting an image of permanence and necessity. My own memories of the border before the boom in policing, fencing, and cross-border commerce in the 1990s are fading, and my students at the University of Texas at Austin, many of whom come from border towns, have never known anything else. For those who live in the successful flood control zones, it is nearly impossible to imagine the devastating inundations of the early twentieth century, just as it is difficult to envision what the border rivers must have looked like before their waters were straightened and diverted to quench sprawling monocultures of nonnative plants. Especially along border water, however, much of the human modification has been earthwork projects or vegetation clearing. In these cases, it can be difficult to recognize that there is a built environment at all. Most people do not know how many bends and meanders the rivers used to have and never sat in the shade of tall cottonwood trees that grew along many of their banks. And just as it is hard to picture southern Arizona in a time before the exceptionally high concentration of both Border Patrol and migrant fatalities, is also a challenge to recall the militarized landscape of the big bend of the Rio Grande, now one of the most placid areas in the whole border region, made all the more so by the largest collection of environmentally protected lands along the international divide: Big Bend Ranch State Park and Big

Bend National Park in Texas, Parque Nacional Cañón de Santa Elena in Chihuahua, and the Área Natural Protegida Maderas del Carmen in Coahuila.[1]

The few people throughout history who developed and maintained a nuanced sense of the border region as a whole, or at least tried to, were the border builders. When the surveyors and cartographers set out onto border land and border water in the nineteenth century, they encountered both people and environments they did not like. They struggled with their equipment through some of the most remote and inhospitable places on the continent, intensely aware of their bodies' susceptibility to the localized threats of heat and dehydration even as they dismissed the ecological adaptations of the indigenous peoples and rural Mexicans who already lived there. But they undertook these expeditions with a larger geography in mind; their efforts were meant to leave physical traces on the earth that could materially delimit the edges of national territories in perpetuity. As disorganized, racist, and inaccurate as these surveys often were, the men who undertook them were some of the very few who possessed intimate and firsthand knowledge of long sections of the border line.

During the Mexican Revolution, US military officials operationalized the territorial sovereignty represented in the maps and markers the nineteenth-century border surveys left behind. The geographic imagination of the armed forces conceived of the international divide as a tactical landscape, and some places within it were easier to navigate than others. The officers and logistics men approached this unevenness through a system logic that tried to balance deployments, transportation, animal power, and machine power with recalcitrant topography, intermittent water supplies, and bad or nonexistent roads along the entire border, from the Pacific Ocean to the Gulf of Mexico. They met with only limited success in their objectives, but in the process they developed a much deeper understanding of border environments, and they left behind both a network of new patrol roads as well as a highly developed border patrol mentality that would come to be adopted by federal law enforcement over the course of the twentieth and twenty-first centuries.

After completing the last major border survey in the 1890s, the American and Mexican sections of the International Boundary Commission dedicated themselves to small land claims arbitrations along the divide. For a generation, officials from the IBC got to know the border region in very small pieces, often only a few acres at a time. The resolutions to these disputes, however, required them to constantly refer to the concept of the border as a whole, a purportedly definitive and continuous dividing line. In the 1930s, the IBC began much larger border construction projects, starting with the straightening of the Rio Grande that formed the West Texas–Chihuahua border and the Western Land Boundary Fence Project, the first long-distance border fence. A 1944 bilateral treaty changed the agency's name to the International Boundary and Water Commission and authorized the two sections to collaborate in building major dam projects on the main channel of the Rio Grande river border. Falcon Dam in 1954 and Amistad Dam in 1969 were the results. To build these, the IBWC expanded its holistic understanding of the border region to include not only the length of the border line but also the multiple and complex hydrological systems that make up the Rio Grande watershed.

The US Border Patrol was created in 1924 and began construction on the border in the 1930s. First it built watchtowers, then its officials collaborated closely with the IBWC in the design and placement of the Western Land Boundary Fence Project, 237 miles long upon its completion in 1951. As immigration law and policing evolved over the course of the twentieth century and into the twenty-first, the Border Patrol developed a more and more detailed conception of the border region. By the 1990s, the agency had taken over from the IBWC as the biggest builder on the international divide, this time focusing on constructing more durable border barriers. As is common for most police, the rank-and-file of border law enforcement relied on an extremely detailed and localized sense of place. However, the larger amalgam of barricade and surveillance infrastructure the Border Patrol spearheaded alongside eager politicians was built according to a holistic vision of the border region that took into account varied topography, climate, a diverse patchwork of land management and tenure, as well as long-distance highway and road systems that carried both unauthorized migrants and contraband. As with the first border patrols carried out by the US Army during the Mexican Revolution, increasing the geographic scope of police maneuvers and the capacity of surveillance did not necessarily translate to operational efficacy. It did mean, however, that border police, like hydrological engineers, were among the few people who imagined the border region both in its entirety and in terms of its myriad local specificities.

Part of what it meant to know the border as these organizations did was to envision it from above and monitor it from the air. This viewpoint, like the holistic conceptions of the border region as a unified space albeit composed of diverse constituent places, was also reserved for very few people. It required the most advanced cartographic and survey technology, which included access to aircraft, radar, the most technologically complex surveillance systems, and eventually extraterrestrial satellites—equipment that is nearly the exclusive purview of either governments or major corporations. The border builders tended to look down at the international divide, as so many of the images reproduced throughout this book attest. This was in part a way to mentally comprehend so vast a space. It was also a technical tool designed to assist with site preparation for construction projects. And the airborne view has been a definitive perspective of both the military and the police on the border, who are always striving to enhance their field of vision and detection capability.

For those of us who look at the border at ground level, we can still learn much from the border builders, especially from their attentiveness to place and the specificity of local environments. This book is an invitation to explore the border region, not as the nineteenth-century explorers did, harboring antipathy for its inhabitants and environments, but rather in the interest of recuperating the history of a region artificially unified through war and political fiat but now concretely united through a string of physical construction projects. An understanding of the history of construction on the border line allows us to imagine counterrepresentations of the border as a whole that do not cast it as either a wasteland or a pathological zone. The attention to detail that so possessed the border builders need not be directed exclusively toward the invasion of deserts, the interruption of watersheds, and coercive force. It can also, I hope, be channeled toward ecological stewardship, deeper cultural understanding, and peace.

ACKNOWLEDGMENTS

The early stages of this book began in graduate school at the University of Chicago. My dissertation committee, Mauricio Tenorio Trillo, Mark Bradley, Ramón Gutiérrez, and Emilio Kourí, taught me how to ask difficult questions, even though I could not yet come up with many answers. I also learned a great deal from Jim Sparrow, a generous interlocutor and mentor. As I developed my thinking about the border, I benefited from the institutional and intellectual support of the Center for International Security and Cooperation at Stanford University, where Tino Cuéllar and Lynn Eden made me feel at home. Roger Waldinger's National Endowment for the Humanities seminar at UCLA introduced me to the California–Baja California border for the first time. Iñigo García-Bryce and Neil Harvey gave me space in the summers to write at the Center for Latin American and Border Studies at New Mexico State University, and at the Newberry Library Borderlands and Latino Studies Seminar, Gerry Cadava and Ben Johnson led some of the best writing workshops I've ever attended.

In the archives, two people stood out: Ketina Taylor at the National Archives branch in Fort Worth, Texas, and Ílian Mendoza Cerriteño at the Archivo Histórico y Biblioteca Central del Agua of the Comisión Nacional del Agua in Mexico City. Both volunteered hours of their time to help me understand the organization and scope of the collections they know so well. Without their expertise and guidance, many of the sources and images in this book that have never been seen before by researchers would still be filed away in obscurity.

I couldn't have asked for more supportive colleagues at the

University of Texas at Austin. They lent me their time and moral support every step of the way. Thanks in particular to Matthew Butler, Karma Chávez, Richard Flores, Laura G. Gutiérrez, John Morán González, and Julie Minich. My students, too, have been an inspiration. I'm always fascinated to hear their border stories. They will find much of the material in this book familiar from long conversations in class and office hours. As I organized my ideas for this project, the discussions I shared with them were more helpful than any of them knew.

Karl Jacoby, Madeline Hsu, Sam Vong, and Laura G. Gutiérrez read parts of an earlier version of the book and helped redirect me when I made a wrong turn. Madeline, Paul Kramer, and Erika Bsumek all read parts of the final manuscript and helped me along in the right direction. Ben Johnson, Eric Meeks, Casey Walsh, Andrew Needham, and one anonymous reviewer all read drafts of the whole thing. Their critiques, perspectives, and suggestions pushed me to write a much better book. Whatever limitations there may be in my analysis, however, are my responsibility alone. Robert Devens and the rest of the folks at the University of Texas Press made the unwieldy and stressful process of putting a book together as easy as it could possibly be. Many thanks to them for their hard work and enthusiasm.

The friends I've had over the years, including Adam Goodman, Diana Schwartz, Luis Francisco, Tessa Murphy, Romina Robles Ruvalcaba, Maru Balandrán Castillo, Erica Kim, and Marisa Bass, have made me a better thinker by far. I've always been able to count on Mike Sulmeyer, Wes Harden, and Tarun Chhabra to make me laugh or lend me a hand. To the people from the old days, Dan Webb, Helen Davis, and Kirstin Valdez Quade, our times back in Arizona and New Mexico were some of the best ever. And to Linda Rodriguez, it was so good to see you here in Texas after all these years. Special thanks to Sarah Lopez, who taught me better than anyone how to see and interpret the built world around me, and to Heather Houser, who was always up for a long conversation about land and water.

Ever since I was a child, my mother was always ready and willing to head out into the backcountry and explore. My sister and Milos have always been ready to listen and are wiser than I am. Thanks, most of all, to my family.

NOTES

INTRODUCTION

1. Most historians who write about the border region use the word "border-lands" to describe the zone around the international divide. This term originated with Herbert Bolton, an early twentieth-century historian who was intent on recovering the influence of Spanish imperial history in the American Southwest. Two generations of scholars followed this trajectory, most notably Francis Bannon and David Weber. By the 1980s, the term had been incorporated into queer feminist theory by Gloria Anzaldúa, as well as updated Spanish viceregal histories revised to focus on gender and sexuality. After that, the term proved particularly useful for historians trying to elucidate the contrasts between imperial systems and the modern nation-state, as well as the conceptual problem of liminality more generally. Historically, however, it is not a term that most people living in the border region would have used to describe the places they lived. My intent in this book is to demonstrate the thoroughness of human intervention on both the western land border as well as the river borders, and the term "borderlands" tends to ignore "borderwaters." To recover the distinctiveness of border spaces, in the pages that follow I use the word "land" to refer to *terra firma*, and "water" to refer to hydrological features. I write "border region" simply to refer to places near the international divide. See Bolton, *Spanish Borderlands*; Bannon, *Spanish Borderlands Frontier*; David J. Weber, *Spanish Frontier in North America*; Anzaldúa, *Borderlands/La Frontera*; Ramón A. Gutiérrez, *When Jesus Came, the Corn Mothers Went Away*; Adelman and Aron, "From Borderlands to Borders"; Hämäläinen and Truett, "On Borderlands."

2. Webster, "Reconnaissance of the Flora and Vegetation."

3. Shelton, "Climate of *La Frontera*," 45–46; Davis, "Deserts," 108–123.

4. Garza Almanza, *Breve historia ambiental*, 28, 33, 43, 49–50.

5. Braudel, "History and the Social Sciences"; Adelman, "Latin American *Longues Durées*."

6. Richard White points out that the transcontinental railroads were in fact a continental system, linking Canada, the United States, and Mexico, all the more so

because they were often capitalized by the same investors. And in the context of the British Isles, Jo Guldi emphasizes the importance of roads in the consolidation of state power. White, *Railroaded*; Guldi, *Roads to Power*.

7. Truett, *Fugitive Landscapes*; John Weber, *From South Texas to the Nation*; Díaz, *Border Contraband*.

8. J. F. Friedkin, Commissioner, "Technical Summaries of Projects along the International Boundary between the United States and Mexico," April 1979, revised January 1981, Box 1, TR 0076–15–0012, Series 902–01b (IBWC Project Planning, Design, and Construction Case Files), Records of the International Boundary and Water Commission, Record Group 76.

9. Timm, *International Boundary Commission*, 11.

10. James Scott has most famously described this as a "high-modern" ideology, common across the globe in the midcentury and across a wide range of bureaucracies. See Scott, *Seeing Like a State*; Mann, *Sources of Social Power*.

11. Reséndez, *Changing National Identities*; Truett, *Fugitive Landscapes*; Mora-Torres, *Making of the Mexican Border*; Jacoby, *Shadows at Dawn*; Johnson, *Revolution in Texas*; Graybill, *Policing the Great Plains*; Lytle Hernández, *Migra!*; St. John, *Line in the Sand*; Chavez, *Latino Threat*; Kang, *INS on the Line*; Cohen, *Braceros*; Loza, *Defiant Braceros*; Rosas, *Abrazando el Espíritu*; Cadava, *Standing on Common Ground*; Andreas, *Border Games*; Dunn, *Militarization of the U.S.-Mexico Border*; Dunn, *Blockading the Border*; Nevins, *Operation Gatekeeper*; Massey, Durand, and Malone, *Beyond Smoke and Mirrors*; Dear, *Why Walls Won't Work*.

12. Sayre, *Ranching, Endangered Species, and Urbanization*; Sayre, *Politics of Scale*; Worster, *Rivers of Empire*; Pisani, *To Reclaim a Divided West*; Pisani, *Water and American Government*; Littlefield, *Conflict on the Rio Grande*; Aboites Aguilar, *La irrigación revolucionaria*; Aboites Aguilar, *El agua de la nación*; Aboites Aguilar, "Historias de ríos"; Boyer, *Political Landscapes*; Teisch, *Engineering Nature*; Olsson, *Agrarian Crossings*; Walsh, *Building the Borderlands*; Needham, *Power Lines*; Masco, *Nuclear Borderlands*; Fiege, *Republic of Nature*.

13. Sassen, *Territory, Authority, Rights*; Maier, *Once Within Borders*; Worster, *Shrinking the Earth*.

14. While many scholars have oriented their narratives around specific built environments such as smelters, irrigation districts, towns, and mines, few focus in sustained ways on the construction process itself.

15. Arreola and Curtis, *Mexican Border Cities*; Martínez, *Border People*.

16. Truett, *Fugitive Landscapes*; Isenberg, *Mining California*; Walsh, *Building the Borderlands*; Mora-Torres, *Making of the Mexican Border*; Aboites Aguilar, *La irrigación revolucionaria*.

17. Kang, *INS on the Line*; Littlefield, *Conflict on the Rio Grande*.

18. Calavita, *Inside the State*; Escobar, *Race, Police, and the Making of a Political Identity*; Weber, *From South Texas to the Nation*; Lytle Hernández, *Migra!*; Jones, *Border Walls*; Andreas, *Border Games*; Mckiernan-González, *Fevered Measures*; Stern, "Buildings, Boundaries, and Blood."

19. Rosas, *Abrazando el Espíritu*; Loza, *Defiant Braceros*; Cohen, *Braceros*; Díaz, *Border Contraband*; Lopez, *Remittance Landscape*; De León, *Land of Open Graves*.

THE BORDER ENVIRONMENT IN THE NINETEENTH CENTURY

1. Werne, *The Imaginary Line*; Rebert, *La Gran Línea*; Werne, "Pedro García Conde"; Werne, "Surveying the Rio Grande"; Hewitt, "Mexican Boundary Survey Team"; Hewitt, "Mexican Commission and Its Survey."

2. Werne, "Redrawing the Southwestern Boundary."

3. Morrissey, "Monuments, Photographs, and Maps"; see also Kelsey, *Archive Style*; Emory, "Running the Line."

4. Griswold del Castillo, *Treaty of Guadalupe Hidalgo*, 188.

5. Ibid., 194.

6. J. F. Friedkin, Commissioner, "Technical Summaries of Projects along the International Boundary between the United States and Mexico," April 1979, revised January 1981, Box 1, TR 0076–15–0012, Series 902–01b (IBWC Project Planning, Design, and Construction Case Files), Records of the International Boundary and Water Commission, Record Group 76; *Report of the Boundary Commission*, Part I, 17; Part II, 178, 173.

7. Marsh, *Man and Nature*, 43.

8. White, *"It's Your Misfortune,"* 222–227, 232–234. See also Isenberg, *Mining California*, 48–51.

9. Coatsworth, *Growth Against Development*, 21–23.

10. Ibid., 35. See also White, *Railroaded*.

11. Coatsworth, *Growth Against Development*, 80, 171.

12. Díaz also established a "free zone" along the international divide in an effort to stimulate border business. See Herrera Pérez, *La zona libre*. This was also a period in which Mexico's internal market drastically expanded and diversified (see Kuntz Ficker, "Mercado interior y vinculación"), and despite hiccups in formal trade agreements, commerce between the two countries advanced inexorably. See Márquez Colín, "El tratado de reciprocidad de 1883."

13. Vanderwood, *Disorder and Progress*, 71.

14. Holden, *Mexico and the Survey of Public Lands*, 11.

15. Ibid., 9, 16–17.

16. Truett, *Fugitive Landscapes*, 67–77.

17. St. John, "Divided Ranges," 123, 127.

18. Ibid., 124.

19. Truett, *Fugitive Landscapes*, 78–103.

20. J. F. Friedkin, Commissioner, "Technical Summaries of Projects along the International Boundary between the United States and Mexico," April 1979, revised January 1981, Box 1, TR 0076–15–0012, Series 902–01b (IBWC Project Planning, Design, and Construction Case Files), Records of the International Boundary and Water Commission, Record Group 76.

21. *Report of the Boundary Commission*, Part II, 155–156.

22. Flores, *Horizontal Yellow*, 135.

23. *Report of the Boundary Commission*, Part II, 30.

24. Ibid., Part I, 49.

25. Ibid., Part I, 34.

26. Ibid., Part I, 34.

27. Ibid., Part II, 18.

28. Ibid., Part II, 20.

29. Ibid., Part II, 23.

30. Ibid., Part II, 10; Part II, 181.

31. Ibid., Part II, 182.

32. Ibid., Part II, 174.

33. *Planos de la línea divisoria entre México y los Estados Unidos*.

34. Morrissey, "Monuments, Photographs, and Maps," 51.

35. Kelsey, *Archive Style*, 37.

36. Ibid., 37.

37. *Report of the Boundary Commission*, Part II, 23–24.

38. Ibid., Part II, 123.

39. Ibid., Part II, 165–166.

40. Ibid., Part II, 30.

41. Ibid., Part II, 30.

42. Ibid., Part I, 40.

43. "Ese tramo desierto . . . fué siempre el lugar predilecto de los apaches en épocas anteriores." *Memoria de la Sección mexicana*, 27.

44. DeLay, *War of a Thousand Deserts*, xv–xvi.

45. Ibid., 318.

46. "Nuestros ingenieros tuvieron que luchar contra todo linaje de inconvenientes; perdieron los caballos y mulas en un asalto dado por los indios bárbaros; la falta de recursos impedia [*sic*] á la pequeña escolta aventurarse en el desierto." Orozco y Berra, *Apuntes para la historia de la geografía*, 481.

47. "Nuestra Comision [*sic*], no obstante, cumplió lealmente su encargo; se portó con dignidad ante los norteamericanos y dejó bien puestos así el honor nacional como la reputación científica de México. . . . Nuestros ingenieros tuvieron que luchar, durante sus tareas científicas, contra todos los peligros de un país inmenso, desierto, falto de agua, recorrido únicamente por tribus broncas y salvajes." Ibid., 482.

48. The United States did not yet use the rank of ambassador in the 1870s; this rank was created in 1898. Foster was the head of the mission for the United States in Mexico, officially holding the rank of Envoy Extraordinary and Minister Plenipotentiary, which meant that he did not represent the head of state (Ulysses S. Grant) but nevertheless had full authority to represent the United States and its interests. The Mexican Secretaría de Relaciones Exteriores is the foreign relations arm of the federal government. Vallarta was Porfirio Díaz's first foreign minister and simultaneously the president of the Supreme Court.

49. "existiendo antiguos odios entre los habitantes de una y otra orilla del Bravo . . ." Legajo L-E-1712, Años 1877–1879; Conferencias Vallarta-Foster, sobre asuntos entre México y los Estados Unidos de América, celebradas en la Ciudad de México, D.F., para tratar el arreglo de varios asuntos sobre límites, reclamaciones, extradiciones, etc. entre el Secretario de Relaciones Exteriores de México y el Representante de los Estados Unidos de América; Secretaría de Relaciones Exteriores, Archivo Histórico Genaro Estrada. See also Mora, *Border Dilemmas*; "Memorandum," el dia 21 de Junio de 1879; Legajo L-E-1712, Años 1877–1879; Conferencias Vallarta-Foster, sobre asuntos entre México y los Estados Unidos de América, celebradas en la Ciudad de México, D.F., para tratar el arreglo de varios asuntos sobre límites, reclamaciones, extradiciones, etc. entre el Secretario de Relaciones Exteriores de México y el Representante de los Estados Unidos de América; Secretaría de Relaciones Exteriores, Archivo Histórico Genaro Estrada.

50. "Segundo Memorandum, México," 23 de Agosto de 1877; Legajo L-E-1712, Años 1877–1879; Conferencias Vallarta-Foster, sobre asuntos entre México y los Estados Unidos de América, celebradas en la Ciudad de México, D.F., para tratar el arreglo de varios asuntos sobre límites, reclamaciones, extradiciones, etc. entre el Secretario de Relaciones Exteriores de México y el Representante de los Estados Unidos de América; Secretaría de Relaciones Exteriores, Archivo Histórico Genaro Estrada.

51. St. John, *Line in the Sand*, 59; Johnson, "Negotiating North America's New National Borders," 31.

52. "War Department Signal Service, U.S. Army, telegram to General Miles Willard," May 4, 1886, Box 3, Department of Arizona, Apache Campaign, 1886, U.S. Army Continental Commands, 1821–1920, Record Group 393; "Compañía del Ferrocarril de Sonora, Linea Telegráfica, telegram from Luis Torres to Gens. Nelson and Miles," May 7, 1886, Box 1, Department of Arizona, Apache Campaign, 1886, U.S. Army Continental Commands, 1821–1920, Record Group 393.

53. *Report of the Boundary Commission*, Part II, 9.

54. Jacoby, *Shadows at Dawn*, 14.

55. *Report of the Boundary Commission*, Part II, 22.

56. Nabhan, *The Desert Smells Like Rain*, 6; Meeks, *Border Citizens*, 19–20; Marak and Tuennerman, *At the Border of Empires*, 13.

57. Morrissey, "Monuments, Photographs, and Maps," 49–50.

58. *Memoria de la Sección mexicana*.

59. *Report of the Boundary Commission*, Part I, 18.

60. Ibid., Part II, 26.

61. *Report of the Boundary Commission*, Album, 55th Cong., 2d sess., Doc. No. 247, 1898.

62. Kelsey, *Archive Style*, 5.

63. *Report of the Boundary Commission*, Part II, 191.

64. Kelsey, *Archive Style*, 28.

65. *Report of the Boundary Commission*, Part II, 27.

66. *Convention between the United States of America and the United States of Mexico*, 2–3.

67. Joseph F. Friedkin, interview by Oscar J. Martinez and Sarah E. John, 1977, "Interview no. 552," Institute of Oral History, 8–9.

68. Morrissey, "Monuments, Photographs, and Maps," 51.

69. Walsh, *Building the Borderlands*, 32–33.

70. Werne, *The Imaginary Line*, 127.

71. Green and Tyler, "Exploring the Rio Grande," 48.

72. Rebert, *La Gran Línea*, 139.

73. Ibid., 179–180.

74. Alexander, *Father of Texas Geology*, 122.

75. Hill, "Running the Cañons of the Rio Grande."

76. Flores, *Horizontal Yellow*, 130.

77. Hill, "Running the Cañons of the Rio Grande," 373.

78. Ibid., 372.

79. Ibid., 371.

80. Ibid., 372.

81. Ibid., 373, 377.

82. Ibid., 372, 373, 377.

83. Ibid., 382.

84. Follansbee and Dean, *Water Resources of the Rio Grande Basin*.

85. Ibid., 9.

86. Walsh, *Building the Borderlands*, 41.

87. Follansbee and Dean, *Water Resources of the Rio Grande Basin*, 27.

88. Green and Tyler, "Exploring the Rio Grande," 46.

89. Ibid., 60.

90. Nichols, "Line of Liberty"; Cornell, "Citizens of Nowhere."

91. Green and Tyler, "Exploring the Rio Grande," 60.

92. Ibid., 50.

93. Hill, "Running the Cañons of the Rio Grande," 378.

94. Ibid., 371–372.

95. Ibid., 376–377.

96. Ibid., 373, 382–383.

THE BORDER AND THE MEXICAN REVOLUTION

1. Womack, "The Mexican Revolution"; Katz, *Life and Times of Pancho Villa*; Womack, *Zapata and the Mexican Revolution*.

2. For a complete explanation of the significance of de facto versus de jure recognition in international law, see Gilderhus, "The United States and Carranza, 1917," and Katz, *Life and Times of Pancho Villa*, 615.

3. Knight, *The Mexican Revolution*; Knight, *U.S.-Mexican Relations;* Gillingham and Smith, *Dictablanda*.

4. Knight, *The Mexican Revolution*, 1:10.

5. Katz, *Life and Times of Pancho Villa*, 14–16, 27–35, 524, xiii.

6. Katz, "Liberal Republic and the Porfiriato."

7. Vanderwood, *Disorder and Progress*; Coatsworth, *Growth Against Development*; Hart, *Empire and Revolution*.

8. Skirius, "Railroad, Oil, and Other Foreign Interests," 25.

9. White, *Railroaded*, xxiii.

10. W. D. Smithers Collection of Photographs, Box 19, Image 2764.

11. Hart, *Empire and Revolution*, 152.

12. Truett, *Fugitive Landscapes*.

13. Hart, *Empire and Revolution*, appendix 1, 511–525.

14. For an overview of US neutrality policy during these years, see Berbusse, "Neutrality-Diplomacy."

15. The Knott Amendment of 1878, more commonly known as the Posse Comitatus Act, stated that "'it shall not be lawful to employ any part of the Army of the United States, as a posse comitatus, or otherwise, for the purposes of executing the laws, except in such cases and under such circumstances as such employment of said force may be expressly authorized by the Constitution or by act of Congress.'" See Coakley, *Role of Federal Military Forces*, 344. Nevertheless, the army operated as such in the enforcement of neutrality laws, and at one point in 1912, explicitly acknowledged that it was in fact being used as a *posse comitatus*. See also "Henry Stimson, Secretary of War to Secretary of Commerce and Labor, quoting Commanding Officer, Fort Bliss," August 23, 1912, Folder 53108/71-D, Box 1110, Records of the Immigration and Naturalization Service, Subject and Policy Files, 1893–1957, Record Group 85. In official military history, this role is rarely mentioned if not completely ignored. Laurie and Cole, for instance, in *Role of Federal Military Forces*, focus exclusively on the army's role in suppressing organized labor during the years of the Mexican Revolution.

16. Rachel St. John also sees a tripartite periodization of the US response to the Mexican Revolution: the first three years (1910–1913), when "both Mexicans and Americans held out the hope that the revolution would be a short-term conflict"; the middle four years (1913–1917), "which saw some of the greatest violence and destruction as the Mexican Revolution devolved into a civil war and the United States and Mexico nearly went to war"; and the last three years (1917–1920), "during which the United States' engagement in World War I led to the creation of new border crossing regulations." See St. John, *Line in the Sand*, 120.

17. *Annual Report of the Secretary of War, United States War Department, 1910*, 3:134, 127, 98.

18. *Annual Report of the Secretary of War, United States War Department, 1911*, 1:1, 12, 238–242.

19. "Correspondence Relating to the Mexican Revolution of 1911," March 6–March 30, 1911, E-290, I-18, Records of the Office of Naval Intelligence, 1887–1927, Record Group 45.

20. "Secretary of the Navy Beekman Winthrop to Thomas, USS California,"

March 7, 1911, Correspondence Relating to the Mexican Revolution of 1911, E-290, I-18, Records of the Office of Naval Intelligence, 1887–1927, Record Group 45.

21. "Wm. H. Carter, Major General, Chief of Staff to Adjutant General," November 17, 1911, Folder 53108/71-B, Box 1110, Records of the Immigration and Naturalization Service, Subject and Policy Files, 1893–1957, Record Group 85.

22. "Revolutions in Mexico," Subcommittee of the Committee on Foreign Relations, US Senate, 62nd Cong., 2nd sess., 1913, 23.

23. Ibid., 109, 124.

24. Ibid., 185.

25. The question of how and from what source the Mexican Revolution was funded has invited much speculation. See Grieb, "Standard Oil and the Financing."

26. "Funsten, Major General Commanding, Brownsville, to F. H. Berkshire, Supervising Inspector of Immigration, El Paso," September 12, 1915, Folder 53108/71-G, Box 1111, Records of the Immigration and Naturalization Service, Subject and Policy Files, 1893–1957, Record Group 85; "Commissioner General of Immigration," April 3, 1911, Folder 53108/71, Box 1110, Records of the Immigration and Naturalization Service, Subject and Policy Files, 1893–1957, Record Group 85; "Commissioner General of Immigration," March 27, 1911, Folder 53108/71, Box 1110, Records of the Immigration and Naturalization Service, Subject and Policy Files, 1893–1957, Record Group 85.

27. "Funsten, Major General Commanding, Brownsville, to F. H. Berkshire, Supervising Inspector of Immigration, El Paso," Record Group 85; "Col. Edgar Z. Steever, 4th Cavalry, Ft. Bliss," August 12, 1912, Folder 53108/71-D, Box 1110, Records of the Immigration and Naturalization Service, Subject and Policy Files, 1893–1957, Record Group 85; "Adjutant General, Department of Texas to Secretary of War Stimson," July 29, 1912, Folder 53108/71-D, Box 1110, Records of the Immigration and Naturalization Service, Subject and Policy Files, 1893–1957, Record Group 85.

28. "Commanding General, Department of Texas, Ft. Bliss to Henry Stimson, Secretary of War," February 13, 1913, Folder 53108/71-E, Box 1110, Records of the Immigration and Naturalization Service, Subject and Policy Files, 1893–1957, Record Group 85.

29. "Adkins Finch, US Attorney to Attorney General," November 20, 1911, Folder 53108/71-B, Box 1110, Records of the Immigration and Naturalization Service, Subject and Policy Files, 1893–1957, Record Group 85. David Work has shown that this military enforcement was often imperfect and confused due to the sometimes vague and arbitrary application of neutrality statutes. See Work, "Enforcing Neutrality."

30. *Annual Report of the Secretary of War, United States War Department, 1912*, 1:9, 3:5.

31. *Annual Report of the Secretary of War, United States War Department, 1914*, 1:136.

32. Harris III and Sadler, *Secret War in El Paso*, 285–293.

33. Wilson, "Mexican Affairs," 4, 7.

34. *Annual Report of the Attorney General of the United States, United States Department of Justice, 1912*, 47.

35. *Annual Report of the Attorney General of the United States, United States Department of Justice, 1913*, 46.

36. *Annual Report of the Secretary of War for the Year 1912*, 9.

37. *Annual Report of the Secretary of War, 1913*, 9–10.

38. *Annual Report of the Secretary of War, 1915*, 1.

39. *Annual Report of the Secretary of War, United States War Department, 1916*, 1:15.

40. *Annual Report of the Secretary of War, United States War Department, 1915*, 1:1; *Annual Report of the Secretary of War, United States War Department, 1919*, 1:54.

41. Carrigan and Webb, *Forgotten Dead*, appendix A.

42. Johnson, *Revolution in Texas*, 120.

43. W. D. Smithers Collection of Photographs, Box 20, Images 2800 and 2804.

44. W. D. Smithers Collection of Photographs, Box 20, Image 2803.

45. W. D. Smithers Collection of Photographs, Box 20, Image 2801.

46. W. D. Smithers Collection of Photographs, Box 20, Image 2802.

47. Tucker and Russell, *Natural Enemy, Natural Ally*.

48. Winters et al., "Heat, Rock, and Sand," 250–251.

49. Jefferson, "The Revolution and the Mexican Plateau," n.p.; italics in original.

50. "The Frontier Region of Mexico," 16–17.

51. Ibid., 16, 20–21.

52. Ibid., 22, 17.

53. Ibid., 25; italics in original.

54. "Report of the Chief of Staff," in *War Department, Annual Reports, 1914*, 1:136.

55. "Report of the Secretary of War," in *War Department, Annual Reports, 1916*, 1:10–11.

56. *Annual Report of the Secretary of War for the Year 1911*, 9.

57. Ibid., 13.

58. *Annual Report of the Secretary of War for the Year 1912*, 9.

59. "Report of the Secretary of War," in *War Department, Annual Reports, 1916*, 1:17–18.

60. "Report of the Quartermaster General," in ibid., 1:384.

61. "Report of the Secretary of War," in ibid., 1:22.

62. "Major P. D. Lockridge, 13th Cavalry to the Commanding General, Second Cavalry Brigade, Military Situation across from This Brigade," El Paso, Texas, August 18, 1913, Folder 16, "Mexican Revolution," Box 3, Correspondence Relating to the Mexican Revolution, 1913–16, Southern Department, 1913–1920, Records of the U.S. Army Continental Commands, 1821–1920, Record Group 393.

63. See also Lewis, *Iron Horse Imperialism*, 51–57.

64. "Major P. D. Lockridge, 13th Cavalry to the Commanding General, Second Cavalry Brigade, Military Situation across from This Brigade," Record Group 393.

65. Folder 1-Maps, doc. #2579, Records of the Ferrocarril Noroeste de México, 1910–1919.

66. Boyer, *Political Landscapes*, 69.

67. Ibid., 44.

68. Box 5, Folder 16, doc. #2607, Records of the Ferrocarril Noroeste de México, 1910–1919.

69. Box 3, Folder 6, doc. #1274, Records of the Ferrocarril Noroeste de México, 1910–1919.

70. Johnson, *Revolution in Texas*, 76, 92, 104.

71. "Commissioner General of Immigration to Lieutenant Colonel M. E. Spalding," July 2, 1919, Folder 54261/202, Box 2864, Records of the Immigration and Naturalization Service, Subject and Policy Files, 1893–1957, Record Group 85.

72. W. D. Smithers Collection of Photographs, Box 20, Image 2909.

73. Ibid., Box 20, Image 2908.

74. Ibid., Box 20, Images 2901 and 2902.

75. Ibid., Box 20, Image 2905.

76. Ibid., Box 20, Image 2923.

77. Huston, *Sinews of War*, 273.

78. Ibid., 296, 298–299.

79. W. D. Smithers Collection of Photographs, Box 51, Image 6001.

80. Ibid., Box 51, Image 6019.

81. Ibid., Box 51, Image 6035.

82. Ibid., Box 51, Image 6020.

83. *Annual Report of the Secretary of War, United States War Department, 1917*, 1:10.

84. W. D. Smithers Collection of Photographs, Box 20, Image 2919.

85. Eisenhower, *At Ease*, 112.

86. Ibid., 120, 126.

87. W. D. Smithers Collection of Photographs, Box 20, Image 2958.

88. Ibid., Box 51, Image 6036.

89. Ibid., Box 20, Image 2960.

90. "Funsten, Major General Commanding, Brownsville, to F. H. Berkshire, Supervising Inspector of Immigration, El Paso," September 12, 1915, Folder 53108/71-G, Box 1111, Record Group 85.

91. "E. P. Reynolds, Inspector in Charge, Immigration Service, Brownsville to Supervising Inspector, Immigration Service, El Paso," September 13, 1915, Folder 53108/71-L, Box 1111, Records of the Immigration and Naturalization Service, Subject and Policy Files, 1893–1957, Record Group 85.

92. Hinkle, *Wings over the Border*, 6, 64.

93. Ibid., 7, 11, 34–35, 17; W. D. Smithers Collection of Photographs, Box 2, Image 143.

94. W. D. Smithers Collection of Photographs, Box 2, Image 157.

95. The relationship between the United States, Mexico, and Germany during the war is a subject that has been well documented. See Katz, *Secret War in Mexico;* Knight, *U.S.-Mexican Relations.* My purpose here is to show the effect the mobilization for the war had on the border region military buildup. In 1919, the secretary of war rightly stated that "during the progress of the war in Europe the work of the United States Army in protecting our southern border received a comparatively small share of the public attention[,] and the importance of this work was not generally understood." See *Annual Report of the Secretary of War, United States War Department, 1919*, 1:469.

96. Annual Report of the Secretary of War, United States War Department, 1919, 1:496.

97. Ibid., 1:410.

98. *Annual Report of the Secretary of War, United States War Department, 1917*, 1:10.

99. *Annual Report of the Secretary of War, United States War Department, 1919*, 1:469–470.

100. Ibid., 469–470.

101. "Benedict Crowell, Acting Secretary of War to the Secretary of Labor," October 8, 1918, Folder 54261/276A, Box 2864, Records of the Immigration and Naturalization Service, Subject and Policy Files, 1893–1957, Record Group 85.

102. "Memorandum for the Acting Secretary in re Proposal to Establish an Immigration Patrol Service on the Land Boundaries," November 8, 1918, Folder 54261/276A, Box 2864, Records of the Immigration and Naturalization Service, Subject and Policy Files, 1893–1957, Record Group 85.

103. Lytle Hernández, *Migra!*, 26.

104. Ngai, *Impossible Subjects*, 67. See also St. John, *Line in the Sand*, 121; Massey, Durand, and Malone, *Beyond Smoke and Mirrors*, 32–33; and Kang, *INS on the Line*.

105. Eisenhower, *At Ease*, 158–159.

POLICE AND WATERWORKS ON THE BORDER: ASPIRATIONS TO CONTROL THROUGH BUILDING

1. Several historians have traced the institutional and legal history of these years. See especially Kang, *INS on the Line*; Lytle Hernández, *Migra!*; and Lim, *Porous Borders*.

2. The few studies that examine this agency tend to focus on its unique bureaucratic and legal aspects. See Littlefield, *Conflict on the Rio Grande*; and Timm, *International Boundary Commission*.

3. Several excellent histories about water development in Northern Mexico have been written, though they do not focus on the CILA, with the notable

exception of Samaniego López, *Ríos internacionales entre México y Estados Unidos*. See also Aboites Aguilar, *La irrigación revolucionaria*; Walsh, *Building the Borderlands*; and Wolfe, *Watering the Revolution*.

4. Two important studies of early border fencing by Mary Mendoza and Rachel St. John make no mention of this fence project, though it was far more substantial in every way than the fences they researched. Mendoza anachronistically refers to a plan put forward in 1910 for forty-five miles of barbed-wire fencing, all in Southern California, as border "fortification." See Mendoza, "Fencing the Line," 78; and St. John, "Divided Ranges."

5. Weber, *From South Texas to the Nation*; Meeks, *Border Citizens*.

6. Border historians have reconstructed many aspects of these years with a vivid clarity. They have recovered personal and collective agency among guest workers previously portrayed to be passive subjects, thereby elucidating the emotional lives of migrants between Mexico and United States. These studies have tended to ignore the collaborations with water engineers, however. See Loza, *Defiant Braceros*; Rosas, *Abrazando el Espíritu*; Cohen, *Braceros*.

7. Some scholars have also pointed to US government attempts to associate pathology and the border. See Mckiernan-González, *Fevered Measures*; Stern, "Buildings, Boundaries, and Blood."

8. Pisani, *Water and American Government*; Donald Worster, *Rivers of Empire*.

9. Gutiérrez, *Walls and Mirrors*, 41.

10. Worster, *Rivers of Empire*, 4, 7.

11. Reisner, *Cadillac Desert*, 251–252; Johnston, "Beyond 'The West,'" 248.

12. Meeks, "Tohono O'odham, Wage Labor, and Resistant Adaptation," 471–472.

13. Foley, *The White Scourge*, 118–140.

14. Worster, *Rivers of Empire*, 310.

15. FitzGerald and Cook-Martín, *Culling the Masses*, 105.

16. Schulman, "Governing Nature, Nurturing Government."

17. "Immigrant Inspector to Commissioner-General of Immigration, U.S. Department of Labor, Washington, D.C.," June 2, 1919, Folder 54261/202-?, Box 2864, Subject and Policy Files, 1893–1957, Records of the Immigration and Naturalization Service, Record Group 85.

18. "Governor of Arizona to Hon. William B. Wilson, Secretary of Labor, Washington, D.C.," June 20, 1919, Folder 54261/202-?, Box 2864, Subject and Policy Files, 1893–1957, Records of the Immigration and Naturalization Service, Record Group 85.

19. "Arizona Cotton Growers Association to Hon. W. D. Wilson, Secretary of Labor, Washington, D.C." June 28, 1919, Folder 54261/202 H, Box 2864, Subject and Policy Files, 1893–1957, Records of the Immigration and Naturalization Service, Record Group 85.

20. "Governor of Texas to Hon. W. B. Wilson, Secretary of Labor, Washington, D.C.," June 28, 1919, Folder 54261/202-?, Box 2864, Subject and Policy Files, 1893–1957, Records of the Immigration and Naturalization Service, Record Group 85.

21. Weber, *From South Texas to the Nation;* Mora-Torres, *Making of the Mexican Border.*

22. Montejano, *Anglos and Mexicans,* 113.

23. "W. W. Follett, Consulting Engineer to General Anson Mills, Commissioner, Washington, D.C.," El Paso, Texas, March 7, 1908, Legajo 177, Expediente 3, Folio 115, Secretaría de Relaciones Exteriores, Archivo Histórico Genaro Estrada.

24. "Sección de Límites, Número 688," México, Enero 20 de 1908, Legajo 177, Expediente 3, Folio 115, Secretaría de Relaciones Exteriores, Archivo Histórico Genaro Estrada.

25. "Obra que indudablemente perjudicaría los seculares derechos preferentes de Ciudad Juárez á las aguas mansas del Rio Bravo." "F. Gamboa, Subsecretario, Sección de Límites," México, Junio 5 de 1908, Legajo 177, Expediente 3, Folio 115, Secretaría de Relaciones Exteriores, Archivo Histórico Genaro Estrada.

26. At the time, this translated to roughly 94,000 acres in New Mexico, 52,000 acres in El Paso, and only around 24,000 acres in the Juárez Valley, which corresponded to both the amount of cultivated land and the capacity of the Acequia Madre according to an 1896 Mexican report. Samaniego López, *Ríos internacionales,* 253–262.

27. "Sección de Límites, Número 566," México, 11 de Diciembre de 1908, Legajo 177, Expediente 3, Folio 115, Secretaría de Relaciones Exteriores, Archivo Histórico Genaro Estrada.

28. Lytle Hernández, *Migra!,* 45–69; Montejano, *Anglos and Mexicans,* 103–155; Escobar, *Race, Police, and the Making of a Political Identity,* 37–52.

29. Joseph F. Friedkin interview by Michelle L. Gomilla, 1994, "Interview no. 837," Institute of Oral History, 1–2.

30. Joseph F. Friedkin interview by Oscar J. Martinez and Sarah E. John, 1977, "Interview no. 552," Institute of Oral History, 5; Hart, *Empire and Revolution,* 131–166.

31. Joseph F. Friedkin interview by Oscar J. Martinez and Sarah E. John, 1977, "Interview no. 552," Institute of Oral History, 6.

32. Minute No. 129, "Report on the Rio Grande Rectification," 5–6.

33. J. F. Friedkin, Commissioner, "Technical Summaries of Projects along the International Boundary between the United States and Mexico," April 1979, revised January 1981, Box 1, TR 0076–15–0012, Series 902–01b (IBWC Project Planning, Design, and Construction Case Files), Records of the International Boundary and Water Commission, Record Group 76.

34. Minute No. 129, "Report on the Rio Grande Rectification," 21; Lawson, "Stabilizing the Rio Grande," 67–68; J. F. Friedkin, Commissioner, "Technical Summaries of Projects along the International Boundary between the United States and Mexico," April 1979, revised January 1981, Box 1, TR 0076–15–0012, Series 902–01b (IBWC Project Planning, Design, and Construction Case Files), Records of the International Boundary and Water Commission, Record Group 76.

35. J. F. Friedkin, Commissioner, "Technical Summaries of Projects along the International Boundary between the United States and Mexico," April 1979,

revised January 1981, Box 1, TR 0076–15–0012, Series 902–01b (IBWC Project Planning, Design, and Construction Case Files), Records of the International Boundary and Water Commission, Record Group 76.

36. Joseph F. Friedkin interview by Oscar J. Martinez and Sarah E. John, 1977, "Interview no. 552," Institute of Oral History, 10, 12.

37. "Nos dijeron que era una obra de defenza [*sic*], pero en el campo de los echos [*sic*] no compredimos [sic] que era lo que se defendia con esa hobra [*sic*]." "No estamos de conformidad con eso travajos [*sic*] porque no hemos tenido havizo [*sic*] de ninguna autoridad." Ejido de Jesús Carranza a Ministro de la Secretaría de Agricultura y Fomento, México Dto. Federal, Agosto 9, 1933, Caja 572, Expediente 6345, Legajo 01, Fojas 14, Fondo Documental Aguas Nacionales, Comisión Nacional del Agua, Archivo Histórico y Biblioteca Central del Agua.

38. Informe sobre escrito de los ejidatarios de "Jesús Carranza," México, D.F., a 9 de septiembre de 1933, Caja 572, Expediente 6345, Legajo 01, Fojas 14, Fondo Documental Aguas Nacionales, Comisión Nacional del Agua, Archivo Histórico y Biblioteca Central del Agua; "Información General, Trabajos de la Comisión Internacional de Límites," C. Juárez, Chih., Diciembre 1, 1933, Caja 572, Expediente 6345, Legajo 01, Fojas 14, Fondo Documental Aguas Nacionales, Comisión Nacional del Agua, Archivo Histórico y Biblioteca Central del Agua.

39. J. F. Friedkin, Commissioner, "Technical Summaries of Projects along the International Boundary between the United States and Mexico," April 1979, revised January 1981, Box 1, TR 0076–15–0012, Series 902–01b (IBWC Project Planning, Design, and Construction Case Files), Records of the International Boundary and Water Commission, Record Group 76; Kang, *INS on the Line;* Balderrama and Rodríguez, *Decade of Betrayal.*

40. Lawson, "Stabilizing the Rio Grande," 67.

41. Act of August 19, 1935, 49 Stat. 660, Public Law 286, 22 U.S.C. 277.

42. St. John, "Divided Ranges," 116.

43. Sayre, *Ranching, Endangered Species, and Urbanization;* Sayre, *Politics of Scale.*

44. Statement: Western Land Boundary Fence Project Estimated Cost of Remaining Construction, July 27, 1953, 901–01 Western Land Boundary Fence Project, Engineering Office Case File, Folder 12, Series 902–01b (IBWC Project Planning, Design, and Construction Case Files), Box 3, TR 076–2013–0020, Records of the International Boundary and Water Commission, Record Group 76.

45. *To Establish a Border Patrol,* April 12 and 19, 1926, 12–13.

46. W. A. Carmichael, District Director [USI&NS], Los Angeles 13, California to Commissioner, Washington 25, DC, "Proposed Fence at Calexico, California," August 24, 1948, Folder 56084/946, Box 2864, Subject and Policy Files, 1893–1957, Records of the Immigration and Naturalization Service, Record Group 85.

47. District Director, USI&NS, Los Angeles, California, Chief Patrol Inspector, El Centro California, "Boundary Fence, Imperial Valley Area," August 19, 1948, Folder 56084/946, Box 2864, Subject and Policy Files, 1893–1957, Records of the Immigration and Naturalization Service, Record Group 85.

48. Ibid.

49. Andrés Jr., *Power and Control in the Imperial Valley*, 68–97.

50. District Director, Los Angeles 13, California, R. L. Williams, Assistant Officer in Charge, Calexico, California, "International Boundary Fence," April 7, 1948, Folder 56084/946, Box 2864, Subject and Policy Files, 1893–1957, Records of the Immigration and Naturalization Service, Record Group 85.

51. District Director, El Paso, Texas, H. D. Nice, Officer in Charge, Nogales, Arizona, "Boundary Fence," December 15, 1947, Folder 56084/946, Box 2864, Subject and Policy Files, 1893–1957, Records of the Immigration and Naturalization Service, Record Group 85.

52. District Director, Imm. & Natzn. Service, El Paso, Texas, G. J. McBee, Chief Patrol Inspector, El Paso, Texas, "Boundary Fence," December 16, 1947, Folder 56084/946, Box 2864, Subject and Policy Files, 1893–1957, Records of the Immigration and Naturalization Service, Record Group 85.

53. Fence Construction by Fiscal Years 1948 through 1950, 901–01 Western Land Boundary Fence Project, Engineering Office Case File, Folder 12, Series 902–01b (IBWC Project Planning, Design, and Construction Case Files), Box 3, TR 076–2013–0020, Records of the International Boundary and Water Commission, Record Group 7.

54. Nogales, Arizona, Oblique Aerial Photos, May 1948, Folder 2.9.2/5C, Box 14, Records of the International Boundary and Water Commission, Record Group 76.

55. Oblique Aerial Photographs, Western Land Boundary, Luna County, New Mexico, Folder 2.9.2/2, Box 14, Records of the International Boundary and Water Commission, Record Group 76.

56. Statement: Western Land Boundary Fence Project Estimated Cost of Remaining Construction, July 27, 1953, 901–01 Western Land Boundary Fence Project, Engineering Office Case File, Folder 12, Series 902–01b (IBWC Project Planning, Design, and Construction Case Files), Box 3, TR 076–2013–0020, Records of the International Boundary and Water Commission, Record Group 76.

57. Fence Construction by Fiscal Years 1948 through 1950, 901–01 Western Land Boundary Fence Project, Engineering Office Case File, Folder 12, Series 902–01b (IBWC Project Planning, Design, and Construction Case Files), Box 3, TR 076–2013–0020, Records of the International Boundary and Water Commission, Record Group 76.

58. [L. M. Lawson, Commissioner of IBWC to] The Honorable T. B. Shoemaker, Acting Commissioner, Immigration and Naturalization Service, Franklin Trust Building, Philadelphia, Pennsylvania, September 18, 1947, Folder 56084/946, Box 2864, Subject and Policy Files, 1893–1957, Records of the Immigration and Naturalization Service, Record Group 85.

59. [Photographs of towers, 1949?], Folder 56084/946-B, Box 2864, Subject and Policy Files, 1893–1957, Records of the Immigration and Naturalization Service, Record Group 85.

60. Edwin M. Reeves interview by Robert H. Novak, 1974, "Interview no. 135," Institute of Oral History, 1–2.

61. Ibid., 3–4.

62. Ibid., 14–15.

63. Ibid., 1–2.

64. Arthur L. Adams interview by Jim Marchant and Oscar J. Martínez, August 10, 1977, "Interview No. 646," Institute of Oral History, 25, 26.

65. Aboites Aguilar, *El agua de la nación*, 60–61.

66. Hundley, *Water and the West*.

67. Reisner, *Cadillac Desert*, 163.

68. Falcon Dam releasing 50,000 c.f.s., 9/20/71, 12:00 noon to 3:00 p.m., Folder 4.5.14–71, Roll 6, Box 30, Aerial Photographs, Records of the International Boundary and Water Commission, Record Group 76.

69. J. F. Friedkin, Commissioner, "Technical Summaries of Projects along the International Boundary between the United States and Mexico," April 1979, revised January 1981, Box 1, TR 0076–15–0012, Series 902–01b (IBWC Project Planning, Design, and Construction Case Files), Records of the International Boundary and Water Commission, Record Group 76.

70. Ibid.

71. Joseph F. Friedkin interview by Oscar J. Martínez and Sarah E. John, 1977, "Interview no. 552," Institute of Oral History, 29, 36.

72. Fiege, *Irrigated Eden*, 45.

73. Joseph F. Friedkin interview by Oscar J. Martínez and Sarah E. John, 1977, "Interview no. 552," Institute of Oral History, 30–31.

74. Ibid., 32.

75. "Ing. Carlos Molina R., gerente general de construcción, Secretaría de Recursos Hidráulicos, Hoja Núm. 3," [1955], Caja 3126, Expediente 43121, Fondo Documental Aguas Nacionales, Comisión Nacional del Agua, Archivo Histórico y Biblioteca Central del Agua.

76. "Dirección General de Aprovechamientos Hidráulicos, presa internacional 'Falcon,' indemnizaciones," Nva. Cd. Guerrero, Tam., Diciembre 31 de 1955, Caja 3126, Expediente 43121, Fondo Documental Aguas Nacionales, Comisión Nacional del Agua, Archivo Histórico y Biblioteca Central del Agua.

77. "[Various kinds of personal property were] invadidos por las aguas del vaso de la Presa Internacional de 'FALCON,'" Eustolio González Treviño al C. Secretario de Recursos Hidráulicos, Nueva Ciudad Guerrero, Tamps., a 14 de junio de 1954, Caja 4693, Expediente 63165, Fondo Documental Aguas Nacionales, Comisión Nacional del Agua, Archivo Histórico y Biblioteca Central del Agua.

78. Lic. Javier Juárez V. al C. Director de Aprovechamientos Hidráulicos, México, D.F. a 28 de Agosto de 1954, Caja 4693, Expediente 63165, Fondo Documental Aguas Nacionales, Comisión Nacional del Agua, Archivo Histórico y Biblioteca Central del Agua.

79. Joseph F. Friedkin interview by Oscar J. Martínez and Sarah E. John, 1977, "Interview no. 552," Institute of Oral History, 33–34.

80. Zapata, Border Patrol Station JTEX 598C, Box TX319 HM 1996, Disposal

Case Files, Records of Federal Property and Resource Management (GSA), Record Group 291.

81. Kang, *INS on the Line*, 157.

82. This was perhaps the most tense moment in US-Mexico relations during the revolution. Pancho Villa and his men attacked a small town in southern New Mexico, which prompted a US armed invasion, led by General Pershing, in an ultimately futile attempt to find and kill Villa. See Katz, "Pancho Villa and the Attack"; Katz, *Life and Times of Pancho Villa*.

83. "Operation Cloud Burst," July 29, 1953, Folder 56363/299, Records of the Immigration and Naturalization Service, Record Group 85.

84. Ibid.

85. Nevins, *Operation Gatekeeper*, appendix F; "Draft of press release, Operation Cloud Burst, Department of Justice, Attorney General Herbert Brownell," 1953, Folder 56363/299, Records of the Immigration and Naturalization Service, Record Group 85.

86. "Operation Cloud Burst," July 29, 1953, Folder 56363/299, Records of the Immigration and Naturalization Service, Record Group 85.

87. "Draft of press release, Operation Cloud Burst, Department of Justice, Attorney General Herbert Brownell," 1953, Folder 56363/299, Records of the Immigration and Naturalization Service, Record Group 85.

88. "Operation Cloud Burst," July 29, 1953, Folder 56363/299, Records of the Immigration and Naturalization Service, Record Group 85.

89. Lytle Hernández, *Migra!*, 171–195; Kang, *INS on the Line*, 139–167; Calavita, *Inside the State*; Cohen, *Braceros*; Fitzgerald, *A Nation of Emigrants*; Aguila, "Mexican/U.S. Immigration Policy."

90. Lytle Hernández, *Migra!*, 184–190; Kang, *INS on the Line*, 159–163.

POLICE AND WATERWORKS ON THE BORDER: SYSTEMIC FLAWS

1. "S. A. Andretta, Adminstrative Assistant Attorney General to Mr. C. Jack Cowart, Regional Director, Utilization and Disposal Service, General Services Adminstration," June 23, 1964, Folder 291–66A1046, FRC 330764, "Border Patrol Sector Towers, JTEX749, 1964–1965," Box TX165, HM1995, Disposal Case Files, El Paso, Texas, Records of the Federal Property Resource Mgt. (GSA), Record Group 291.

2. "W. K. Duckworth, Assistant Regional Commissioner, Administrative Services, INS to General Services Adminstration," January 8, 1965, Folder 291–66A1046, FRC 330764, "Border Patrol Sector Towers, JTEX749, 1964–1965," Box TX165, HM1995, Disposal Case Files, El Paso, Texas, Records of the Federal Property Resource Mgt. (GSA), Record Group 291; Edwin M. Reeves interview by Robert H. Novak, 1974, "Interview no. 135," Institute of Oral History, 15.

3. "S. A. Andretta, Adminstrative Assistant Attorney General to Mr. C. Jack

Cowart, Regional Director, Utilization and Disposal Service, General Services Adminstration," June 23, 1964, Folder 291–66A1046, FRC 330764, "Border Patrol Sector Towers, JTEX749, 1964–1965," Box TX165, HM1995, Disposal Case Files, El Paso, Texas, Records of the Federal Property Resource Mgt. (GSA), Record Group 291.

4. "J. F. Friedkin, Commissioner, IBWC to O. W. Lucas, Realty Officer, Real Property Division, General Services Adminstration," December 30, 1964, Folder 291–66A1046, FRC 330764, "Border Patrol Sector Towers, JTEX749, 1964–1965," Box TX165, HM1995, Disposal Case Files, El Paso, Texas, Records of the Federal Property Resource Mgt. (GSA), Record Group 291; "O. W. Lucas, Realty Officer, Real Property Division, GSA, Inspection Report," March 15, 1965, Folder 291–66A1046, FRC 330764, "Border Patrol Sector Towers, JTEX749, 1964–1965," Box TX165, HM1995, Disposal Case Files, El Paso, Texas, Records of the Federal Property Resource Mgt. (GSA), Record Group 291.

5. Bustamante, "El programa fronterizo de maquiladoras," 185.

6. Ericson, "Analysis of Mexico's Border Industrialization Program," 33.

7. Bob Ybarra interview by Michelle L. Gomilla, 1994, "Interview no. 847," Institute of Oral History, 13.

8. Schulze, "The Chamizal Blues"; Lamborn and Mumme, *Statecraft, Domestic Politics, and Foreign Policy Making*; Kramer, "A Border Crosses."

9. Bob Ybarra interview by Michelle L. Gomilla, 1994, "Interview no. 847," Institute of Oral History, 5–6.

10. Nestor Valencia interview by Michelle L. Gomilla, 1994, "Interview no. 844," Institute of Oral History, 4–5.

11. "Bridges Relocations Chamizal," August 1966, Folder 34, Series 902–01b (IBWC Project Planning, Design, and Construction Case Files), Box 4, TR 076–2013–0026, Records of the International Boundary and Water Commission, Record Group 76.

12. J. F. Friedkin, Commissioner, "Technical Summaries of Projects along the International Boundary between the United States and Mexico," April 1979, revised January 1981, Box 1, TR 0076–15–0012, Series 902–01b (IBWC Project Planning, Design, and Construction Case Files), Records of the International Boundary and Water Commission, Record Group 76.

13. J. Samuel Moore interview by Michelle L. Gomilla, 1994, "Interview no. 842," Institute of Oral History, 11.

14. Bob Ybarra interview by Michelle L. Gomilla, 1994, "Interview no. 847," Institute of Oral History, 14.

15. "Peyton Packing Company, Fixed Equipment," 1965, Folder 26, Series 902–01b (IBWC Project Planning, Design, and Construction Case Files), Box 4, TR 076–2013–0026, Records of the International Boundary and Water Commission, Record Group 76.

16. Joseph F. Friedkin interview by Michelle L. Gomilla, 1994, "Interview no. 837," Institute of Oral History, 15.

17. Nestor Valencia interview by Michelle L. Gomilla, 1994, "Interview no. 844," Institute of Oral History, 26.

18. William Bass interview by Michelle L. Gomilla, 1994, "Interview no. 834," Institute of Oral History, 15.

19. Ibid., 1–2, 5–6, 10, 18.

20. Feliciano Hinojosa interview by Michelle L. Gomilla, 1994, "Interview no. 841," Institute of Oral History, 8.

21. William E. Wood interview by Michelle L. Gomilla, 1994, "Interview no. 846," Institute of Oral History, 14–15.

22. "Chamizal Maps-Properties to Be Acquired," February 25, 1966, Folder 2, Series 902–01b (IBWC Project Planning, Design, and Construction Case Files), Box 4, TR 076–2013–0026, Records of the International Boundary and Water Commission, Record Group 76.

23. Joaquín Bustamante interview by Michelle L. Gomilla, 1994, "Interview no. 835," Institute of Oral History, 22–23.

24. "Chamizal Project-General Relocation Plan Drawings," January 1966, Folder 12, Series 902–01b (IBWC Project Planning, Design, and Construction Case Files), Box 4, TR 076–2013–0026, Records of the International Boundary and Water Commission, Record Group 76.

25. Nestor Valencia interview by Michelle L. Gomilla, 1994, "Interview no. 844," Institute of Oral History, 34–37. See also Cadava, "Borderlands of Modernity and Abandonment," 370, 380.

26. Nestor Valencia interview by Michelle L. Gomilla, 1994, "Interview no. 844," Institute of Oral History, 35.

27. Bob Ybarra interview by Michelle L. Gomilla, 1994, "Interview no. 847," Institute of Oral History, 32.

28. "Nosotros no más vimos que fueron levantado unos monstruos que nos han separado, que nos han dividido, que nos han distanciado." René Mascarenas Miranda interview by Oscar J. Martínez, 1976, "Interview no. 234," Institute of Oral History, 246.

29. Ray Daguerre interview by Oscar J. Martínez, 1975, "Interview no. 185," Institute of Oral History, 33.

30. *Convention between the United States of America and the United States of Mexico Touching the International Boundary Line Where It Follows the Bed of the Rio Colorado,* concluded at Washington, DC, November 12, 1884.

31. Joseph F. Friedkin interview by Oscar J. Martínez and Sarah E. John, 1977, "Interview no. 552," Institute of Oral History, 52–59.

32. "Chamizal Relocation Plan," November 25, 1966, Folder 7, Series 902–01b (IBWC Project Planning, Design, and Construction Case Files), Box 4, TR 076–2013–0026, Records of the International Boundary and Water Commission, Record Group 76.

33. Ray Daguerre interview by Oscar J. Martínez, 1975, "Interview no. 185," Institute of Oral History, 36–38.

34. Joseph F. Friedkin interview by Oscar J. Martínez and Sarah E. John, 1977, "Interview no. 552," Institute of Oral History, 68–69.

35. Nestor Valencia interview by Michelle L. Gomilla, 1994, "Interview no. 844," Institute of Oral History, 34.

36. Ray Daguerre interview by Oscar J. Martínez, 1975, "Interview no. 185," Institute of Oral History, 39.

37. Joseph F. Friedkin interview by Oscar J. Martínez and Sarah E. John, 1977, "Interview no. 552," Institute of Oral History, 67.

38. J. F. Friedkin, Commissioner, "Technical Summaries of Projects along the International Boundary between the United States and Mexico," April 1979, revised January 1981, Box 1, TR 0076–15–0012, Series 902–01b (IBWC Project Planning, Design, and Construction Case Files), Records of the International Boundary and Water Commission, Record Group 76.

39. Ibid.

40. Johnson, "Remarks in El Paso at the Inauguration of the New River Channel."

41. Ibid.

42. Joseph F. Friedkin interview by Oscar J. Martínez and Sarah E. John, 1977, "Interview no. 552," Institute of Oral History, 42.

43. Ibid., 45.

44. Ibid., 42.

45. Richard Nixon, "Remarks at the Dedication of the Amistad Dam on the Rio Grande," September 8, 1969, http://www.presidency.ucsb.edu/ws/?pid=2224.

46. J. F. Friedkin, Commissioner, "Technical Summaries of Projects along the International Boundary between the United States and Mexico," April 1979, revised January 1981, Box 1, TR 0076–15–0012, Series 902–01b (IBWC Project Planning, Design, and Construction Case Files), Records of the International Boundary and Water Commission, Record Group 76.

47. Joseph F. Friedkin interview by Oscar J. Martínez and Sarah E. John, 1977, "Interview no. 552," Institute of Oral History,46, 48.

48. Jesús Ma. Ramón Cantú a C. Ing. Oscar González Lugo, Gerente Gral. de Recursos Hidráulicos en el Edo. De Coah., Cd. Acuña, agosto 17 de 1967, Caja 2812, Expediente 39295, Fojas 207, Fondo Documental Aguas Nacionales, Comisión Nacional del Agua, Archivo Histórico y Biblioteca Central del Agua.

49. Ing. Oscar González Lugo a C. Ing. Antonio Rodríguez L., Campto, "El Mirador", Coah., agosto 23, 1967, Caja 2812, Expediente 39295, Fojas 207, Fondo Documental Aguas Nacionales, Comisión Nacional del Agua, Archivo Histórico y Biblioteca Central del Agua.

50. Officials from Recursos Hidráulicos produced elaborate studies of these four houses in an effort to precisely tabulate the indemnities that would be paid. They photographed them from every angle, itemized all the building materials, and reproduced floor plans to calculate square footage. Based on these calculations, the four owners were compensated $49,373 pesos in total. María Salas's house was

the simplest, so she received the least, $7,086 pesos. Domingo Franco Robles lived in the largest and most structurally complicated house. For it, he got $22,125 pesos. Fojas 4–42, Caja 2812, Expediente 39295, Fojas 207, Fondo Documental Aguas Nacionales, Comisión Nacional del Agua, Archivo Histórico y Biblioteca Central del Agua.

51. "View looking southeast showing diversion and 1st stage construction," August 23, 1965, Folder "Amistad Dam Construction Photos," Series 902–01b (IBWC Project Planning, Design, and Construction Case Files), Box 8, TR 076–13–0014, Records of the International Boundary and Water Commission, Record Group 76.

52. "Amistad Dam, Site Plan," March 1965, Box 281, E. FW8, Records of the Army Corps of Engineers, Fort Worth Division, Record Group 77.

53. J. F. Friedkin, Commissioner, "Technical Summaries of Projects along the International Boundary between the United States and Mexico," April 1979, revised January 1981, Box 1, TR 0076–15–0012, Series 902–01b (IBWC Project Planning, Design, and Construction Case Files), Records of the International Boundary and Water Commission, Record Group 76.

54. "Amistad Dam, Areal Geography," March 1965, Box 285, E. FW8, Records of the Army Corps of Engineers, Fort Worth Division, Record Group 77.

55. "Quarry Site No. 2, Profile of Borings," March 1965, Box 285, E. FW8, Records of the Army Corps of Engineers, Fort Worth Division, Record Group 77.

56. "Construction Schedule," March 1965, Box 281, E. FW8, Records of the Army Corps of Engineers, Fort Worth Division, Record Group 77.

57. "Amistad Dam, Concrete Dam, Scope of Work, Plan and Elevation," March 1965, Box 282, E. FW8, Records of the Army Corps of Engineers, Fort Worth Division, Record Group 77.

58. "Amistad Dam, Reservoir Area Plan," March 1965, Box 281, E. FW8, Records of the Army Corps of Engineers, Fort Worth Division, Record Group 77.

59. J. F. Friedkin, Commissioner, "Technical Summaries of Projects along the International Boundary between the United States and Mexico," April 1979, revised January 1981, Box 1, TR 0076–15–0012, Series 902–01b (IBWC Project Planning, Design, and Construction Case Files), Records of the International Boundary and Water Commission, Record Group 76.

60. Johnson, "Remarks in El Paso at the Inauguration of the New River Channel."

61. Reisner, *Cadillac Desert*, 104.

62. J. F. Friedkin, Commissioner, "Technical Summaries of Projects along the International Boundary between the United States and Mexico," April 1979, revised January 1981, Box 1, TR 0076–15–0012, Series 902–01b (IBWC Project Planning, Design, and Construction Case Files), Records of the International Boundary and Water Commission, Record Group 76.

63. Ibid.

64. Aerial Photographs, "Colorado River Clearing Project-1965," 1965, Folder

3.9.1.1, Box 27, Records of the International Boundary and Water Commission, Record Group 76.

65. Ibid.

66. Ibid.

67. Ibid.

68. J. F. Friedkin, Commissioner, "Technical Summaries of Projects along the International Boundary between the United States and Mexico," April 1979, revised January 1981, Box 1, TR 0076–15–0012, Series 902–01b (IBWC Project Planning, Design, and Construction Case Files), Records of the International Boundary and Water Commission, Record Group 76.

69. Worster, *Rivers of Empire*, 319–324; Reisner, *Cadillac Desert*, 460–464.

70. Niemeyer, "Personal Diplomacy," 173, 176.

71. Worster, *Rivers of Empire*, 321.

72. "Location & General Description," Wellton-Mohawk Irrigation and Drainage District, http://www.wmidd.org/general.html, accessed February 18, 2018.

73. J. F. Friedkin, Commissioner, "Technical Summaries of Projects along the International Boundary between the United States and Mexico," April 1979, revised January 1981, Box 1, TR 0076–15–0012, Series 902–01b (IBWC Project Planning, Design, and Construction Case Files), Records of the International Boundary and Water Commission, Record Group 76.

74. "Challenges," Wellton-Mohawk Irrigation and Drainage District, http://www.wmidd.org/challenges.html, accessed February 18, 2018.

75. Ibid.; J. F. Friedkin, Commissioner, "Technical Summaries of Projects along the International Boundary between the United States and Mexico," April 1979, revised January 1981, Box 1, TR 0076–15–0012, Series 902–01b (IBWC Project Planning, Design, and Construction Case Files), Records of the International Boundary and Water Commission, Record Group 76.

76. Johnson, "Remarks in El Paso at the Inauguration of the New River Channel."

77. J. F. Friedkin, Commissioner, "Technical Summaries of Projects along the International Boundary between the United States and Mexico," April 1979, revised January 1981, Box 1, TR 0076–15–0012, Series 902–01b (IBWC Project Planning, Design, and Construction Case Files), Records of the International Boundary and Water Commission, Record Group 76; "History: El Morillo Drain," Rio Grande Regional Water Authority, http://rgrwa.org/index.php/projects/el-morillo-drain, accessed February 7, 2018.

78. "Challenges," Wellton-Mohawk Irrigation and Drainage District, http://www.wmidd.org/general.html, accessed February 18, 2018.

79. Writing about drug-related topics presents special challenges to historians. Chief among them is the fact that illegal psychoactive substances are very often produced and consumed clandestinely. This means that many aspects of drug commodity chains are illegible in official archives and difficult to recover through oral history. To complicate matters further, both conservative and liberal policy and

social science literature are laced with statistics, tables, and graphs meant to represent some aspect of the illicit drug market, lending a quantitative authority to a fundamentally unknowable phenomenon. The political scientist Peter Andreas, for instance, points out that "official" estimates of the value of the global illegal drug trade are often based on slipshod methodology that results in comically disparate figures that swing wildly from $45 billion to $500 billion dollars annually. In any other data-driven analysis, a margin of error hovering above 1,000 percent is preposterous, yet the grave tone that inflects most high-level drug talk helps obscure the fundamental epistemological problem of drug history: there is an enormous amount of information that scholars and policymakers alike simply cannot know. See Andreas, "Politics of Measuring Illicit Flows and Effectiveness," 24–25.

80. Craig, "Operation Intercept," 571.

81. Another challenging aspect of drug history is the vague and arbitrary nature of categories of psychoactive substances. The historian Paul Gootenberg warns of the analytic trap of "talking like a state" or of unselfconsciously using the same vocabulary and categories that government bodies and agencies use when they discuss outlawed drugs. Histories of commodities, too, remind us that alkaloids such as caffeine were once demonized for their psychoactive properties, and the well-trod story of Prohibition's backfire does not vouch for the salubriousness of alcohol, only the impotence of criminalizing it. Gootenberg, "Talking about the Flow," 13; Pendergrast, *Uncommon Grounds*; Mintz, *Sweetness and Power*; Courtwright, *Forces of Habit*; and Okrent, *Last Call*.

82. Doyle, "Operation Intercept."

83. The studies I have drawn on the most to inform my understanding of drug history are Gootenberg, *Andean Cocaine*; McCoy, *Politics of Heroin*; Campos, *Home Grown*; Frydl, *Drug Wars in America*; Andreas, *Border Games*; and Andreas and Nadelmann, *Policing the Globe*.

84. See Dunn, *Militarization of the U.S.-Mexico Border*.

85. "Mexico Is Asked to Help Combat Drug Smuggling," *New York Times*, September 9, 1969.

86. The intuitive, seemingly "self-evident" nature of policing strategies has been a core characteristic of criminal justice paradigms since the 1970s and 1980s. See Garland, *Culture of Control*.

87. "Drive on Border Smuggling Begun," *Los Angeles Times*, September 22, 1969.

88. Ibid.

89. Belair, "Operation Intercept."

90. "Mexico Is Asked to Help Combat Drug Smuggling," *New York Times*, September 9, 1969.

91. "Border Searches and the Fourth Amendment," 1007–1010.

92. "Dope Checks at Border Will Go On Indefinitely," *Los Angeles Times*, September 29, 1969.

93. Ibid.

94. Belair, "U.S. Bows to Mexican Demands."

95. "Drive on Border Smuggling Begun," *Los Angeles Times*, September 22, 1969.

96. Belair, "Operation Intercept."

97. "Drug Drive Opens at Mexico Border," *New York Times*, September 22, 1969.

98. Salinas Alvarez, *Historia de los caminos de México*, 3:212, 222.

99. Here I am using the idea of uneven development to describe the concrete imbalances of transportation infrastructure in Mexico. David Harvey has a much more complex, though related, discussion of his "theory of uneven geographical development" under capitalism. See Harvey, *Spaces of Global Capitalism*, 71–116; and *A Brief History of Neoliberalism*, 87–119.

100. Salinas Alvarez, *Historia de los caminos de México*, 4:33.

101. Díaz, *Border Contraband*; Andreas, *Smuggler Nation*.

102. In the case of illicit drugs in particular, Alfred McCoy distinguishes between "perfect" and "imperfect" coercion by states. He argues that in heavily managed economies, as in the case of certain European colonial holdings and certain communist and authoritarian regimes, perfect coercion, that is, draconian and deeply illiberal police responses to drug trafficking, have been effective at stamping out contraband markets, though with steep costs to human rights and basic freedoms. See McCoy, *Politics of Heroin*, 455–459.

103. Lawrence, "History from Below," 269.

104. The historian of US foreign relations Gaddis Smith notes that after World War II, Mexico existed entirely outside the threat of intervention under the Monroe Doctrine precisely because conditions in the United States were so dependent on Mexican labor markets and resource exchange. See Smith, *Last Years of the Monroe Doctrine*, 220–221, 225, and especially 228.

105. Lorey, *United States-Mexico Border Statistics*, Table 900, pg. 183.

106. Domínguez and Fernández de Castro, *United States and Mexico*, 138.

107. Lorey, *United States-Mexico Border Statistics*, Table 1500, pg. 329.

108. Ibid., Table 604, pg. 124.

109. Ibid., Table 1701, pg. 367. This number pales in comparison to today's post-NAFTA trade relationship. In 2012, for instance, the United States imported $277 billion worth of goods from Mexico and exported $216 billion, making Mexico the United States' third-largest trading partner.

110. Ibid., Table 105, pg. 30.

111. Craig, "Operation Intercept," 567. One theory of Operation Intercept's strategic motivation maintains that it was designed precisely to provoke the Mexican government to "do something" about drug production there. Though probably partially true, this perspective still did not recognize that one cannot hurt commerce in Mexico without eventually wounding commerce in the United States.

112. Robert T. Hudgins interview by Oscar J. Martínez and James Merchant, 1977, "Interview no. 425," Institute of Oral History, 8–9.

113. Ibid., 24.

114. Bob Ybarra interview by Michelle L. Gomilla, 1994, "Interview no. 847," Institute of Oral History, 42–43.

115. Arthur L. Adams interview by Jim Marchant and Oscar J. Martínez, August 10, 1977, "Interview No. 646," Institute of Oral History, 464, 69.

116. Héctor Chánez Aragón interview by Margarita Cázares, 1977, "Interview no. 545," Institute of Oral History, 1–2, 4, 10–12.

117. René Mascarenas Miranda interview by Oscar J. Martínez, 1976, "Interview no. 234," Institute of Oral History, 230–232.

118. Belair, "Operation Intercept."

119. Onis, "U.S. Drug Search Irks Diaz Ordaz."

120. "Mexican President Calls Searches at Border a 'Mistake.'"

121. "Secret Memorandum, Operation Intercept," Folder (Mexico-Operation Intercept), Box 3, Records of the Department of State, Bureau of Inter-American Affairs, Deputy Assistant Secretary, Subject and Country Files, 1968–1975, Department of State Central Files, Record Group 59.

BUILDING THE BORDER OF TODAY

1. This physical infrastructure constituted one part of a strategic plan developed in 1993 by the Border Patrol El Paso Sector Chief Silvestre Reyes, then adopted by San Diego Sector Chief Gustavo de la Viña in 1994. It was based on increases in manpower and the "forward deployment" of Border Patrol agents to the international border. This all amounted to a strategy of "prevention through deterrence." See Dunn, *Blockading the Border*; Nevins, *Operation Gatekeeper*; *2012–2016 Border Patrol Strategic Plan*, 4.

2. Waterhouse, *Lobbying America*; Cameron and Tomlin, *The Making of NAFTA*.

3. Dunn, *Militarization of the U.S.-Mexico Border*; Dunn, *Blockading the Border*; Andreas, *Border Games*; Nevins, *Operation Gatekeeper*; De León, *Land of Open Graves*; Escalante Gonzalbo, *El homicidio en México*; Massey, Durand, and Malone, *Beyond Smoke and Mirrors*; Nadelmann, *Cops across Borders*.

4. Sassen, *Territory, Authority, Rights*; Sassen, *Expulsions*; Brown, "American Nightmare"; Brown, *Walled States, Waning Sovereignty*; Garland, *Culture of Control*; Balko, *Rise of the Warrior Cop*; Harvey, *Spaces of Global Capitalism*.

5. Dear, *Why Walls Won't Work*; Dunn, *Militarization of the U.S.-Mexico Border*; Dunn, *Blockading the Border*; Nevins and Dunn, "Barricading the Border"; Martínez, "Border Conflict, Border Fences"; Jones, *Border Walls*; Rael, *Borderwall as Architecture*.

6. McCoy, *Politics of Heroin*; Frydl, *Drug Wars in America*; Campos, *Home Grown*; Astorga Almanza, *Drogas sin fronteras*; Astorga Almanza, *El siglo de las drogas*; Astorga Almanza, "Cocaine in Mexico"; Astorga Almanza, *Seguridad, traficantes y militares*; Gootenberg, *Andean Cocaine*; Maier, "Consigning the Twentieth

Century to History"; Maier, "Transformations of Territoriality"; Maier, *Once Within Borders*.

7. "Invasive Species Summary Project: Saltcedar (*Tamarix ramosissima*)," http://www.columbia.edu/itc/cerc/danoff-burg/invasion_bio/inv_spp_summ/Tamarix_ramosissima.html.

8. J. F. Friedkin, Commissioner, "Technical Summaries of Projects along the International Boundary between the United States and Mexico," April 1979, revised January 1981, Box 1, TR 0076–15–0012, Series 902–01b (IBWC Project Planning, Design, and Construction Case Files), Records of the International Boundary and Water Commission, Record Group 76.

9. "Minute No. 262, Recommendations for Works to Preserve for the Rio Grande Its Character as the International Boundary in the Reach from Cajoncitos, Chihuahua to Haciendita, Texas," International Boundary and Water Commission United States and Mexico, December 26, 1979, Ciudad Juárez, Chih., https://www.ibwc.gov/Files/Minutes/Min262.pdf.

10. Treaty to Resolve Pending Boundary Differences and Maintain the Rio Grande and Colorado River as the International Boundary between the United States of America and Mexico, signed at México, November 23, 1970, T.I.A.S. 7313.

11. J. F. Friedkin, Commissioner, "Technical Summaries of Projects along the International Boundary between the United States and Mexico," April 1979, revised January 1981, Box 1, TR 0076–15–0012, Series 902–01b (IBWC Project Planning, Design, and Construction Case Files), Records of the International Boundary and Water Commission, Record Group 76.

12. Ibid.

13. Ibid.

14. Ibid.

15. Ibid.

16. Johnson, *Revolution in Texas*; Foley, *The White Scourge*; Montejano, *Anglos and Mexicans*; Weber, *From South Texas to the Nation*; Carrigan and Webb, *Forgotten Dead*.

17. J. F. Friedkin, Commissioner, "Technical Summaries of Projects along the International Boundary between the United States and Mexico," April 1979, revised January 1981, Box 1, TR 0076–15–0012, Series 902–01b (IBWC Project Planning, Design, and Construction Case Files), Records of the International Boundary and Water Commission, Record Group 76.

18. "Brownsville Port of Entry." Map.

19. J. F. Friedkin, Commissioner, "Technical Summaries of Projects along the International Boundary between the United States and Mexico," April 1979, revised January 1981, Box 1, TR 0076–15–0012, Series 902–01b (IBWC Project Planning, Design, and Construction Case Files), Records of the International Boundary and Water Commission, Record Group 76.

20. "San Ysidro Port of Entry." Map.

21. J. F. Friedkin, Commissioner, "Technical Summaries of Projects along the International Boundary between the United States and Mexico," April 1979,

revised January 1981, Box 1, TR 0076–15–0012, Series 902–01b (IBWC Project Planning, Design, and Construction Case Files), Records of the International Boundary and Water Commission, Record Group 76.

22. There is no discussion in this document of how they arrived at this sinister number.

23. J. F. Friedkin, Commissioner, "Technical Summaries of Projects along the International Boundary between the United States and Mexico," April 1979, revised January 1981, Box 1, TR 0076–15–0012, Series 902–01b (IBWC Project Planning, Design, and Construction Case Files), Records of the International Boundary and Water Commission, Record Group 76.

24. Ibid.

25. Martínez, "Border Conflict, Border Fences," 270.

26. Nevins and Dunn, "Barricading the Border," 22.

27. Martínez, "Border Conflict, Border Fences," 270–271; Crewdson, "Plans for 'Berlin Wall.'"

28. "Western Boundary Fence Project, Engineering Office, Case File," [1978?], Box 1, TR 0076–2013–0020, Series 902–01 (IBWC Project Planning, Design, and Construction Case Files), Records of the International Boundary and Water Commission, Record Group 76.

29. Ibid.

30. Ibid.

31. Ibid.

32. Ibid.

33. Ibid.

34. Ibid.

35. De León, *Land of Open Graves*, 31–37; Regan, *The Death of Josseline*, 148–166.

36. Andreas, *Border Games*; Nevins, *Operation Gatekeeper*; Massey, Durand, and Malone, *Beyond Smoke and Mirrors*; Andreas and Nadelmann, *Policing the Globe*; De León, *Land of Open Graves*.

37. Box 3, Folder 6, doc. #1274, Records of the Ferrocarril Noroeste de México, 1910–1919.

38. Nevins, *Operation Gatekeeper*, 151–164; Chavez, *The Latino Threat*, 21–43; Jones, *Border Walls*, 31–45; Astorga Almanza, "Cocaine in Mexico."

39. Brown, *Walled States, Waning Sovereignty*, 24.

40. Ibid., 8–19, 24.

41. Nevins, *Operation Gatekeeper*.

42. Haddal, Kim, and Garcia, *Border Security*, 2.

43. Ibid., 22.

44. Ibid., 26; *Fencing the Border*, 2–3.

45. *Fencing the Border*, 2–3.

46. Jones, *Border Walls*, 31–45.

47. Kang, *INS on the Line*, 168–180.

48. Haddal, Kim, and Garcia, *Border Security*, 6–7.

49. *Fencing the Border*, 25–26.

50. Ibid., 11–12, 63–64.

51. Ibid., 28–29.

52. Haddal, Kim, and Garcia, *Border Security*, 18.

53. *Fencing the Border*, 67; Haddal, Kim, and Garcia, *Border Security*, 20.

54. "Border Fence K, El Paso," n.p.

55. *Securing the Border*.

56. Photograph by the author.

57. Photograph by the author.

58. *Fencing the Border*, 49, 53.

59. Photograph by the author.

60. De León, *Land of Open Graves*, 23–37.

61. Jackson, *A Sense of Place, a Sense of Time*, 5.

62. Flores, *Horizontal Yellow*, 125–165.

63. Haddal, Kim, and Garcia, *Border Security*, 17.

64. Jackson, *Discovering the Vernacular Landscape*, 133–134.

65. Bergeron, "Carrizo Cane Might Stem Illegal Crossings," n.p.

66. Dunn, *Militarization of the U.S.-Mexico Border*, 183.

67. *2012–2016 Border Patrol Strategic Plan*, 14.

68. Ibid., 15; Masco, *The Nuclear Borderlands*, 10, 94.

69. *Project 28*, 6; *Secure Border Initiative*.

70. *Border Patrol*, 2, 5, 22–23.

71. Haddal, Kim, and Garcia, *Border Security*. See also Massey, Durand, and Malone, *Beyond Smoke and Mirrors*.

72. Garland, *Culture of Control*, 157.

73. Gavrilis, *Dynamics of Interstate Boundaries*, 5.

74. W. D. Smithers Collection of Photographs, Box 20, Image 2923.

75. Haber et al., *Mexico since 1980*, 66–77.

76. Salinas Alvarez, *Historia de los caminos de México*, 4:119–121; "Programa nacional de modernización de la infraestructura del transporte," 185–190.

77. *United States-Mexico Cross-Border Long-Haul Trucking Pilot Program Report to Congress*, 4.

78. Ibid., 1, 3.

79. Overall, the number of Mexican-domiciled and Mexican-owned-but-US-domiciled motor carriers with authority to operate in the United States was much higher. As of 2014, there were some 7,586 carriers with the license to operate in the commercial zone, though just over 4,000 were active, while another 1,660 were permitted to operate in other parts of United States, though just under 1,000 were active. Ibid., 3.

80. Federal Motor Carrier Safety Administration, *United States-Mexico Cross-Border Long-Haul Trucking Pilot Program*.

81. Jackson, *A Sense of Place, a Sense of Time*, 189–190.

82. "International Bridges and Border Crossing United States Names." Map.

International Boundary & Water Commission, United States and Mexico, United States Section, April 27, 2017, https://www.ibwc.gov/Files/Bridge_Border_Crossings_.pdf.

83. "Texas-Mexico International Bridges and Border Crossings, Existing and Proposed 2015," ii.

84. Geller, "Anzalduas Bridge Is a Go"; Lorena Figueroa, "Road Work Begins."

85. "Santa Teresa Port of Entry, NM, 1985." Map; "Santa Teresa Port of Entry, NM, 2014." Map.

86. Post, "San Ysidro Land Port's Team Tames the Logistical Monster."

87. Jackson, *Discovering the Vernacular Landscape*, 23.

88. Ibid., 24.

89. For detailed descriptions of how migrants blaze unauthorized trails through remote landscapes, see Urrea, *The Devil's Highway*, and De León, *Land of Open Graves*.

90. Jackson, *Discovering the Vernacular Landscape*, 22.

91. Haddal, Kim, and Garcia, *Border Security*, 33.

92. De León, *Land of Open Graves*, 3.

93. Haddal, Kim, and Garcia, *Border Security*, 33.

94. Andreas, *Border Games*, 93.

95. Maier, *Once Within Borders*; Maier, "Transformations of Territoriality"; Maier, "Consigning the Twentieth Century to History"; Sassen, *Territory, Authority, Rights*.

96. Garland, *Culture of Control*.

97. Brown, "American Nightmare."

EPILOGUE

1. It is worth pointing out here, however, that a construction company was instrumental in consolidating this ecozone. CEMEX, a Mexican multinational corporation that is the third-largest cement producer in the world, acquired 195,000 acres of land as part of the preserve. See Robles Gil, "El Carmen," 38–39.

BIBLIOGRAPHY

ARCHIVAL SOURCES

Archivo Histórico Genaro Estrada, Secretaría de Relaciones Exteriores, Mexico City.

Fondo Documental Aguas Nacionales, Comisión Nacional del Agua (CONAGUA), Archivo Histórico y Biblioteca Central del Agua, Mexico City.

Institute of Oral History, University of Texas at El Paso.

Record Group 45: Records of the Office of Naval Intelligence, 1887–1927, National Archives at Washington, DC.

Record Group 59: Department of State Central Files, National Archives at College Park, MD.

Record Group 76: Records of the International Boundary and Water Commission, National Archives at Fort Worth.

Record Group 77: Records of the Army Corps of Engineers, Fort worth Division, National Archives at Fort Worth.

Record Group 85: Records of the Immigration and Naturalization Service, 1787–2004, National Archives at Washington, DC.

Record Group 85: Records of the Immigration and Naturalization Service, Subject and Policy Files, 1893–1957, National Archives at Washington, DC.

Record Group 291: Records of the Federal Property and Resource Management (GSA), National Archives at Fort Worth.

Record Group 393: Records of United States Army Continental Commands, 1821–1920, National Archives at Washington, DC.

Records of the Ferrocarril Noroeste de México, 1910–1919, Benson Latin American Collection, University of Texas Libraries, University of Texas at Austin.

W. D. Smithers Collection of Photographs, Harry Ransom Center, University of Texas at Austin.

PUBLISHED PRIMARY SOURCES

Act of August 19, 1935, 49 Stat. 660, Public Law 286, 22 U.S.C. 277.

Annual Report of the Attorney General of the United States, United States Department of Justice, 1912. Washington, DC: Government Printing Office, 1912.

Annual Report of the Attorney General of the United States, United States Department of Justice, 1913. Washington, DC: Government Printing Office, 1913.

Annual Report of the Secretary of War for the Year 1911.

Annual Report of the Secretary of War for the Year 1912.

Annual Report of the Secretary of War, 1913. Washington, DC: Government Printing Office, 1913.

Annual Report of the Secretary of War, 1915. Washington, DC: Government Printing Office, 1915.

Annual Report of the Secretary of War, United States War Department, 1910. Washington, DC: Government Printing Office, 1910.

Annual Report of the Secretary of War, United States War Department, 1911. Washington, DC: Government Printing Office, 1911.

Annual Report of the Secretary of War, United States War Department, 1912. Washington, DC: Government Printing Office, 1912.

Annual Report of the Secretary of War, United States War Department, 1914. Washington, DC: Government Printing Office, 1914.

Annual Report of the Secretary of War, United States War Department, 1915. Washington, DC: Government Printing Office, 1915.

Annual Report of the Secretary of War, United States War Department, 1916. Washington, DC: Government Printing Office, 1916.

Annual Report of the Secretary of War, United States War Department, 1917. Washington, DC: Government Printing Office, 1917.

Annual Report of the Secretary of War, United States War Department, 1919. Washington, DC: Government Printing Office, 1919.

Belair, Felix, Jr. "Operation Intercept: Success on Land, Futility in the Air." *New York Times,* October 2, 1969.

———. "U.S. Bows to Mexican Demands; Drug Smuggling Drive Is Eased; U.S. to Ease Drive on Illicit Drugs." *New York Times,* October 11, 1969.

Bergeron, Angelle. "Carrizo Cane Might Stem Illegal Crossings along the Rio Grande, but the 'Natural Barrier' Is Unwelcome in Texas." *Texas Construction* 17, no. 4 (2009): N.p.

"Binational Trade Corridors (Mexico-United States) from Binational Border Transportation Planning and Programming Study, Task 2, 1998 (U.S. Department of Transportation, Federal Highway Administration)." Map. Perry-Castañeda Library Map Collection, University of Texas Libraries, University of Texas at Austin.

"Border Fence K, El Paso." *Texas Construction* 17, no. 12 (2009): N.p.

Border Patrol: Available Data on Interior Checkpoints Suggest Differences in Sector Performance. Washington, DC: U.S. Government Accountability Office, 2005.

"Brownsville Port of Entry." Map. United States-Mexico Border, Color Image Map Series, US Geological Survey and US Customs Service, 1979–1983. Perry-Castañeda Library Map Collection, University of Texas Libraries, University of Texas at Austin.

"Challenges." Wellton-Mohawk Irrigation and Drainage District, http://www.wmidd.org/challenges.html, accessed February 18, 2018.

Convention between the United States of America and the United States of Mexico Touching the International Boundary Line Where It Follows the Bed of the Rio Grande and the Rio Colorado. Concluded at Washington, November 12, 1884. https://www.loc.gov/law/help/us-treaties/bevans/b-mx-ust000009-0865.pdf.

Crewdson, John M. "Plans for 'Berlin Wall.'" *New York Times*, November 7, 1978.

"Dope Checks at Border Will Go On Indefinitely." *Los Angeles Times*, September 29, 1969.

"Drive on Border Smuggling Begun." *Los Angeles Times*, September 22, 1969.

"Drug Drive Opens at Mexico Border." *New York Times*, September 22, 1969.

Eisenhower, Dwight D. *At Ease: Stories I Tell to Friends*. N.p.: Eastern Acorn Press, 1967.

Federal Motor Carrier Safety Administration. *United States-Mexico Cross-Border Long-Haul Trucking Pilot Program: Aggregate Data Chart through 10/10/2014–Revised 10/24/2014*, 2014. https://www.fmcsa.dot.gov/sites/fmcsa.dot.gov/files/docs/US-Mexico%20Cross-Border%20Long-Haul%20Trucking%20Pilot%20Program%20Report%20FINAL%20January%202015.pdf.

Fencing the Border: Construction Options and Strategic Placement. Hearing Before the Subcommittee on Economic Security, Infrastructure Protections, and Cybersecurity of the Committee on Homeland Security and the Subcommittee on Criminal Justice, Drug Policy, and Human Resources of the Committee on Government Reform, US House of Representatives, 109th Cong., 2nd sess., July 20, 2006.

Figueroa, Lorena. "Road Work Begins on Mexican Side of Tornillo-Guadalupe International Bridge." *El Paso Times*, May 17, 2015.

Follansbee, Robert, and H. J. Dean. *Water Resources of the Rio Grande Basin, 1888–1913.* Water Supply Paper 358, Department of the Interior, United States Geological Survey. Washington, DC: Government Printing Office, 1915.

"The Frontier Region of Mexico: Notes to Accompany a Map of the Frontier." *Geographical Review* 3, no. 1 (January 1917): 16–27.

Geller, Marc B. "Anzalduas Bridge Is a Go." *The Monitor*, March 22, 2006.

Green, Duff C., and Ronnie C. Tyler. "Exploring the Rio Grande: Lt. Duff C. Green's Report of 1852." *Arizona and the West* 10, no. 1 (Spring 1968): 43–60.

Haddal, Chad C., Yule Kim, and Michael John Garcia. *Border Security: Barriers along the U.S. International Border*. Washington, DC: Congressional Research Service, 2009.

Hill, Robert T. "Running the Cañons of the Rio Grande: A Chapter of Recent Exploration." *Century Magazine*, January 1901, 371–387.

Hinkle, Stacy C. *Wings over the Border: The Army Air Service Armed Patrol of the United States-Mexico Border, 1919–1921*. El Paso: Texas Western Press, 1970.

"History: El Morillo Drain." Rio Grande Regional Water Authority. http://rgrwa. org/index.php/projects/el-morillo-drain, accessed February 7, 2018.

Huston, James A. *The Sinews of War: Army Logistics, 1775–1953*. Washington, DC: Office of the Chief of Military History, United States Army, 1966.

"Invasive Species Summary Project: Saltcedar *(Tamarix ramosissima)*." http://www. columbia.edu/itc/cerc/danoff-burg/invasion_bio/inv_spp_summ/Tamarix_ ramosissima.html, accessed September 1, 2018.

Jefferson, Mark. "The Revolution and the Mexican Plateau." *Bulletin of the American Geographic Society* 46, no. 6 (1914): 436–437.

Lawson, L. M. "Stabilizing the Rio Grande." *Scientific American* 155, no. 2 (1936): 66–68.

"Location & General Description." Wellton-Mohawk Irrigation and Drainage District. http://www.wmidd.org/general.html, accessed February 18, 2018.

Lorey, David E., ed. *United States–Mexico Border Statistics since 1900*. Los Angeles: UCLA Latin American Center Publications, 1990.

Memoria de la Sección mexicana de la Comisión Internacional de Límites entre México y los Estados Unidos que restableció los monumentos de El Paso al Pacífico; bajo la dirección por parte de México del ingeniero Jacobo Blanco, jefe de la Comisión Mexicana. New York: Imprenta de John Polhemus, 1901.

"Mexican President Calls Searches at Border a 'Mistake.'" *Los Angeles Times*, October 1, 1969.

"Mexico Is Asked to Help Combat Drug Smuggling." *New York Times*, September 9, 1969.

Convention between the United States of America and the United States of Mexico Touching the International Boundary Line Where It Follows the Bed of the Rio Colorado. Concluded at Washington, DC, November 12, 1884, by the president of the United States.

Minute No. 129: "Report on the Rio Grande Rectification/Informe sobre rectificación del Río Bravo." Mexico City: International Boundary Commission/ Comisión Internacional de Límites, July 31, 1930.

Nixon, Richard. "Remarks at the Dedication of the Amistad Dam on the Rio Grande." September 8, 1969. No. 354. Online by Gerhard Peters and John T. Woolley, *The American Presidency Project*. http://www.presidency.ucsb.edu/ ws/?pid=2224.

Onis, Juan de. "U.S. Drug Search Irks Diaz Ordaz; Mexican Hails Astronauts, Notes 'Wall of Suspicion.'" *New York Times*, September 30, 1969.

Orozco y Berra, Manuel. *Apuntes para la historia de la geografía en México*. Mexico City: Imp. de F. Díaz de León, 1881.

Planos de la línea divisoria entre México y los Estados Unidos del Norte al oeste de El Paso, levantados bajo la dirección por parte de México del Ingeniero Jacobo Blanco, jefe de la comisión mexicana, 1891–1896. New York: Impr. de J. Polhemus, 1901.

Post, Nadine M. "San Ysidro Land Port's Team Tames the Logistical Monster." *Engineering News-Record*, December 31. 2014.

"Programa nacional de modernización de la infraestructura del transporte,

1990–1994." *Revista de Adminstración Pública* (Universidad Nacional Autónoma de México) 79 (1991): 181–213.

Project 28: Lessons Learned and the Future of SBINET. Subcommitte on Border, Maritime, and Global Counterterrorism and the Subcommittee on Management, Investigations, and Oversight of the Committee on Homeland Security, House of Representatives, February 27, 2008.

Report of the Boundary Commission upon the Survey and Re-Marking of the Boundary between the United States and Mexico West of the Rio Grande, 1891–1896. Washington, DC: Government Printing Office, 1898.

Revolutions in Mexico. Subcommittee of the Committee on Foreign Relations, US Senate, 62nd Cong., 2nd sess., 1913.

"San Ysidro Port of Entry." Map. United States-Mexico Border, Color Image Map Series, U.S. Geological Survey and U.S. Customs Service, 1979–1983. Perry-Castañeda Library Map Collection, University of Texas Libraries, University of Texas at Austin.

"Santa Teresa Port of Entry, NM, 1985." Map. Google Earth Pro, October 23, 2017.

"Santa Teresa Port of Entry, NM, 2014." Map. Google Earth Pro, October 23, 2017.

Secure Border Initiative: DHS Needs to Strengthen Management and Oversight of Its Prime Contractor. Washington, DC: United States Government Accountability Office, 2010.

Securing the Border: Fencing, Infrastructure, and Technology Force Multipliers. Committee on Homeland Security and Govermental Affairs, U.S. Senate, 114th Cong., 1st sess., May 13, 2015.

"Texas-Mexico International Bridges and Border Crossings, Existing and Proposed 2015." Austin: International Relations Section of the Governmental Relations Division, Texas Department of Transportation, 2015.

To Establish a Border Patrol. Committee on the Judiciary, House of Representatives, 69th Congress, First Session on H.R. 9731, April 12 and 19, 1926. Washington, DC: U.S. Government Printing Office, 1926.

Treaty to Resolve Pending Boundary Differences and Maintain the Rio Grande and Colorado River as the International Boundary between the United States of America and Mexico, signed at México, November 23, 1970. T.I.A.S. 7313.

2012–2016 Border Patrol Strategic Plan. U.S. Customs and Border Protection, U.S. Department of Homeland Security, May 9, 2012. https://nemo.cbp.gov/obp/bp_strategic_plan.pdf.

United States-Mexico Cross-Border Long-Haul Trucking Pilot Program Report to Congress. Washington, DC: U.S. Department of Transportation and the Federal Motor Carrier Safety Adminstration, January 2015.

PUBLISHED SOURCES

Aboites Aguilar, Luis. *El agua de la nación: Una historia política de México (1888–1946).* Mexico City: CIESAS, 1998.

———. "Historias de ríos: Un modo de hacer historia agraria en México." In *Agua y tierra en México, siglos XIX y XX*, 2 vols., edited by Antonio Escobar Ohmstede, Martín Sánchez Rodríguez, and Ana María Gutiérrez Rivas, 1:85–102. Zamora, Michoacán: El Colegio de Michoacán, El Colegio de San Luis, 2008.

———. *La irrigación revolucionaria: Historia del sistema nacional de riego del Río Conchos, Chihuahua, 1927–1938*. Mexico City: SEP/CIESAS, 1988.

Adelman, Jeremy. "Latin American *Longues Durées*." *Latin American Research Review* 39, no. 1 (2004): 223–237.

Adelman, Jeremy, and Stephen Aron. "From Borderlands to Borders: Empires, Nation-States, and the Peoples in between in North American History." *The American Historical Review* 104, no. 3 (June 1999): 814–841.

Aguila, Jaime R. "Mexican/U.S. Immigration Policy prior to the Great Depression." *Diplomatic History* 31, no. 2 (April 2007): 207–225.

Alexander, Nancy. *Father of Texas Geology: Robert T. Hill*. Dallas: SMU Press, 1976.

Andreas, Peter. *Border Games: Policing the U.S.-Mexico Divide*. Ithaca, NY: Cornell University Press, 2000.

———. *Border Games: Policing the U.S.-Mexico Divide*. 2nd ed. Ithaca: Cornell University Press, 2009.

———. "The Politics of Measuring Illicit Flows and Policy Effectiveness." In *Sex, Drugs, and Body Counts*, edited by Peter Andreas and Kelly M. Greenhill, 23–45. Ithaca, NY: Cornell University Press, 2010.

———. *Smuggler Nation: How Illicit Trade Made America*. New York: Oxford University Press, 2014.

Andreas, Peter, and Ethan Avram Nadelmann. *Policing the Globe: Criminalization and Crime Control in International Relations*. Oxford: Oxford University Press, 2006.

Andrés, Benny J., Jr. *Power and Control in the Imperial Valley: Nature, Agribusiness, and Workers on the California Borderland, 1900–1940*. College Station: Texas A&M University Press, 2015.

Anzaldúa, Gloria. *Borderlands/La Frontera: The New Mestiza*. San Francisco: Aunt Lute Books, 1999 [1987].

Arreola, Daniel D., and James R. Curtis. *The Mexican Border Cities: Landscape Anatomy and Place Personality*. Tucson: University of Arizona Press, 1994.

Astorga Almanza, Luis. "Cocaine in Mexico: A Prelude to 'Los Narcos.'" In *Cocaine: Global Histories*, edited by Paul Gootenberg, 183–191. New York: Routledge, 1999.

———. *Drogas sin fronteras*. Línea Académica. Mexico City: Grijalbo Mondadori, 2003.

———. *El siglo de las drogas: El narcotráfico, del Porfiriato al nuevo milenio*. Mexico City: Plaza y Janés, 2005.

———. *Seguridad, traficantes y militares: El poder y la sombra*. Mexico City: Tusquets, 2012.

Balderrama, Francisco E., and Raymond Rodríguez. *Decade of Betrayal: Mexican Repatriation in the 1930s*. Albuquerque: University of New Mexico Press, 2006.

Balko, Radley. *Rise of the Warrior Cop: The Militarization of America's Police Forces.* New York: PublicAffairs, 2014.

Bannon, John Frances. *The Spanish Borderlands Frontier, 1513–1821.* Histories of the American Frontier series. Albuquerque: University of New Mexico Press, 1974.

Berbusse, Edward J. "Neutrality-Diplomacy of the United States and Mexico, 1910–1911." *The Americas* 12, no. 3 (January 1956): 265–283.

Bolton, Herbert E. *The Spanish Borderlands: A Chronicle of Old Florida and the Southwest.* Albuquerque: University of New Mexico Press, 1996 [1919].

"Border Searches and the Fourth Amendment." *Yale Law Journal* 77, no. 5 (April 1968): 1007–1018.

Boyer, Christopher. *Political Landscapes: Forests, Conservation, and Community in Mexico.* Durham: Duke University Press, 2015.

Braudel, Fernand. "History and the Social Sciences: The Longue Durée." *Review (Fernand Braudel Center)* 32, no. 2 (2009 [1958]): 171–203.

Brown, Wendy. "American Nightmare: Neoliberalism, Neoconservatism, and De-Democratization." *Political Theory* 34, no. 6 (December 2006): 690–714.

———. *Walled States, Waning Sovereignty.* Cambridge, MA: Zone Books, 2010.

Bustamante, Jorge A. "El programa fronterizo de maquiladoras: Observaciones para una evaluación." *Foro Internacional* 16, no. 2 (1975): 183–204.

Cadava, Geraldo L. "Borderlands of Modernity and Abandonment: The Lines within Ambos Nogales and the Tohono O'odham Nation." *Journal of American History* 98, no. 2 (September 2011): 362–383.

———. *Standing on Common Ground: The Making of a Sunbelt Borderland.* Cambridge, MA: Harvard University Press, 2013.

Calavita, Kitty. *Inside the State: The Bracero Program, Immigration, and the I.N.S.* New Orleans: Quid Pro Books, 2010.

Cameron, Maxwell A., and Brian W. Tomlin. *The Making of NAFTA: How the Deal Was Done.* Ithaca, NY: Cornell University Press, 2000.

Campos, Isaac. *Home Grown: Marijuana and the Origins of Mexico's War on Drugs.* Chapel Hill: University of North Carolina Press, 2012.

Carrigan, William D., and Clive Webb. *Forgotten Dead: Mob Violence against Mexicans in the United States, 1848–1928.* New York: Oxford University Press, 2013.

Chavez, Leo R. *The Latino Threat: Constructing Immigrants, Citizens, and the Nation.* Stanford, CA: Stanford University Press, 2008.

Coakley, Robert W. *The Role of Federal Military Forces in Domestic Disorders, 1789–1878.* Washington, DC: Center of Military History, United States Army, 2011.

Coatsworth, John H. *Growth against Development: The Economic Impact of Railroads in Porfirian Mexico.* DeKalb: Northern Illinois University Press, 1981.

Cohen, Deborah. *Braceros: Migrant Citizens and Transnational Subjects in the Postwar United States and Mexico.* Chapel Hill: University of North Carolina Press, 2011.

Cornell, Sarah E. "Citizens of Nowhere: Fugitive Slaves and Free African

Americans in Mexico, 1833–1857." *Journal of American History* 100, no. 2 (September 2013): 351–374.

Courtwright, David T. *Forces of Habit: Drugs and the Making of the Modern World.* Cambridge: Harvard University Press, 2001.

Craig, Richard B. "Operation Intercept: The International Politics of Pressure." *Review of Politics* 42, no. 4 (October 1980): 556–580.

Davis, Diana K. "Deserts." In *The Oxford Handbook of Environmental History*, edited by Andrew C. Isenberg, 108–132. New York: Oxford University Press, 2014.

Dear, Michael. *Why Walls Won't Work: Repairing the US-Mexico Divide.* New York: Oxford University Press, 2013.

DeLay, Brian. *War of a Thousand Deserts: Indian Raids and the U.S.-Mexican War.* New Haven: Yale University Press, 2008.

De León, Jason. *The Land of Open Graves: Living and Dying on the Migrant Trail.* Berkeley: University of California Press, 2015.

Díaz, George T. *Border Contraband: A History of Smuggling across the Rio Grande.* Austin: University of Texas Press, 2015.

Domínguez, Jorge I., and Rafael Fernández de Castro. *The United States and Mexico: Between Partnership and Conflict.* Contemporary Inter-American Relations Series. New York: Routledge, 2009.

Doyle, Kate. "Operation Intercept: The Perils of Unilateralism." *The National Security Archive* (2003). https://nsarchive2.gwu.edu/NSAEBB/NSAEBB86/, accessed May 1, 2018.

Dunn, Timothy J. *Blockading the Border and Human Rights: The El Paso Operation That Remade Immigration Enforcement.* Austin: University of Texas Press, 2009.

———. *The Militarization of the U.S.-Mexico Border, 1978–1992: Low-Intensity Conflict Doctrine Comes Home.* CMAS Border and Migration Studies Series. Austin: Center for Mexican American Studies, University of Texas at Austin, 1996.

Emory, Deborah Carley. "Running the Line: Men, Maps, Science, and Art of the United States and Mexico Boundary Survey, 1849–1856." *New Mexico Historical Review* 75, no. 2 (April 2000): 221–265.

Ericson, Anna-Stina. "An Analysis of Mexico's Border Industrialization Program." *Monthly Labor Review* 93, no. 5 (May 1970): 33–40.

Escalante Gonzalbo, Fernando. *El homicidio en México entre 1990 y 2007: Aproximación estadística.* Mexico City: El Colegio de México; Secretaría de Seguridad Pública Federal, 2009.

Escobar, Edward J. *Race, Police, and the Making of a Political Identity: Mexican Americans and the Los Angeles Police Department, 1900–1945.* Berkeley: University of California Press, 1999.

Fiege, Mark. *Irrigated Eden: The Making of an Agricultural Landscape in the American West.* Seattle: University of Washington Press, 1999.

———. *The Republic of Nature: An Environmental History of the United States.* Seattle: University of Washington Press, 2013.

Fitzgerald, David. *A Nation of Emigrants: How Mexico Manages Its Migration.* Berkeley: University of California Press, 2009.

FitzGerald, David Scott, and David Cook-Martín. *Culling the Masses: The Democratic Origins of Racist Immigration Policy in the Americas*. Cambridge, MA: Harvard University Press, 2014.

Flores, Dan. *Horizontal Yellow: Nature and History in the Near Southwest*. Albuquerque: University of New Mexico Press, 1999.

Foley, Neil. *The White Scourge: Mexicans, Blacks, and Poor Whites in Texas Cotton Culture*. Berkeley: University of California Press, 1997.

Frischmann, Brett M. *Infrastructure: The Social Value of Shared Resources*. New York: Oxford University Press, 2012.

Frydl, Kathleen J. *The Drug Wars in America, 1940–1973*. New York: Cambridge University Press, 2013.

Garland, David. *The Culture of Control: Crime and Social Order in Contemporary Society*. Chicago: University of Chicago Press, 2001.

Garza Almanza, Victoriano. *Breve historia ambiental de la frontera México-Estados Unidos, 1889–2010*. Torreón, Coahuila: Talleres de Carmona Impresores, 2011.

Gavrilis, George. *The Dynamics of Interstate Boundaries*. New York: Cambridge University Press, 2008.

Gilderhus, Mark T. "The United States and Carranza, 1917: The Question of *De Jure* Recognition." *The Americas* 29, no. 2 (October 1972): 214–231.

Gillingham, Paul, and Benjamin T. Smith, eds. *Dictablanda: Politics, Work, and Culture in Mexico, 1938–1968*. Durham, NC: Duke University Press, 2014.

Gootenberg, Paul. *Andean Cocaine: The Making of a Global Drug*. Chapel Hill: University of North Carolina Press, 2008.

———. "Talking about the Flow: Drugs, Borders, and the Discourse of Drug Control." *Cultural Critique*, no. 71 (Winter 2009): 13–46.

Graybill, Andrew R. *Policing the Great Plains: Rangers, Mounties, and the North American Frontier, 1875–1910*. Lincoln: University of Nebraska Press, 2007.

Grieb, Kenneth J. "Standard Oil and the Financing of the Mexican Revolution." *California Historical Quarterly* 50, no. 1 (March 1971): 59–71.

Griswold del Castillo, Richard. *The Treaty of Guadalup Hidalgo: A Legacy of Conflict*. Norman: University of Oklahoma Press, 1990.

Guldi, Jo. *Roads to Power: Britain Invents the Infrastructure State*. Cambridge, MA: Harvard University Press, 2012.

Gutiérrez, David. *Walls and Mirrors: Mexican Americans, Mexican Immigrants, and the Politics of Ethnicity*. Berkeley: University of California Press, 1995.

Gutiérrez, Ramón A. *When Jesus Came, the Corn Mothers Went Away: Marriage, Sexuality, and Power in New Mexico, 1500–1846*. Stanford, CA: Stanford University Press, 1991.

Haber, Stephen, Herbert S. Klein, Noel Maurer, and Kevin J. Middlebrook. *Mexico since 1980*. Cambridge: Cambridge University Press, 2008.

Hämäläinen, Pekka, and Samuel Truett. "On Borderlands." *Journal of American History* 98, no. 2 (September 2011): 338–361.

Harris, Charles H., III, and Louis R. Sadler. *The Secret War in El Paso: Mexican*

Revolutionary Intrigue, 1906–1920. Albuquerque: University of New Mexico Press, 2009.

Hart, John Mason. *Empire and Revolution: The Americans in Mexico since the Civil War*. Berkeley: University of California Press, 2002.

Harvey, David. *A Brief History of Neoliberalism*. Oxford: Oxford University Press, 2005.

———. *Spaces of Global Capitalism: Towards a Theory of Uneven Geographical Development*. London: Verso, 2006.

Herrera Pérez, Octavio. *La zona libre: Excepción fiscal y conformación histórica de la frontera norte de México*. Mexico City: Secretaría de Relaciones Exteriores, 2004.

Hewitt, Harry P. "The Mexican Boundary Survey Team: Pedro García Conde in California." *Western Historical Quarterly* 21, no. 2 (May 1990): 171–196.

———. "The Mexican Commission and Its Survey of the Rio Grande River Boundary, 1850–1854." *Southwestern Historical Quarterly* 94, no. 4 (April 1991): 555–580.

Holden, Robert H. *Mexico and the Survey of Public Lands: The Management of Modernization, 1876–1911*. DeKalb: Northern Illinois University Press, 1994.

Hundley, Norris, Jr. *Water and the West: The Colorado River Compact and the Politics of Water in the American West*. 2nd ed. Berkeley: University of California Press, 2009.

Isenberg, Andrew C. *Mining California: An Ecological History*. New York: Hill and Wang, 2006.

Jackson, John Brinckerhoff. *Discovering the Vernacular Landscape*. New Haven, CT: Yale University Press, 1984.

———. *A Sense of Place, a Sense of Time*. New Haven, CT: Yale University Press, 1994.

Jacoby, Karl. *Shadows at Dawn: A Borderlands Massacre and the Violence of History*. New York: Penguin Press, 2008.

Johnson, Benjamin H. "Negotiating North America's New National Borders." In *Borderlands in World History, 1700–1914*, edited by Paul Readman, Cynthia Radding, and Chad Bryant, 27–45. New York: Palgrave Macmillan, 2014.

Johnson, Benjamin H. *Revolution in Texas: How a Forgotten Rebellion and Its Bloody Supression Turned Mexicans into Americans*. New Haven, CT: Yale University Press, 2005.

Johnson, Lyndon B. "Remarks in El Paso at the Inauguration of the New River Channel Completing the Chamizal Boundary Change." December 13, 1968. Online by Gerhard Peters and John T. Woolley, *The American Presidency Project*. http://www.presidency.ucsb.edu/ws/?pid=29275.

Johnston, Robert D. "Beyond 'The West': Regionalism, Liberalism, and the Evasion of Politics in the New Western History." *Rethinking History* 2, no. 2 (1998): 239–277.

Jones, Reece. *Border Walls: Security and the War on Terror in the United States, India, and Israel*. New York: Zed Books, 2012.

Kang, S. Deborah. *The INS on the Line: Making Immigration Law on the US-Mexico Border, 1917–1954*. New York: Oxford University Press, 2017.

Katz, Friedrich. "The Liberal Republic and the Porfiriato, 1867–1910." In *Mexico since Independence*, edited by Leslie Bethell, 49–124. Cambridge: Cambridge University Press, 1991.

———. *The Life and Times of Pancho Villa*. Stanford, CA: Stanford University Press, 1998.

———. "Pancho Villa and the Attack on Columbus, New Mexico." *American Historical Review* 83, no. 1 (February 1978): 101–130.

———. *The Secret War in Mexico: Europe, the United States, and the Mexican Revolution*. Chicago: University of Chicago Press, 1981.

Kelsey, Robin. *Archive Style: Photographs and Illustrations for U.S. Surveys, 1850–1890*. Berkeley: University of California Press, 2007.

Knight, Alan. *The Mexican Revolution*. 2 vols. Cambridge: Cambridge University Press, 1986.

———. *U.S.-Mexican Relations, 1910–1940: An Interpretation*. Monograph Series Book 28/Center for U.S.-Mexican Studies. La Jolla, CA: Center for U.S.-Mexican Studies, University of California, San Diego, 1987.

Kramer, Paul. "A Border Crosses." *New Yorker*, September 20, 2014.

Kuntz Ficker, Sandra. "Mercado interior y vinculación con el exterior: El papel de los ferrocarriles en la economía del Porfiriato." *Historia Mexicana* 45, no. 1 (1995): 39–66.

Lamborn, Alan C., and Stephen P. Mumme. *Statecraft, Domestic Politics, and Foreign Policy Making: The El Chamizal Dispute*. Boulder, CO: Westview Press, 1988.

Laurie, Clayton D., and Ronald H. Cole. *The Role of Federal Military Forces in Domestic Disorders, 1877–1945*. Washington, DC: Center for Military History, 1995.

Lawrence, Mark Atwood. "History from Below: The United States and Latin America in the Nixon Years." In *Nixon in the World: American Foreign Relations, 1969–1977*, edited by Frederick Logevall and Andrew Preston, 269–288. New York: Oxford University Press, 2008.

Lewis, Daniel. *Iron Horse Imperialism: The Southern Pacific of Mexico, 1880–1951*. Tucson: University of Arizona Press, 2007.

Lim, Julian. *Porous Borders: Multiracial Migrations and the Law in the U.S.-Mexico Borderlands*. Chapel Hill: University of North Carolina Press, 2017.

Littlefield, Douglas R. *Conflict on the Rio Grande: Water and the Law, 1879–1939*. Norman: University of Oklahoma Press, 2008.

Lopez, Sarah Lynn. *The Remittance Landscape: Spaces of Migration in Rural Mexico and Urban USA*. Chicago: University of Chicago Press, 2015.

Loza, Mireya. *Defiant Braceros: How Migrant Workers Fought for Racial, Sexual, and Political Freedom*. Chapel Hill: University of North Carolina Press, 2016.

Lytle Hernández, Kelly. *Migra! A History of the U.S. Border Patrol*. Berkeley: University of California Press, 2010.

Maier, Charles S. "Consigning the Twentieth Century to History: Alternative Narratives for the Modern Era." *American Historical Review* 105, no. 3 (June 2000): 807–831.

———. *Once Within Borders: Territories of Power, Wealth, and Belongning since 1500*. Cambridge, MA: Belknap Press of Harvard University Press, 2016.

———. "Transformations of Territoriality, 1600–2000." In *Transnationale Geschichte: Themen, Tendenzen und Theorien*, edited by Gunilla Budde, Sebastian Conrad, and Janz Oliver, 32–55. Göttingen, Germany: Vandenhoeck and Ruprecht, 2010.

Mann, Michael. *The Sources of Social Power*. Vol. 2, *The Rise of Classes and Nation-States, 1760–1914*. New York: Cambridge University Press, 1993.

Marak, Andrae M., and Laura Tuennerman. *At the Border of Empires: The Tohono O'odham, Gender, and Assimilation, 1880–1934*. Tucson: University of Arizona Press, 2013.

Márquez Colín, Graciela. "El tratado de reciprocidad de 1883: ¿Una oportunidad perdida?" *Historia Mexicana* 61, no. 4 (January 2012): 1413–1459.

Marsh, George Perkins. *Man and Nature*. Seattle: University of Washington Press, 2003 [1864].

Martínez, Oscar J. "Border Conflict, Border Fences, and the 'Tortilla Curtain' Incident of 1978–1979." *Journal of the Southwest* 50, no. 3 (Autumn 2008): 263–278.

———. *Border People: Life and Society in the U.S.-Mexico Borderlands*. Tucson: University of Arizona Press, 1994.

Masco, Joseph. *The Nuclear Borderlands: The Manhattan Project in Post–Cold War New Mexico*. Princeton, NJ: Princeton University Press, 2006.

Massey, Douglas S., Jorge Durand, and Nolan J. Malone. *Beyond Smoke and Mirrors: Mexican Immigration in an Era of Economic Integration*. New York: Russell Sage Foundation, 2002.

McCoy, Alfred W. *The Politics of Heroin: CIA Complicity in the Global Drug Trade*. Chicago: Lawrence Hill Books, 2003.

Mckiernan-González, John. *Fevered Measures: Public Health and Race at the Texas-Mexico Border, 1848–1942*. Durham, NC: Duke University Press, 2012.

Meeks, Eric V. *Border Citizens: The Making of Indians, Mexicans, and Anglos in Arizona*. Austin: University of Texas Press, 2007.

———. "The Tohono O'odham, Wage Labor, and Resistant Adaptation, 1900–1930." *Western Historical Quarterly* 34, no. 4 (2003): 468–489.

Mendoza, Mary E. "Fencing the Line: Race, Environment, and the Changing Visual Landscape at the U.S.-Mexico Divide." In *Border Spaces: Visualizing the U.S.-Mexico Frontera*, edited by Katherine G. Morrissey and John-Michael H. Warner, 66–85. Tucson: University of Arizona Press, 2018.

Mintz, Sidney W. *Sweetness and Power: The Place of Sugar in Modern History*. New York: Viking, 1985.

Montejano, David. *Anglos and Mexicans in the Making of Texas, 1836–1986*. Austin: University of Texas Press, 1987.

Mora, Anthony P. *Border Dilemmas: Racial and National Uncertainties in New Mexico, 1848–1912*. Durham, NC: Duke University Press, 2011.

Mora-Torres, Juan. *The Making of the Mexican Border: The State, Capitalism, and Society in Nuevo León, 1848–1910*. Austin: University of Texas Press, 2001.

Morrissey, Katherine G. "Monuments, Photographs, and Maps: Visualizing the U.S.-Mexico Border in the 1890s." In *Border Spaces: Visualizing the U.S.-Mexico Frontera*, edited by Katherine G. Morrissey and John-Michael H. Warner, 39–65. Tucson: University of Arizona Press, 2018.

Nabhan, Gary Paul. *The Desert Smells Like Rain: A Naturalist in Papago Indian Country*. San Francisco, CA: North Point Press, 1982.

Nadelmann, Ethan A. *Cops across Borders: The Internationalization of U.S. Criminal Law Enforcement*. University Park: Penn State University Press, 1993.

Needham, Andrew. *Power Lines: Phoenix and the Making of the Modern Southwest*. Princeton, NJ: Princeton University Press, 2014.

Nevins, Joseph. *Operation Gatekeeper: The Rise of the "Illegal Alien" and the Making of the U.S.-Mexico Boundary*. New York: Routledge, 2002.

Nevins, Joseph, and Timothy Dunn. "Barricading the Border." *NACLA Report on the Americas* (November/December 2008): 21–42. https://nacla.org/sites/default/files/A04106023_1.pdf.

Ngai, Mae. *Impossible Subjects: Illegal Aliens and the Making of Modern America*. Princeton, NJ: Princeton University Press, 2004.

Nichols, James David. "The Line of Liberty: Runaway Slaves and Fugitive Peons in the Texas-Mexico Borderlands." *Western Historical Quarterly* 44, no. 4 (November 2013): 413–433.

Niemeyer, E. V., Jr. "Personal Diplomacy: Lyndon B. Johnson and Mexico, 1963–1968." *Southwestern Historical Quarterly* 90, no. 2 (October 1986): 159–186.

Okrent, Daniel. *Last Call: The Rise and Fall of Prohibition*. New York: Scribner, 2010.

Olsson, Tore C. *Agrarian Crossings: Reformers and the Remaking of the US and Mexican Countryside*. Princeton, NJ: Princeton University Press, 2017.

Pendergrast, Mark. *Uncommon Grounds: The History of Coffee and How It Transformed Our World*. New York: Basic Books, 1999.

Pisani, Donald J. *To Reclaim a Divided West: Water, Law, and Public Policy, 1848–1902*. Albuquerque: University of New Mexico Press, 1992.

———. *Water and American Government: The Reclamation Bureau, National Water Policy, and the West, 1902–1935*. Berkeley: University of California Press, 2002.

Rael, Ronald. *Borderwall as Architecture: A Manifesto for the U.S.-Mexico Boundary*. Berkeley: University of California Press, 2017.

Rebert, Paula. *La Gran Línea: Mapping the United States–Mexico Boundary, 1849–1857*. Austin: University of Texas Press, 2001.

Regan, Margaret. *The Death of Josseline: Immigration Stories from the Arizona Borderlands*. Boston: Beacon Press, 2010.

Reisner, Marc. *Cadillac Desert: The American West and Its Disappearing Water*. New York: Penguin Books, 1993 [1986].

Reséndez, Andrés. *Changing National Identities at the Frontier: Texas and New Mexico, 1800–1850*. Cambridge: Cambridge University Press, 2004.

Robles Gil, Patricio. "El Carmen: The First Wilderness Designation in Latin America." *International Journal of Wilderness* 12, no. 2 (August 2006): 36–40.

Rosas, Ana Elizabeth. *Abrazando el Espíritu: Bracero Families Confront the US-Mexico Border.* Berkeley: University of California Press, 2014.

Salinas Alvarez, Samuel (text). *Historia de los caminos de México.* Vol. 2 of 4. El Marqués, Querétaro: Banco Nacional de Obras y Servicios Públicos; Gráficas Monte Albán, 1994.

Samaniego López, Marco Antonio. *Ríos internacionales entre México y Estados Unidos: Los tratados de 1906 y 1944.* Mexico City: El Colegio de México, Centro de Estudios Históricos, Universidad Autónoma de Baja California, 2006.

Sassen, Saskia. *Expulsions: Brutality and Complexity in the Global Economy.* Cambridge, MA: Harvard University Press, 2014.

———. *Territory, Authority, Rights: From Medieval to Global Assemblages.* Princeton, NJ: Princeton University Press, 2006.

Sayre, Nathan F. *The Politics of Scale: A History of Rangeland Science.* Chicago: University of Chicago Press, 2017.

———. *Ranching, Endangered Species, and Urbanization in the Southwest: Species of Capital.* Tucson: University of Arizona Press, 2002.

Schulman, Bruce J. "Governing Nature, Nurturing Government: Resource Management and the Development of the American State, 1900–1912." *Journal of Policy History* 17, no. 4 (Fall 2005): 375–403.

Schulze, Jeffrey M. "The Chamizal Blues: El Paso, the Wayward River, and the Peoples in Between." *Western Historical Quarterly* 43, no. 3 (September 2012): 301–322.

Scott, James C. *Seeing Like a State: How Certain Schemes to Improve the Human Condition Have Failed.* New Haven, CT: Yale University Press, 1998.

Shelton, M. L. "Climate of *La Frontera.*" In *Changing Plant Life of La Frontera: Observations on Vegetation in the United States/Mexico Borderlands,* edited by Grady L. Webster and Conrad J. Bahre, 39–55. Albuquerque: University of New Mexico Press, 2001.

Skirius, John. "Railroad, Oil and Other Foreign Interests in the Mexican Revolution, 1911–1914." *Journal of Latin American Studies* 35, no. 1 (February 2003): 25–51.

Smith, Gaddis. *The Last Years of the Monroe Doctrine, 1945–1993.* New York: Hill and Wang, 1994.

St. John, Rachel. "Divided Ranges: Trans-border Ranches and the Creation of National Space along the Western Mexico–U.S. Border." In *Bridging National Borders in North America,* edited by Benjamin H. Johnson and Andrew R. Graybill, 116–140. Durham, NC: Duke University Press, 2010.

———. *Line in the Sand: A History of the Western U.S.–Mexico Border.* Princeton, NJ: Princeton University Press, 2011.

Stern, Alexandra Minna. "Buildings, Boundaries, and Blood: Medicalization and Nation-Building on the U.S.-Mexico Border, 1910–1930." *Hispanic American Historical Review* 79, no. 1 (February 1999): 41–81.

Teisch, Jessica B. *Engineering Nature: Water, Development, and the Global Spread of American Environmental Expertise.* Chapel Hill: University of North Carolina Press, 2011.

Timm, Charles A. *The International Boundary Commission: United States and Mexico.* Austin: University of Texas, 1941.

Truett, Samuel. *Fugitive Landscapes: The Forgotten History of the U.S.-Mexico Borderlands.* New Haven, CT: Yale University Press, 2006.

Tucker, Richard P., and Edmund Russell, eds. *Natural Enemy, Natural Ally: Toward an Environmental History of War.* Corvallis: Oregon State University Press, 2004.

Urrea, Luis Alberto. *The Devil's Highway: A True Story.* New York: Back Bay Books, 2004.

Vanderwood, Paul. *Disorder and Progress: Bandits, Police, and Mexican Development.* New York: Rowman and Littlefield, 1981.

Walsh, Casey. *Building the Borderlands: A Transnational History of Irrigated Cotton along the Mexico-Texas Border.* College Station: Texas A&M University Press, 2008.

Waterhouse, Benjamin C. *Lobbying America: The Politics of Business from Nixon to NAFTA.* Princeton, NJ: Princeton University Press, 2014.

Weber, David J. *The Spanish Frontier in North America.* New Haven, CT: Yale University Press, 1992.

Weber, John. *From South Texas to the Nation: The Exploitation of Mexican Labor in the Twentieth Century.* Chapel Hill: University of North Carolina Press, 2015.

Webster, Grady L. "Reconnaissance of the Flora and Vegetation of *La Frontera.*" In *Changing Plant Life of La Frontera: Observations on Vegetation in the United States/Mexico Borderlands,* edited by Grady L. Webster and Conrad J. Bahre, 6–38. Albuquerque: University of New Mexico Press, 2001.

Werne, Joseph Richard. *The Imaginary Line: A History of the United States and Mexican Boundary Survey, 1848–1857.* Forth Worth: Texas Christian University Press, 2007.

———. "Pedro García Conde: El trazado de límites con Estados Unidos desde el punto de vista mexicano (1848–1853)." *Historia Mexicana* 36, no. 1 (July–September 1986): 113–129.

———. "Redrawing the Southwestern Boundary, 1891–1896." *Southwestern Historical Quarterly* 104, no. 1 (July 2000): 1–20.

———. "Surveying the Rio Grande, 1850–1853." *Southwestern Historical Quarterly* 94, no. 4 (April 1991): 535–554.

White, Richard. *"It's Your Misfortune and None of My Own": A History of the American West.* Norman: University of Oklahoma Press, 1991.

———. *Railroaded: The Transcontinentals and the Making of Modern America.* New York: W. W. Norton, 2011.

Wilson, Woodrow. "Mexican Affairs: Address of the President of the United States Delivered at a Joint Session of the Two Houses of Congress." Washington, DC: Government Printing Office, 1913.

Winters, Harold A., Gerald E. Galloway Jr., William J. Reynolds, and David W.

Rhyne. "Heat, Rock, and Sand: The Western Desert and the Sinai." In *Battling the Elements: Weather and Terrain in the Conduct of War*, 248–265. Baltimore, MD: Johns Hopkins University Press, 1998.

Wolfe, Mikael D. *Watering the Revolution: An Environmental and Technological History of Agrarian Reform in Mexico*. Durham, NC: Duke University Press, 2017.

Womack, John, Jr. "The Mexican Revolution, 1910–1920." In *Mexico since Independence*, edited by Leslie Bethell, 79–154. Cambridge: Cambridge University Press, 1991.

———. *Zapata and the Mexican Revolution*. New York: Vintage Books, 1970.

Work, David K. "Enforcing Neutrality: The Tenth U.S. Cavalry on the Mexican Border, 1913–1919." *Western Historical Quarterly* 40, no. 2 (Summer 2009): 179–200.

Worster, Donald. *Rivers of Empire: Water, Aridity, and the Growth of the American West*. New York: Oxford University Press, 1992.

———. *Shrinking the Earth: The Rise and Decline of American Abundance*. New York: Oxford University Press, 2016.

INDEX